Principles of optical
disc systems.

Principles of Optical Disc Systems

Principles of Optical Disc Systems

G Bouwhuis, J Braat, A Huijser, J Pasman, G van Rosmalen and K Schouhamer Immink

Philips Research Laboratories, Eindhoven

Adam Hilger Ltd, Bristol and Boston

British Library Cataloguing in Publication Data
Principles of optical disc systems.
  1. Optical data processing
  I. Bouwhuis, G.
  621.36   TA1630

  ISBN 0-85274-785-3

Consultant Editor: **Dr E R Pike** RSRE, Malvern

First published 1985
Reprinted 1986
Reprinted 1987

Published by Adam Hilger Ltd
Techno House, Redcliffe Way, Bristol BS1 6NX
PO Box 230, Accord, MA 02018, USA

Typeset by Mathematical Composition Setters Ltd, Salisbury, UK
Printed in Great Britain by J W Arrowsmith Ltd, Bristol

Contents

1 Introduction

G Bouwhuis

During the past decade the optical disc has found various applications. The small 12 cm diameter version, prerecorded with a digitally-encoded audio program is rapidly penetrating the consumer market. The larger version with video information is used in home entertainment and in education. The high information capacity together with the ease of replication make the optical disc well suited for these applications. In the field of data storage the direct optical recording system is becoming popular as a computer peripheral.

At read-out the simple scanning of a flat disc allows for fast random access, an important feature in data storage. An additional advantage of optical discs is the absence of physical contact between the reading head and the information layer because of the existing simple ways to focus radiation in the optical region of the electromagnetic spectrum. A transparent film covering the information may even protect the fine details from damage and from shadowing particles.

As in a conventional gramophone record the information is stored in a spiral, called the track, though in many cases neither a groove nor a continuous line is present but only marks forming a spiralling broken line (figure 1.1). The marks are small areas showing optical contrast with respect to the surrounding mirror surface, for example black line-shaped elements or oblong depressions (pits) in the surface. This causes the reflection to change along the track according to the marks. The optical pick-up which replaces the mechanical stylus of the gramophone converts the variation of the reflection into an electrical signal. The lens of the pick-up focuses a laser beam to a small spot of light on the track and sends the light reflected off the disc to a photodetector. The photo signal thus varies in time according to the marks along the track of the rotating disc.

1

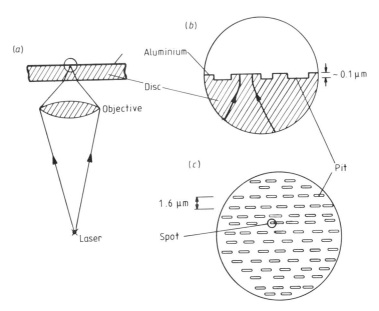

Figure 1.1   The disc and the reading spot. (*a*) The spot is formed at the reflecting rear side. (*b*) The pits in the surface. (*c*) The pits form tracks. The half-width of the spot is somewhat larger than the pit width.

The high information density is achieved with an optical arrangement which resembles a medium power scanning optical microscope. The limit is set by the diffraction of light resulting in a minimum diameter of the spot, formed at the focal point, of about $\lambda/2\text{NA}$ where λ is the wavelength and NA is the numerical aperture of the focused beam. Consequently the information density is approximately $(\text{NA}/\lambda)^2$ corresponding to 10^9-10^{11} bits on a disc. This means that the whole text of this book can be stored along 25 tracks of a video disc, occupying a ring with a width of 40 μm. Figure 1.2 shows the basic optical elements of the reading head. The (semiconductor) laser is imaged through the substrate onto the rear side of the disc with a microscope-type objective. The part of the reflected light which is gathered by the same objective is sent to the detector. In figure 1.2(*a*) a tilting mirror corrects radial errors of the spot with respect to the track for errors smaller than the field of view of the objective. In order to scan the complete disc the whole arrangement has been mounted on a carriage. In figure 1.2(*b*) the whole arrangement, though compact, has also to follow the small but rapid radial tracking errors. The control loops which serve radial and vertical tracking need, of course, error signals. This means that in general one auxiliary optical element has to be added in front of the detector and that the detector must be composite.

The choice of a modulating reflection rather than transmission has various grounds. Firstly, a reflecting disc is approached optically from one side only which simplifies the player construction. Secondly, a protective layer has to be present on only one side of the information layer whereas in transmission a two-sided protection is needed. This would pose severe problems in disc production because in the frequently occurring case of relief information structures the optical contrast should not be lost. Thirdly, relief structures in reflection have to be a factor of $4n$ ($\simeq 6 \times$) shallower which facilitates mass replication. Finally, it turns out that for focus control more, and simpler, methods are possible in reflection than in transmission.

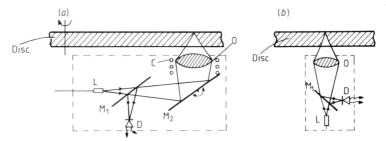

Figure 1.2 Basic player optics. (*a*) The beam from the laser, L, is focused by the objective, O, via the tilting mirror, M_2. The objective has been mounted in a loudspeaker coil, C, such that the spot is maintained in focus at the information layer. The returning light is reflected by the semitransparent mirror, M_1, to the detector, D. The whole arrangement slides radially under the disc. (*b*) Compact set-up (finger) without tilting mirror. The whole finger follows the small high frequency track displacements.

The nature of the contrast of the marks may be due to changes in the intensity–reflection coefficient, changes in the phase of the reflected light (relief structures) or changes in the state of polarisation at reflection. Because mass production of video and audio discs is most easily performed by replication, a relief structure is the obvious choice. The disc surface then contains pits or bumps (see figure 1.1). When the light spot hits a pit the reflected light undergoes a phase change over a part of the spot resulting in light scattering out of the returning beam and a decrease in the photo signal. The variations of the photo signal contain the information to regain the audio, video or data signal. Audio signals are stored digitally on the disc. Sound samples are taken at a rate of 44.1 kHz and the level of each sample of an audio channel is converted into a numerical value which is represented in a binary codeword of 16 bits. After addition of extra bits, and rearranging for the purpose of modulation and error correction, a bit stream of 4.3218 MHz is stored on the disc. With 'zeros' represented by low photo signal levels and 'ones' by high levels the track will consist of pits and spaces of discrete lengths. At read-out the transition from pit to space has to be located in a window of 0.3 μm in order to achieve a playing time of one hour. Video signals on the other hand are stored in analog form because digital storage requires too high bandwidths. The composite video signal (luminance and chroma) is frequency modulated (FM) around a carrier frequency of about 7.5 MHz and sound is added as a duty cycle modulation. This causes the centre-to-centre distance of the pits to vary according to the FM frequency and the ratio of pit length to space length to vary according to the sound content.

Although the optical principles have been well known for more than a century it is only since the 1970s that the applications of optical discs have been developed extensively. An important quantity in data storage, in addition to the bit density, is the bit rate, and before the laser no suitable light source yielded a satisfactory signal-to-noise ratio from a detector illuminated through an area of less than 1 μm^2 for less than 1 μs. At present a wealth of lasers is available among which the small semiconductor lasers lend themselves very well to optical disc read-out; the power may even be amply sufficient to burn holes in a metal layer at megahertz frequencies. Related modern developments include simple and cheap silicon photodetectors and electro-optic and acousto-optic modulators for real-time production of master discs. Materials for home recording have recently been developed which combine high efficiency with a long lifetime. Improvements in erasable materials are the subject of many current research programmes.

It is the purpose of this book to describe the physical and engineering principles used in the construction of optical discs. Various disciplines play an important role and teamwork of optical, electronic, mechanical and chemical scientists and engineers has been vital. The authors of this book worked in such a team and each gives an account of his particular area. The reader can therefore learn about the subject from different viewpoints and gain insight into the links between the different branches of research.

Though the book directs its attention primarily to the application of physics to optical disc systems, some authors devote ample space to treatment of the relevant background knowledge which is of much broader interest.

The non-ideal circumstances encountered in practice determine the limits of the system performance against price. Thus much attention is paid to aberrations in the optics, defects in the disc such as drop-outs, warping and eccentric spinning.

The second chapter concerns the optical aspects. Only one spot (resolved point) for information transfer is considered whereas a well designed lens is able to carry 10^8 channels. The available light power, however, limits the number of channels and, moreover, the first action of the electronic engineer is to generate one time-sequential data stream.

The spot quality is crucial in pushing the system close to the fundamental limits and hence diffraction theory is given much attention, in particular in the discussion of the interaction of the scanning beam with the specific disc structures: optical amplitude modulations along the track may need a different detection mode to that for phase structures. Besides the main signal the generation of error signals needed for control of focusing and of trackfollowing is considered.

Though the approximations made in the treatment of diffraction are fully adequate for geometries of the object which are larger than the wavelength of the radiation, the small pits in the disc with dimensions down to 0.6 μm need different approximations. In the third chapter the scalar treatment is compared with a rigorous vectorial calculation showing that errors up to 15% may occur in the scalar approximation.

In order to properly record and read the information the system has to fulfil the additional conditions for focusing and trackfollowing. The theory of the electromechanics of the control loops is found in Chapter 4. In actuator design long experience is of great value. The author has been involved in optical disc servo systems since the start of the development at Philips and in that time has constructed many types of actuators. The examples given of realised servo systems are very instructive.

The next chapter describes the transfer of information onto the master disc in the case of read-only memories. The quality of the mastering of video and of audio programmes should be well above that of the player so that the contribution to any degradation of the signal due to the master disc is negligible. High level engineering in many disciplines including precision mechanics and photochemistry is needed.

In Chapter 6 direct recording is discussed. The recording is performed by locally changing the reflectivity of a thin layer by means of modulation of the power focused in a spot on the rotating disc. Media that change an optical property such as reflectivity under heating are of interest for on-the-spot storage of large amounts of data. The requirements on error probability, even after years of storage, are extreme.

The properties of the optical disc as a channel for electronic signals are different from magnetic and other conventional media especially with respect to noise and defects. The search for modulation and coding systems together with error correction schemes led to novel formats for analog video, for digital audio and for direct data storage. In Chapter 7 the adaptation to the optical channel and to the material properties in recording is explained. Much attention is paid to restoration of the data stream in the case of corrupted signals. In optics it is well known that destruction of the information due to damage of the storage medium can be prevented by holographic storage. The error correction scheme of the digital disc systems, however, is of such a strength and elegance that it does away with any doubt an optical engineer might have that holographic discs are preferable.

The final chapter gives examples of the design of marketed systems and of the particular applications.

Since the paper by Compaan and Kramer (1973) much has been published on optical disc theories and applications. Korpel (1980) gave an historical background and general view of research and development by various companies. Many papers are still appearing on optical discs, mostly concerning materials for direct recording and erasable materials. The chief points of the subject, however, are fundamental and the technology has now stabilised enough to make it worthwhile compiling a text on optical disc systems, which seem to have a promising future.

References

Compaan K and Kramer P 1973 The Philips 'VLP' system *Philips Tech. Rev.* **33** 178–80
Korpel A 1980 Laser applications: video disc in *Laser Applications* Vol. 4 71–123 (New York: Academic)

2 Read-out of Optical Discs

J Braat

2.1 Introduction

The type of optical disc system that has been widely adopted and that will be described in this chapter relies on the read-out of a relief pattern in a pressed disc (video and audio disc) or on the read-out of an amplitude pattern e.g. burned holes in a digital data disc (Bouwhuis and Braat 1978 and 1983). The information is stored as a sequence of depressions or holes along a spiral track. This track is scanned by a tiny light spot and the optical read-out system should generate a detector signal that is a reliable copy of the signal that was originally recorded on the disc.

It will be clear that the transformation of the surface height of a relief pattern into a varying light intensity on the detector is principally a non-linear process. Even the reflectivity variations of a pattern of burned holes are not translated linearly into intensity variations on the detector. The optical read-out step inevitably introduces a squaring operation when going from the amplitude of the light to the light intensity that is finally transformed into the detector current.

Following the concepts of linear systems theory the frequency response of an optical system has been defined. The frequency to be considered is a spatial frequency (in mm^{-1}) and it is represented by a one-dimensional grating structure. The loss of modulation depth in the grating as it is imaged by the optical system is a measure for the frequency response at that special spatial frequency. The object grating should be weakly modulated (small signal approximation) in order to apply the principle of linear superposition when imaging more complicated objects.

For optical disc systems it is also possible to define some kind of frequency response (or transfer function). But due to the strong modulation on an optical disc, signal distortion will not be negligible. That is why a complete description of the signal includes subjects like intersymbol interference on digital discs and intermodulation on video discs. Moreover crosstalk will be treated since that is likely to occur because of the dense packing of the tracks.

The subjects of frequency response and signal quality will be considered in the next three sections of this chapter together with signal-to-noise calculations and the case of an imperfect optical system. In the fifth section it is shown how the optimum read-out conditions are maintained by proper focusing and tracking of the information with the aid of servo systems that are steered by optically derived error signals. In the sixth section an example of an optical read-out system (the optical pick-up) is briefly described.

2.2 Scanning spot microscopy

The optical read-out method adopted in optical disc systems is that of the scanning microscope (figure 2.1(*a*)). In its simplest form, a point source P is imaged by an objective O_S onto the moving object M. The light diffracted by the object is partly captured by the detector D. It was recognised early on that this set-up closely resembles that of the classical microscope (figure 2.1(*b*)). Welford (1960) showed that the spatial intensity distribution in the image plane of a classical microscope is comparable with the time dependent detector signal that is obtained when scanning the same object with a scanning microscope. For the sake of clarity both microscopes are shown operating in transmission but they can equally be used in reflection.

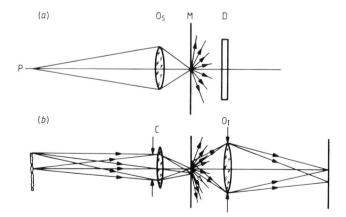

Figure 2.1 Schematic view of a scanning microscope (*a*) and of a classical microscope (*b*).

The analogy between the classical microscope and the scanning microscope concerns the role of the scanning objective O_S and the imaging objective O_I and secondly the detector D in the scanning microscope and the condenser C in the classical microscope. It is known from the theory of image formation in the classical microscope (Zernike 1938) that the condenser determines by its numerical aperture only the coherence of the object illumination and that the condenser lens does not need to be well corrected. However, the objective O_I should be well corrected and focused onto the object in order to obtain maximum resolution. In §2.2.1 it is shown that in the scanning microscope comparable reasoning can be used with respect to the detector D and the scanning objective O_S.

2.2.1 Frequency response of the scanning microscope

A grating and its diffracted orders. In order to study the frequency response of an optical system we use as input a weakly modulated amplitude pattern (grating) with a certain spatial frequency f_{sp} that is the inverse of the period of the grating

$$f_{sp} = \frac{1}{p}.$$

The intensity transmission function of the grating $I(u)$ is given as

$$I(u) = a[1 + m \cos(2\pi u/p] \qquad (m \ll 1) \qquad (2.1)$$

and the amplitude transmission function

$$A(u) = \sqrt{I(u)}$$
$$\approx \sqrt{a}[1 + \tfrac{1}{2}m \cos(2\pi u/p)]. \qquad (2.2)$$

A plane wave incident on the grating (angle α_0) will be split up into a strong zeroth-order plane wave and two weak first-order plane waves whose directions α_N are given by the grating law (figure 2.2)

$$\sin \alpha_N - \sin \alpha_0 = N\lambda/p \qquad (N = -1, 0, +1) \qquad (2.3)$$

where λ is the wavelength of the light.

The amplitude and phase of the diffracted orders depend on the geometry of the grating and on its position. Figure 2.3 shows the grating with its diffracted orders and the phase of the diffracted orders is measured with respect to a certain reference point R (for the sake of simplicity normal incidence is considered). The wavefronts of the diffracted orders are represented by W_0, W_{-1} and W_{+1}. When the reference point R is in a symmetrical position with respect to the grating the wavefronts W_{-1} and W_{+1} must have equal phase. A displacement of the grating (or a displacement of the reference point R) affects the phase of the wavefronts W_{-1} and W_{+1}

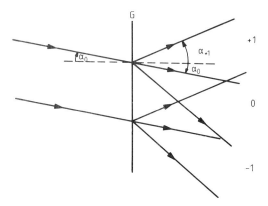

Figure 2.2 Diffraction of a plane wave (labelled 0) by a grating G. Two diffracted orders ($+1$ and -1) are generated by the grating.

but not the phase of the zeroth-order wavefront W_0. In figure 2.3(b) the extra optical pathlength of the order $+1$ equals $+\Delta d$ and for the order -1 we obtain $-\Delta d$. From the figure it is seen that

$$\Delta d = u_0 \sin \alpha = u_0 \lambda / p \qquad (2.4)$$

where $u_0 = RR'$ is the grating displacement.

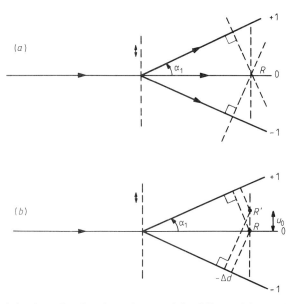

Figure 2.3 (a), (b) The phase change of the diffracted first orders with respect to the zeroth order due to a grating displacement u_0.

The phase change of the orders thus equals

$$\Delta\phi = \pm 2\pi\,\Delta d/\lambda = \pm 2\pi\,u_0/p. \qquad (2.5)$$

In general for an Nth diffracted order we obtain

$$\Delta\phi_N = 2\pi\,Nu_0/p. \qquad (2.6)$$

We notice that the position of a grating thus influences the phase of the diffracted orders but not their amplitude. Phase changes are optically detected by interference experiments. Interference of the constant zeroth order with phase-shifted first diffracted orders thus yields information about the grating position.

Interference of diffracted orders. In a scanning microscope a spherical wave is focused onto the test grating. We decompose this spherical wave into a set of plane waves with varying angles of incidence (angular spectrum of plane waves (Goodman 1968)). The light diffracted by the grating will consist of three spherical waves according to figure 2.4 and they are seen to partly overlap each other.

It will be useful to suppose that the light is projected onto a hollow spherical screen with a radius of curvature R_0 and centred on the grating. When the height h is measured on the screen from the axis and h is divided by R_0 a quantity

$$x = h/R_0 = \sin\alpha \qquad (2.7)$$

is obtained. The grating law, represented by equation (2.3), is linear in the sine of the angles of incidence (the sine of the angle that is present between the marginal ray and the central ray of a spherical wave is frequently called the numerical aperture (NA) of the wave and this quantity is used to characterise, for example, microscope objectives).

When we normalise x with respect to the numerical aperture $\mathrm{NA} = \sin\alpha_s$ of the incident spherical wave, we obtain

$$x' = \frac{\sin\alpha}{\sin\alpha_s} = \frac{h/R_0}{\mathrm{NA}}. \qquad (2.8)$$

Expressed in this coordinate x' and the corresponding coordinate y', the zeroth order fills the unit circle and the diffracted orders remain unit circles merely shifted over a distance $\Delta x'$ given by

$$\Delta x' = \frac{\lambda/p}{\mathrm{NA}} = \frac{\lambda f_{sp}}{\mathrm{NA}}. \qquad (2.9)$$

The detector D of the scanning microscope can also be ascribed a certain extent expressed by the coordinates $(x',\,y')$. In a reflective scanning microscope the detector area will generally be equal to the unit circle.

The regions that yield information about the grating position are the regions where zeroth and first orders overlap and interfere with each other. Equation (2.6) stated that the phase difference between zeroth and higher orders varies linearly with u, the grating displacement. In the case of a linear movement of the grating at a speed s, we obtain

$$\Delta\phi_N = 2\pi \, Nst/p = 2\pi \, N\nu t \tag{2.10}$$

where ν is a time frequency equal to s/p.

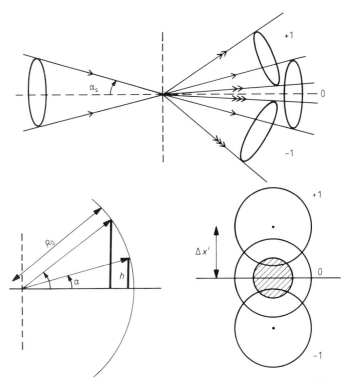

Figure 2.4 An incident spherical wave is split into spherical diffracted waves that partly overlap. Part of the diffracted light is captured by a detector whose area has been hatched in the figure.

The mixing of three diffraction orders A_0, A_{+1} and A_{-1} with a phase difference $\Delta\phi_{+1}$ and $\Delta\phi_{-1}$ gives rise to a time dependent intensity $I(t)$. When $\Delta\phi_{+1} = -\Delta\phi_{-1}$ and $A_{-1} = A_{+1}$ we obtain

$$I(t) = |A_0 + A_{+1} \exp(i\,\Delta\phi_{+1}) + A_{+1} \exp(-i\,\Delta\phi_{+1})|^2$$

$$= A_0^2 + 4A_0 A_{+1} \cos(\Delta\phi_{+1}) + 2A_{+1}^2 + 2A_{+1}^2 \cos(2\,\Delta\phi_{+1}) \tag{2.11}$$

$$\approx A_0^2 \left(1 + \frac{4A_{+1}}{A_0} \cos(2\pi\nu t) \right)$$

where the complex notation for optical amplitudes has been used. The ratio A_{+1}/A_0 follows from equation (2.2) and is equal to $m/4$ while $A_0 = \sqrt{a}$; so the final expression for the time dependent intensity is

$$I(t) \approx a[1 + m \cos(2\pi\nu t)]. \qquad (2.12)$$

Equation (2.12) represents the local intensity in the detector plane and to obtain the final signal this intensity has to be integrated over the detector area. The size and the position of the detector thus influence the variation of the modulation index m with the spatial frequency of the object (frequency response of the scanning microscope).

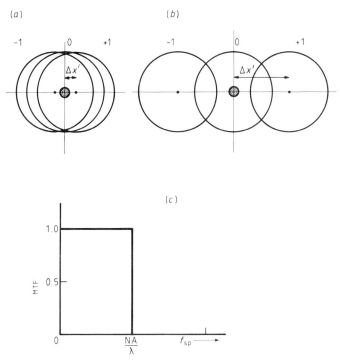

Figure 2.5 Coherent detection in the scanning microscope by using a detector with a small angular extent (a). The corresponding modulation transfer function (MTF) is shown in (c).

For a centred detector with very small dimensions (figure 2.5(a)), the signal will equally be small but fairly independent of the spatial frequency of the grating. However, as soon as the shift $|\Delta x'|$ of the first orders is greater than 1, no area common to the zeroth and first orders covers the detector anymore and the frequency response becomes zero (figure 2.5(b)).

Using equation (2.10) we encounter the following situations

$$|\Delta x'| \leqslant 1 \qquad \text{or} \qquad f_{sp} \leqslant \frac{NA}{\lambda} \qquad MTF = 1$$

$$f_{sp} \geqslant \frac{NA}{\lambda} \qquad MTF = 0 \tag{2.13}$$

and the frequency response or modulation transfer function (MTF) is as indicated in figure 2.5(c).

When the detector D captures exactly the entire zeroth order, the signal on the detector will be proportional to the size of the overlapping region of a zeroth and a first order and decrease monotonically for increasing values of $|\Delta x'|$. When $|\Delta x'|$ is greater than 2 there are no longer any overlapping regions. The modulation transfer function MTF is obtained by taking the ratio of an overlapping region B and the full unit circle. It can be shown that

$$MTF = \frac{2}{\pi} \arccos\left(\frac{\Delta x'}{2}\right) - \frac{\Delta x'}{\pi}\left(1 - \frac{(\Delta x')^2}{4}\right)^{1/2} \qquad f_{sp} \leqslant \frac{2NA}{\lambda}$$

$$MTF = 0 \qquad f_{sp} > \frac{2NA}{\lambda}. \tag{2.14}$$

For intermediate sizes of the detector D it is useful to define the ratio

$$\gamma = \frac{NA_D}{NA}$$

where NA_D stands for the sine of the angle the detector subtends at the object plane. Varying γ from 0 to (theoretically) ∞ we obtain MTF curves such as shown in figure 2.6. The limiting transmitted frequency f_c (cut-off frequency) is given by

$$f_c = (1 + \gamma)\frac{NA}{\lambda} \qquad 0 \leqslant \gamma \leqslant 1$$

$$= 2\frac{NA}{\lambda} \qquad \gamma \geqslant 1 \tag{2.15}$$

In comparison with the classical light microscope, the situation when $\gamma = 0$ is called the coherent situation while $\gamma \rightarrow \infty$ yields the fully incoherent case. Standard operation of a scanning microscope is done with $\gamma = 1$ which corresponds to the partially coherent case. Although the MTF does not change further in going from $\gamma = 1$ to infinity, it will be seen later that non-linearities in the optical detection are still a function of γ.

For $\gamma = 0$, the optical system is a linear system with respect to the complex amplitude of the light. For $\gamma = \infty$, the optical system is linear in light intensity. All intermediate cases require a more detailed analysis.

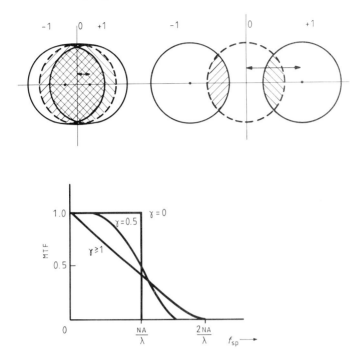

Figure 2.6 A detector configuration that is typical for the reflective scanning microscope (the detector extent is such that the entire zeroth order is captured). The curves show the influence of the coherence ratio γ on the MTF.

2.2.2 *Impulse and step response of a scanning microscope*

The modulation transfer function described in the preceding section is in principle not applicable when strongly modulated amplitude objects are imaged. Therefore it is useful to consider also the impulse and step response of an optical system

In an electronic circuit the impulse response is observed at the output when a short voltage peak (Dirac delta-function) is applied at the input. For an optical system we have to take the spatial equivalent of a time impulse and this is approximated by a very small pinhole in the object plane. The impulse response of a scanning microscope is obtained by translating this tiny pinhole through the object (disc) plane and the time dependent detector current now will be simply proportional to a cross section of the intensity of the scanning spot. In the case of a perfect optical system this will be a section of the intensity of the Airy diffraction pattern (Goodman 1968) as depicted in figure 2.7(a).

The step response of the scanning microscope is obtained by translating a black half-plane (knife edge) in the object plane. An interesting feature of the step (or edge) response is its value when the edge is exactly centred on the scanning spot. The spherical wave focused on this edge is composed of a set of plane waves with varying angles of incidence. Each portion of the plane waves incident on the black half-plane is absorbed. In the fully incoherent case (infinitely large detector) it may simply be stated that the intensities of the truncated plane waves are added and thus yield a detector current that equals half of its maximum value. For the fully coherent case (very small detector, figure 2.7(*b*)) it can be said that half of the amplitudes of the plane waves are added together which leads after the squaring operation to a detector current that is $\frac{1}{4}$ of the maximum. Because of the small detector dimension, the maximum itself has also decreased with respect to the fully incoherent case. In the case of practical interest with $\gamma = 1$, the value of the detector current equals 1/3, a value that has been derived theoretically (Zernike 1934) for the classical light microscope.

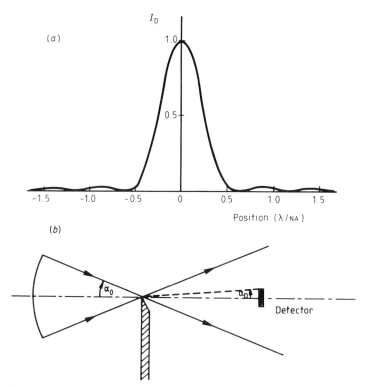

Figure 2.7   (*a*) A cross section of the intensity distribution of the ideal (circularly symmetrical) scanning spot. The width at half intensity is approximately 0.5 λ/NA. (*b*) The scanning spot is incident on a knife edge. The scattered light is captured by a detector whose dimensions are determined by the coherence ratio.

In figure 2.8 the more detailed step responses of a scanning microscope are shown for different values of γ. Note that only in the incoherent case ($\gamma = \infty$) is the optical system linear in intensity such that responses from adjacent edges may simply be added in intensity.

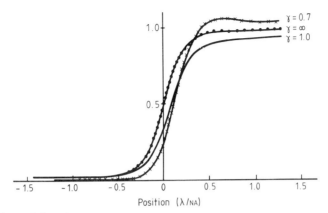

Figure 2.8 The step response of the scanning microscope in the case of a black and white edge as an input. A shift of the detected edge is observed when the detection is performed under not fully incoherent conditions. The shift is approximately equal to 0.1 λ/NA when the coherence ratio γ is 1.0.

2.2.3 *The complex amplitude grating*

Up to now it has been supposed that a grating introduces only a spatially varying transmission or reflection of the incident light. When the optical pathlength nd (with n equal to the refractive index of the medium) is equally modulated by the grating it is called a complex amplitude grating. Both the modulus and the phase of the complex light amplitude are altered by such a grating. In the case of pressed or replicated optical discs, there is no absorption at all and only the phase of the light is influenced by such a 'grating', that is a pure phase structure.

In figure 2.9(a) a cross section of a groove or pit on an optical disc is shown. The phase change of the light incident on such a structure depends on the optical contrast and thus on the way the pit is read. In figure 2.9(b), the structure is read in transmission and the optical path difference (OPD) between light striking a pit and light striking the environment of a pit is equal to

$$\mathrm{OPD} = (n - 1)d$$

and the phase difference is

$$\phi_{\mathrm{tr}} = \frac{2\pi}{\lambda}\,\mathrm{OPD} = 2\pi(n - 1)\frac{d}{\lambda}. \tag{2.16}$$

In figure 2.9(c) the disc is read in reflection from the air side and the OPD is seen to be

$$OPD = 2d$$

$$\phi_{ra} = \frac{2\pi}{\lambda} OPD = 4\pi \frac{d}{\lambda}. \tag{2.17}$$

Finally figure 2.9(d) shows a read-out in reflection from the substrate side and we obtain

$$OPD = 2nd$$

$$\phi_{rs} = \frac{2\pi}{\lambda} OPD = 4\pi n \frac{d}{\lambda}. \tag{2.18}$$

For plastic substrates with a refractive index of approximately 1.5, the OPD varies from $0.5d$ to $3d$, depending on the read-out mode.

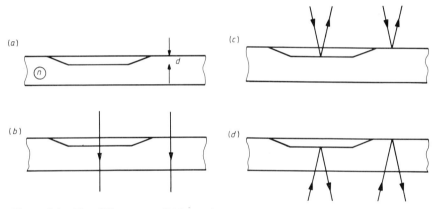

Figure 2.9   The different possibilities of optical read-out of a phase structure (a). The optical contrast may vary by a factor of 6 going from the situation depicted in (b) to that of (d). n is the refractive index of the medium and d the pit depth.

Some quick conclusions can be drawn about the effect of a phase structure on the incident light. When the light reflected by a pit is approximately in antiphase with the light reflected by the surrounding area, a maximum extinction of the light is obtained, which can reach the value of zero when the amplitudes that are in phase opposition are properly balanced. Putting ϕ equal to π in equations (2.16), (2.17) and (2.18) we find for the optimum depth d of a pit ($\lambda = 800$ nm, $n = 1.5$)

$$d = 800 \text{ nm} \qquad \text{(transmission)}$$

$$d = 200 \text{ nm} \qquad \text{(air reflection)}$$

$$d = 135 \text{ nm} \qquad \text{(substrate reflection).}$$

It will be clear that the formation of pits with a depth, for example, of 0.8 μm and width 0.5 μm is not easy. A departure from the optimum depth thus imposes itself when discs are read in transmission and the read-out in these conditions has to be optimised. Before going into detail the amplitude and phase of the orders diffracted by a phase grating will be considered. Once the complex amplitude of the orders is known optimisation of the read-out for different pit sizes is a simple matter.

The diffraction orders of a phase grating. In figure 2.10 the cross section of a phase grating with grooves (depth d) is shown. We consider the transmissive situation. A plane wave incident on the grating has uniform amplitude and phase. The phase of the light is represented by a vector and, for the incident wave, all vectors are in phase. The zeroth order of the transmitted light takes on the average phase of the light distribution

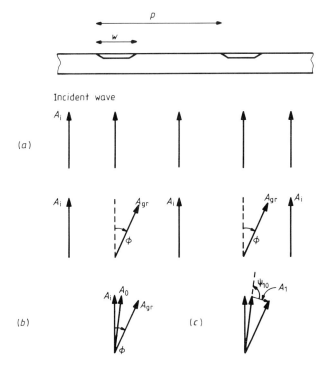

Figure 2.10 The cross section of an optical disc containing depressions (pits). (*a*) A vector diagram of the phase of the incoming wave and the transmitted wave that has suffered an average phaseshift of ϕ at the location of the pits. (*b*) The phaseshift of the transmitted zeroth order A_0 with respect to the phase of the incoming wave A_i. (*c*) Graphical representation of the phaseshift ψ_{10} between the zeroth and first diffracted orders.

immediately behind the grating, which is the sum A_0 of the amplitudes transmitted by the grooves and by their surroundings, each weighted by the relative areas w and p (figure 2.10(b)). There are first diffracted orders because of the amplitude deviations from the average value A_0, that are caused by the grooves. Figure 2.10(c) shows that the phase of these periodic deviations is given by the difference vector A_1 of the vectors A_0 and A_{gr}. From the figure it is seen that the phase difference between the zeroth and first diffracted orders is represented by the angle ψ_{10}.

There is a relation between ϕ, the phase depth of the groove and ψ_{10}. In the limiting case when ϕ is very small, ψ_{10} tends to $\pi/2$; for larger values of ϕ, ψ_{10} increases and attains the value of π when ϕ also equals π.

The phase of the first diffracted orders also depends on the position of the grating as was shown in §2.2.1. This leads to the following expression for the time dependent phase difference between zeroth and first diffracted orders of a phase grating (with period p and translated at linear speed s)

$$\Delta\phi_{+1} = \psi_{10} + 2\pi\nu t$$

$$\Delta\phi_{-1} = \psi_{10} - 2\pi\nu t.$$

Interference of diffracted orders.   The time dependent signal is generated by the interference of zeroth and first diffracted orders in the regions of overlap on the detector. In the case of an amplitude grating whose first orders are in antiphase with the zeroth order ($\psi_{10} = \pi$), the signals from the two overlapping regions (figure 2.6) are in phase and algebraically added by the detector that integrates the whole light flux passing through the unit circle (integral detection). In the case of a phase grating we write for the intensity in the area $D_{0,+1}$ common to the zeroth and $+1$ order

$$I_{0,+1}(t) = |A_0 + A_1 \exp(+i\,\Delta\phi_{+1})|^2$$

$$= A_0^2 + A_1^2 + 2A_0A_1 \cos(\psi_{10} + 2\pi\nu t) \qquad (2.19)$$

and equally for the area $D_{0,-1}$

$$I_{0,-1}(t) = |A_0 + A_1 \exp(+i\,\Delta\phi_{-1})|^2$$

$$= A_0^2 + A_1^2 + 2A_0A_1 \cos(\psi_{10} - 2\pi\nu t) \qquad (2.20)$$

where A_0^2 and A_1^2 are the intensities of the diffracted orders and where we have put $A_{+1} = A_{-1}$ which holds for a grating with a symmetrical profile. The addition of the two signals yields the final detector signal

$$I_D(t) \approx A_0^2 + 2A_1^2 + 2A_0A_1[\cos(\psi_{10} + 2\pi\nu t) + \cos(\psi_{10} - 2\pi\nu t)]\,\text{MTF}(\nu)$$

$$= A_0^2 + 2A_1^2 + 4A_0A_1\,\text{MTF}(\nu)\cos\psi_{10}\cos(2\pi\nu t) \qquad (2.21)$$

where $\text{MTF}(\nu)$ has been defined by equation (2.14) and is seen to be proportional to the overlapping area $D_{0,+1}$.

The time dependent part of the detector signal $I_D(t)$ is seen to be proportional to $\cos(\psi_{10})$. When $\psi_{10} = k\pi$, maximum modulation is obtained but for intermediate values the modulation depth decreases and even becomes zero when ψ_{10} is $\pi/2$. This means that shallow phase gratings ($d/\lambda \ll 1$) are 'invisible' under the scanning microscope when observed with integral detection.

Zernike (1934) invented phase contrast microscopy in order to improve the visibility of weak phase objects. For the scanning microscope a different detection scheme has been developed to enhance the contrast in the case of weak objects (Broussaud 1974, Dekkers and de Lang 1974). In figure 2.11 the detector area (unit circle) is shown with the diffracted orders projected onto it. Instead of a single detector, we now use a split detector and calculate the signals I_{DL} and I_{DR} delivered by these detectors. The common areas are indicated by D_A and D_B for the left- and right-hand detector halves. For the right-hand detector the signal equals

$$I_{DR}(t) = A_0^2{}_{[\text{half circle}]} + A_1^2{}_{[D_{AR}+D_{BR}]} + A_1^2{}_{[D_{BR}]}$$
$$+ 2A_0A_1{}_{[D_{AR}+D_{BR}]} \cos(\psi_{10} + 2\pi\nu t)$$
$$+ 2A_0A_1{}_{[D_{BR}]} \cos(\psi_{10} - 2\pi\nu t) \tag{2.22}$$

and for the left-hand detector we may write

$$I_{DL}(t) = A_0^2{}_{[\text{half circle}]} + A_1^2{}_{[D_{AL}+D_{BL}]} + A_1^2{}_{[D_{BR}]}$$
$$+ 2A_0A_1{}_{[D_{AL}+D_{BL}]} \cos(\psi_{10} - 2\pi\nu t)$$
$$+ 2A_0A_1{}_{[D_{BL}]} \cos(\psi_{10} + 2\pi\nu t). \tag{2.23}$$

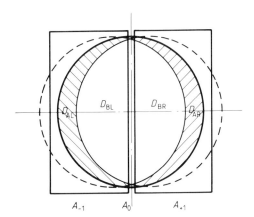

Figure 2.11 Detection of the signal with the aid of a split detector. The regions of overlap between the zeroth and first orders have each been divided in two sections (e.g. D_{AR} and D_{BR}) and the useful signal is obtained from the shaded areas labelled D_{AR} and D_{AL}.

Noting that the regions D_{AR} and D_{AL} are equal as well as D_{BR} and D_{BL}, the addition of the two detector currents would simply yield the result of equation (2.21). However, when subtracting the two detector currents we get the expression

$$\begin{aligned}
I_D(t) &= 2A_0 A_{1[D_{AR}+D_{BR}]} \left[\cos(\psi_{10} + 2\pi\nu t) - \cos(\psi_{10} - 2\pi\nu t)\right] \\
&+ 2A_0 A_{1[D_{BR}]} \left[\cos(\psi_{10} - 2\pi\nu t) - \cos(\psi_{10} + 2\pi\nu t)\right] \qquad (2.24) \\
&= 2A_0 A_{1[D_{AR}]} \left[\cos(\psi_{10} + 2\pi\nu t) - \cos(\psi_{10} - 2\pi\nu t)\right] \\
&= -4A_0 A_{1[D_{AR}]} \sin(\psi_{10}) \sin(2\pi\nu t).
\end{aligned}$$

The area D_{AR} (shaded in figure 2.11) can be expressed in terms of the modulation transfer function $\text{MTF}(\nu)$ by

$$D_{AR} \propto \text{MTF}(\nu) - \text{MTF}(2\nu) \qquad (2.25)$$

because $D_{BL} + D_{BR} + D_{AR}$ is equal to $\text{MTF}(\nu)$ and $D_{BL} + D_{BR}$ to $\text{MTF}(2\nu)$.

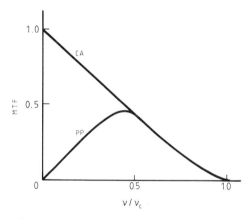

Figure 2.12 The modulation transfer function (MTF) in the case of central aperture (CA) and push–pull detection (PP). The maximum transfer of the PP detection method is found at approximately 0.45 of the optical cut-off frequency ν_c.

In figure 2.12 the standard modulation transfer function $\text{MTF}(\nu)$ and the transfer function according to equation (2.25) are shown. The detection method described above works most effectively when $\psi_{10} = \pi/2$ (sin $\psi_{10} = 1$). The useful signals on the two detector halves, $\cos(\psi_{10} + 2\pi\nu t)$ and $\cos(\psi_{10} - 2\pi\nu t)$, have a phase difference of $2\psi_{10}$ and, for $\psi_{10} = \pi/2$ the signals are exactly in phase opposition. In figure 2.13 the light distribution on the detector at different moments ($2\pi\nu t = 0$, $\pi/2$, π and $3\pi/2$) is shown.

Observing this pattern, the name push–pull (PP), as in electronics, has been suggested for this detection arrangement. The standard detection method (integral detection) has received the name 'central aperture' (CA) detection.

When the angle ψ_{10} is neither $\pi/2$ nor π, both detection schemes are possible. But the PP method yields a signal transfer that is poor at low frequencies and thus offers a somewhat smaller optical bandwidth than the CA method.

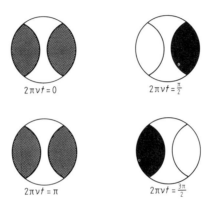

Figure 2.13 The intensity distribution over the detector area in the case of an object with a shallow phase structure on it. Only the relative changes in light intensity in the overlapping areas are indicated. Generally the central area is almost as bright as the regions of overlap so the modulation depth of the signal is small.

2.3 Mathematical model of the read-out of optical discs

The image formation in the classical microscope under different conditions of coherence of the object illumination has been described in a basic article by Hopkins (1953). His analysis of image formation was based on the frequency response of an optical system and in order to account for the influence of the degree of coherence on the image formation he defined a mutual intensity function which is the average value of the product of the complex amplitudes present in two arbitrarily chosen points. In most optical systems the mutual intensity function depends only on the distance between these two points. In the limiting case of fully incoherent object illumination the mutual intensity function is proportional to a Dirac delta-function. The spatial frequency content (spectrum) of the image intensity distribution is then simply equal to the object spectrum multiplied by the frequency response (MTF) of the optical system. In the more general situation of partial coherence in the object illumination the evaluation of the image intensity is more complicated and mostly has to be carried out numerically.

Hopkins's interest in optical disc systems made him adapt his microscope theory to the scanning mode of operation and then to the specific object that is submitted to such a scanning microscope, the optical disc (Hopkins 1979). An optical disc has a surface with a regularly repeating structure in the radial direction (the sequence of tracks) and a more complicated structure in the track direction. In the case of video discs there is a main carrier frequency present in the signal which yields a fairly well defined period of the pits (or depressions) in the track direction. In the case of digital audio discs, the sequence of pits in the track direction appears quite random as regards length and position.

It has proved useful to study the frequency response (in amplitude and phase) of the optical disc system making use of Fourier series analysis of periodic structures. The radial periodicity is always there on an optical disc. In the track direction we deal either with pure frequencies (identical pits at fixed distances) or we take a model with a sequence of random pits that is repeated periodically. Although the numerical work seems elaborate, the advantage is that the signal is now fully determined for any position of the scanning spot on the disc. The evaluation of the detector signal then merely asks for the multiplication of the known Fourier components with cosine and sine functions whose arguments are modified according to the spot position along the track and also perpendicular to the track (tracking error).

In the following paragraphs Hopkins's analysis will be reproduced. It will then be applied to the calculation of the frequency response of the optical read-out system in various cases (off-track movements, different pit geometries, imperfections of the optical light path).

2.3.1 *Outline of Hopkins's analysis*
The goal of the mathematical analysis is to find an expression for the detector signal. Starting with the light amplitude distribution emitted by the source one first calculates the amplitude distribution of the scanning spot in the focal plane of the scanning objective. Next the diffraction of light by the disc structure is studied. At this stage the supposed periodic structure of the disc greatly simplifies the analysis. Part of the light diffracted (or scattered) by the disc is captured by a detector (or by a set of detectors) with finite dimensions. The detector signal is finally expressed as a Fourier series on the basis of the radial and tangential periodicity.

Figure 2.14(a) shows the schematic light path of an optical read-out system. Although most optical disc systems are reflective systems we have shown here a transmission system in order to simplify the diagram. A point source S is focused by the scanning objective O_S onto the disc D. The objective is described by its complex pupil function $a(h_x, h_y)$ that accounts for

local absorption and phase changes (e.g. aberrations) introduced by the
objective. The focusing action of the objective is included by adding a
'spherical' phase factor to the pupil function. The real space coordinates
(h_x, h_y) are normalised with respect to the pupil radius R of the objective
according to

$$x = \frac{h_x}{R} \qquad y = \frac{h_y}{R}. \qquad (2.26)$$

The complex amplitude distribution in the disc plane is obtained by
applying Kirchhoff's diffraction integral (Goodman 1968) where the diffracting structure is the pupil rim (stop) of the objective lens. Applying the
diffraction integral we obtain the complex amplitude in a certain point P in
the disc plane by summing all optical disturbances arriving at this point P
from the diffracting aperture bounded by the lens stop. The optical
pathlength OPD from each point in the diffracting aperture to P determines
the phases of the disturbances in P. In figure 2.14(b) the spherical wave is
shown which leaves the objective aperture and propagates to the disc plane.

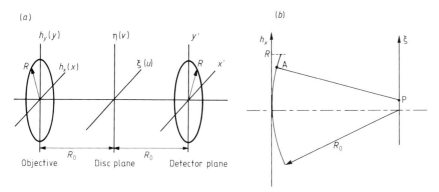

Figure 2.14 (a) The propagation of the light from the objective via the disc to the
detector plane. The real-space coordinates are indicated together with the reduced
coordinates (in brackets). (b) The optical pathlength (OPD) from a general point in
the diffracting aperture to a point P in the plane of the disc.

The complex amplitude $A(\xi, \eta)$ in the plane of the disc thus equals

$$A(\xi, \eta) \propto \int \int_{\substack{\text{diffracting} \\ \text{aperture}}} a(h_x, h_y) \exp\left(\frac{2\pi i}{\lambda} \text{OPD}(h_x, h_y; \xi, \eta)\right) dh_x \, dh_y. \qquad (2.27)$$

In a good approximation, the OPD from a point (h_x, h_y) in the diffracting aperture to a point $P(\xi, \eta)$ in the disc plane is equal to

$$\text{OPD} = AP = [(h_x - \xi)^2 + (h_y - \eta)^2 + R_0^2 - h_x^2 - h_y^2]^{1/2}$$

$$\approx R_0 + \frac{\xi^2 + \eta^2}{2R_0} - \frac{h_x\xi + h_y\eta}{R_0} \tag{2.28}$$

where R_0 denotes the distance from the aperture to the disc plane. Substitution of the expression for the OPD into equation (2.27) yields

$$A(\xi, \eta) \propto \exp\left(\frac{\pi i}{\lambda R_0}(\xi^2 + \eta^2)\right) \int\int_{\substack{\text{diffracting} \\ \text{aperture}}} a(h_x, h_y) \exp\left(-\frac{2\pi i}{\lambda R_0}(h_x\xi + h_y\eta)\right) dh_x\, dh_y \tag{2.29}$$

where the constant term R_0 has been dropped from equation (2.28).

When the disc plane coordinates (ξ, η) are scaled by the factor

$$\lambda \frac{R_0}{R} = \frac{\lambda}{\text{NA}} \tag{2.30}$$

according to

$$u = \frac{\xi}{(\lambda/\text{NA})} \qquad v = \frac{\eta}{(\lambda/\text{NA})} \tag{2.31}$$

equation (2.29) is transformed into

$$A(u, v) \propto \exp\left(\frac{\pi i(u^2 + v^2)\lambda}{R_0 \text{NA}^2}\right) \int\int_{\substack{\text{diffracting} \\ \text{aperture}}} a(x, y) \exp[-2\pi i(ux + vy)]\, dx\, dy \tag{2.32}$$

which is similar to a two-dimensional Fourier transform from the co-ordinates (x, y) to the system (u, v), apart from the phase factor in front of the integral. This phase factor shows that the Fourier transform is projected onto a sphere with radius R_0. We will drop this irrelevant phase factor in the following. The function $A(u, v)$ and its squared modulus $|A(u, v)|^2$ describe the amplitude and intensity distribution of the scanning spot. Although these quantities are not used explicitly in the analysis, we will later show some examples of scanning spot shapes in order to illustrate the effects of aberrations, for example.

The disc D can be attributed a complex reflection (or transmission) function $R(u, v)$ that comprises the local reflectivity and phase changes caused by the information on the disc. The function $R(u, v)$ is supposed to be periodic with periods p' and q' in the u- and v-direction. The real space periods thus equal

$$p = p'(\lambda/\text{NA}) \qquad q = q'(\lambda/\text{NA}). \tag{2.33}$$

Because of the periodicity of $R(u, v)$ we may write this function as a double Fourier series

$$R(u, v) = \sum_{m,n} R_{m,n} \exp\left[2\pi i\left(\frac{m}{p'}u + \frac{n}{q'}v\right)\right] \qquad (2.34)$$

with the coefficients $R_{m,n}$ given by

$$R_{m,n} = \frac{1}{p'q'} \int_{-p'/2}^{+p'/2} \int_{-q'/2}^{+q'/2} R(u, v) \exp\left[-2\pi i\left(\frac{m}{p'}u + \frac{n}{q'}v\right)\right] du\, dv. \quad (2.35)$$

The amplitude distribution $A'(u, v)$ in the plane of the disc immediately after reflection is given by a simple multiplication of the incident light distribution with the disc function $R(u, v)$

$$A'(u, v) = A(u, v)R(u, v). \qquad (2.36)$$

(In Chapter 3 a more detailed treatment of the diffraction of light by the disc will show that the simple relation of equation (2.36) is an approximation that gives satisfactory results but cannot explain all observed phenomena. When it is thought necessary the values of diffracted orders calculated according to the vectorial diffraction theory can be substituted here.)

A displacement of the disc over a distance (u_0, v_0) is accounted for by the transformation

$$u \to u - u_0$$
$$v \to v - v_0 \qquad (2.37)$$

and, in equation (2.34) for the disc reflection function, this introduces a phase factor

$$R(u - u_0, v - v_0) =$$

$$\sum_{m,n} \exp\left[-2\pi i\left(\frac{m}{p'}u_0 + \frac{n}{q'}v_0\right)\right] R_{m,n} \exp\left[2\pi i\left(\frac{m}{p'}u + \frac{n}{q'}v\right)\right] \quad (2.38)$$

according to the Fourier shift theorem.

The final step to be accomplished now is the light propagation from the disc plane to the detector plane and this step again resembles a Fourier transformation. Denoting the normalised detector coordinates by x' and y' (normalised with respect to the objective radius), the complex amplitude $A(x', y')$ is represented by

$$A(x', y') = \int\int_{\text{disc plane}} A'(u, v) \exp[-2\pi i(x'u + y'v)]\, du\, dv. \qquad (2.39)$$

The complex amplitude $A'(u, v)$ is the product of the incident amplitude $A(u, v)$ and the disc reflection function $R(u, v)$. According to the Fourier convolution theorem we write equation (2.39) as

$$A(x', y') = \int\int_{-\infty}^{+\infty} a(x, y) \, r(x - x', y - y') \, dx \, dy \qquad (2.40)$$

where $r(x, y)$ is the Fourier transform of the disc reflection function $R(u - u_0, v - v_0)$. Because of the periodicity of $R(u - u_0, v - v_0)$ (see equation (2.34)) its Fourier transform consists of a set of Dirac delta-functions multiplied with the complex values $R_{m,n}$ that are given by equation (2.35) and with the phase factor of equation (2.38). The substitution of $r(x, y)$ into equation (2.40) yields the expression

$$A(x', y') = \int\int_{-\infty}^{+\infty} a(x, y) \sum_{m,n} \exp\left[-2\pi i \left(\frac{m}{p'} u_0 + \frac{n}{q'} v_0\right)\right]$$

$$\times R_{m,n} \, \delta\left(x - x' - \frac{m}{p'}, y - y' - \frac{n}{q'}\right) dx \, dy \qquad (2.41)$$

$$= \sum_{m,n} \exp\left[-2\pi i \left(\frac{m}{p'} u_0 + \frac{n}{q'} v_0\right)\right] R_{m,n} \, a\left(x' + \frac{m}{p'}, y' + \frac{n}{q'}\right).$$

Equation (2.41) confirms some results which have been obtained in a more approximate way in §2.2.3. The light amplitude after diffraction by the disc consists of diffracted orders $R_{m,n}$ that partly overlap on the detector. The diffraction orders arise because of the supposed periodicity of the disc structure. The amplitude and phase distribution over each circular diffraction order are equal to the amplitude and phase distribution of the incident converging wave. There is an extra phaseshift added to each diffraction order and the value of this shift depends on the order number and on the relative position of the scanning spot and the disc. Figure 2.15 illustrates the diffraction pattern on the detector. The detector signal is proportional to the light intensity integrated over the detector area

$$S(u_0, v_0) = \int\int_{\substack{\text{detector} \\ \text{area}}} g(x', y') \, |A(x', y')|^2 \, dx' \, dy' \qquad (2.42)$$

where a detector sensitivity function $g(x', y')$ has been introduced (Velzel 1978) that can, for example, become locally positive and negative when signals from a detector array are added or subtracted.

The excursion u_0 in the track direction with

$$u_0 = \frac{\xi_0}{(\lambda/\text{NA})}$$

is a linear function of time when the disc rotates uniformly and this yields a basic temporal frequency ν_0

$$\xi_0 = st \qquad \nu_0 = \frac{s}{p'} \qquad (2.43)$$

the number of periods p' scanned per second. The temporal signal is generated by interference of the diffraction orders in overlapping regions (see figure 2.15). The phaseshift $\Delta\phi$ between diffracted orders $R_{m,n}$ and $R_{m',n'}$ is

$$\Delta\phi = -2\pi i(m' - m)\nu_0 t - 2\pi i(n' - n)\frac{\nu_0}{q'} + \arg(R_{m',n'}) - \arg(R_{m,n}). \qquad (2.44)$$

Equation (2.44) shows that harmonics of ν_0 arise when $\mu = (m' - m) > 1$. This harmonic $\mu\nu_0$ will be present in the detector signal when the overlapping region of two such orders still covers the detector.

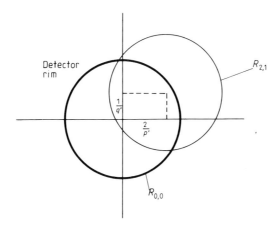

Figure 2.15 The light amplitude on the detector is the sum of the zeroth order $R_{0,0}$ and a certain number of diffracted orders. The order $R_{2,1}$ is shown here with its midpoint located at $(2/p', 1/p')$.

Hopkins has shown that by a proper arrangement of the interfering orders the detector signal is written

$$S(t, \nu_0) = \sum_{\mu} [A_{\mu}(\nu_0) \cos(2\pi\mu\nu_0 t) + B_{\mu}(\nu_0) \sin(2\pi\mu\nu_0 t)] \qquad (2.45)$$

and once the coefficients $A_{\mu}(\nu_0)$ and $B_{\mu}(\nu_0)$ have been evaluated, the detector signal is completely known at whatever time t and for whatever radial displacement (tracking error) ν_0.

From the values of the coefficients A and B one can derive certain properties of the detector signal. The coefficient $A_0(\nu_0)$ yields the variation of the DC content of the signal as a function of the tracking error. $A_1(\nu_0)$ and

$B_1(\nu_0)$ give the amplitude of the fundamental frequency of the signal and their ratio is a measure for the phaseshift in the detected signal due to an asymmetrical scanning spot, for example. The second harmonic content of the signal is given by $A_2(\nu_0)$ and $B_2(\nu_0)$ and gives some information on the effective duty-cycle of the pit and land portions on an optical disc.

2.3.2   Scanning spot and disc geometry

When calculating and comparing the performance of optical read-out systems it is important to be able to simulate the generally non-ideal play-back conditions. A very important parameter is the quality of the scanning objective and the correct focusing of the scanning spot on the optical disc. The different angular light distribution of certain types of lasers also influences the final detector signal. The manufacturing process of the optical disc itself leads to certain possible shapes of pits and to a certain spread of the dimensions of the pits during the mastering process. When the effects of the pit size variations on the detector signal are known one can try to minimise them in order to make the mastering and disc manu-facturing process as reliable as possible.

In this section it will be indicated how aberrations and amplitude variations of the light beam are taken into account. Next the most probable pit model and the corresponding dimensions of the pits are described.

Beam parameters and scanning spot geometry.   The complex pupil or transmission function $a(x, y)$ defines the amplitude over the cross section of the beam incident on the optical disc. Because of the circular shape of the beam it is useful to change to polar coordinates and one obtains

$$a(r, \phi) = t(r, \phi) \exp(2\pi i W(r, \phi)) \tag{2.46}$$

where $a(r, \phi)$ has been written as the product of an amplitude and a phase part. The function $t(r, \phi)$ defines the amplitude variation and would be equal to

$$t(r, \phi) = \exp\left(-\frac{\sigma}{2}r^2\right) \tag{2.47}$$

in the case of a Gaussian laser beam that has an intensity $\exp(-\sigma)$ at the rim of the objective. The phase part $W(r, \phi)$ describes the wavefront aberrations (in units of λ) of the incoming beam. In terms of the primary aberrations $W(r, \phi)$ is written

$$W(r, \phi) = W_{40}r^4 + W_{31}r^3 \cos(\phi - \phi_1)$$
$$+ W_{22}r^2 \cos^2(\phi - \phi_2) + W_{20}r^2 + W_{11}r \cos(\phi - \phi_1) \tag{2.48}$$

where W_{40} represents the spherical aberration, W_{31} the coma and W_{22} the astigmatic term of the wavefront aberration. Defocusing (W_{20}) and tilt (W_{11}) of the wavefront have also been added.

When numerical calculations are carried out, the function $a(r, \phi)$ is sampled at a sufficient number of points (typically a thousand) and deviations from circular symmetry, for example, as with semiconductor lasers, can easily be incorporated.

As was stated before, the analysis does not explicitly use the amplitude or the intensity of the scanning light spot. However, it is interesting to know the complex amplitude and intensity distribution of the scanning spot for some examples.

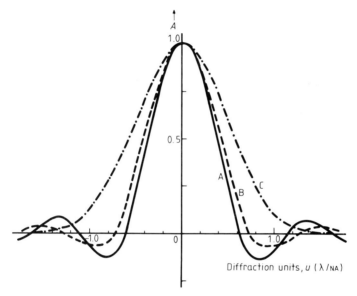

Figure 2.16 A plot of the light amplitude cross section of a scanning spot (no aberrations). The different curves apply to values of the Gaussian parameter σ equal to (A) 0, (B) 1.5 and (C) 8. The relative intensity at the rim of the aperture is respectively equal to 1.00, 0.22 and 0.0003. With increasing values of σ the central lobe of the scanning spot tends to broaden while the relative intensity of the luminous rings of the diffraction spot becomes less. At a σ value of 8.0 the aperture rim is hardly illuminated by the incoming beam and the diffraction spot is virtually Gaussian without any diffraction rings.

In figure 2.16 the complex amplitude of an aberration-free scanning spot is shown for different values of the Gaussian parameter σ. The horizontal scale is in 'diffraction units' equal to λ/NA. For a video-disc player ($\text{NA} = 0.40$) equipped with a HeNe laser, this quantity is equal to 1.6 μm.

Figure 2.17 shows a three-dimensional plot of the intensity of an aberration-free scanning spot (figure 2.17(a)) and some aberrated spots (figures 2.17(b)–2.17(d)).

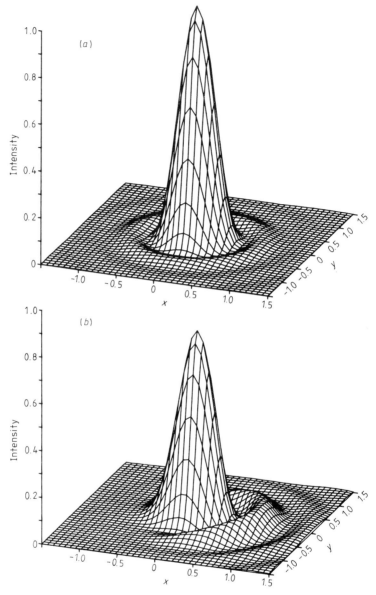

Figure 2.17 A three-dimensional plot of the intensity of the scanning spot. The x and y values are expressed in diffraction units of magnitude λ/NA. In the case of a Compact Disc player ($\lambda = 800$ nm and $\mathrm{NA} = 0.45$) one diffraction unit equals $1.78~\mu\mathrm{m}$. (a) The focused wave is completely free of aberrations and the plotted pattern is the Airy intensity pattern. The intensity on axis is normalised to 1. (b) The incoming wave suffers from comatic aberration and is just 'diffraction limited'. The intensity on axis is 0.80. (c) The incoming wave is astigmatic and is focused on

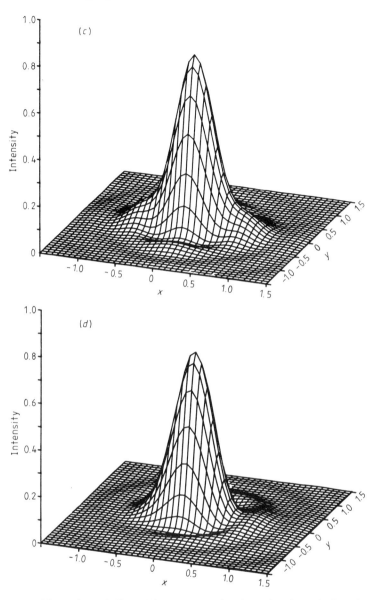

one of its astigmatic lines. The amount of astigmatism is such that the diffraction spot could be again just 'diffraction limited'. By focusing on an astigmatic line the intensity on axis of the spot drops to 0.70. (*d*) The incoming wave shows several residual aberrations (see figure 2.29) and is one focal depth out of focus. The axial intensity is 0.64. Such a deterioration of the scanning spot can occur accidentally during play-back.

The effect of aberrations on the scanning spot intensity is to remove light power from the central lobe of the spot to the bright rings. When the aberrations are sufficiently small there exists a simple relationship between the central peak intensity (also called Strehl-intensity) and the variance V_W of the wavefront aberration as it is measured over the pupil cross section of the objective (Maréchal 1947). Defining V_W by

$$V_W = \overline{W^2} - (\overline{W})^2$$

the normalised axial intensity of the scanning spot equals

$$I_0 = 1 - 4\pi^2 V_W$$

where V_W is expressed in units of λ^2.

When there are no aberrations, the scanning spot does not have the infinitely small size predicted by the ray optics approximation. The still finite scanning spot is commonly called diffraction-limited, the phenomenon of diffraction being the reason for its size. A scanning spot is 'just' diffraction-limited when on top of the diffraction effects there are aberrations of a magnitude such that the on-axis intensity I_0 has dropped to 0.8 or

$$4\pi^2 V_W = 0.2 \rightarrow V_W = 0.005 \, \lambda^2. \tag{2.49}$$

The square root of V_W is the root mean square (RMS) value of the wavefront aberration W (or OPD) and its value should not exceed

$$\text{OPD}_{\text{RMS}} < (0.005 \, \lambda^2)^{1/2} = 0.07 \, \lambda. \tag{2.50}$$

Optical disc players will inevitably show aberrations due to the fairly high power objectives that have to be used (NA $\geqslant$ 0.40) but the RMS value of the aberrations should definitely be smaller than this diffraction limit of 0.07 λ. During play-back the scanning spot is further degraded due to defocusing and disc imperfections. When the initial aberrations show an RMS value that is already close to the diffraction limit the operation of the disc player is likely to become unreliable.

Disc geometry.   Figure 2.18 shows an electron micrograph of the surface of a digital audio disc with pits of varying length. The line diagram shows a pit of the form used in the following numerical model. A pit is centred in its cell with dimensions $p \times q$ and has a length of β measured at the disc surface. The width of the pit equals γ. The end sections of the pits are circular ($\gamma/2 = \delta/2$) or ellipsoidal with an eccentricity $\varepsilon = \delta/\gamma$. A cross section of a pit shows the geometrical depth d of the pit and the slope angle θ of the pit walls. The angle θ will be variable over the circumference of the pit when the pit ends are not circular. The case of a pure relief structure can be satisfactorily treated with this model. Burnt holes and structures due to phase transitions in a recording material are more complicated. They have to be described by a combined amplitude and phase profile of the recorded

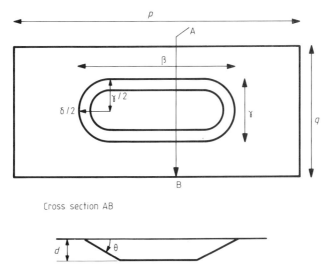

Cross section AB

Figure 2.18 The photograph shows a scanning electron microscope picture of an optical disc with digital music information on it (Compact Disc). The diagram shows a model of the depressions on an optical disc as used in the numerical model. Scale: one white line segment represents 1 μm.

effect and one generally requires a knowledge of the changes in the complex refractive index of the material.

In the simplest disc model the neighbouring tracks are copies of the central track although the pits may be shifted in position. In the more complicated disc model used for cross-talk calculations, the neighbouring tracks contain completely different frequencies.

2.3.3. Diffracted orders

Generally the amplitude and phase of the diffracted orders $R_{m,n}$ is evaluated numerically with the aid of equation (2.35). When the depressions are modelled according to figure 2.19 with a rectangular shape and uniform depth, calculation of the values of $R_{m,n}$ can be carried out analytically. The optical depth of the pits (read-out in reflection through a substrate with refractive index n) is

$$\phi = 4\pi n \frac{d}{\lambda}$$

where λ is the wavelength of the light in air. The zeroth order now equals

$$R_{0,0} = 1 + [\exp(i\phi) - 1] \frac{\beta}{p} \frac{\gamma}{q} \qquad (2.51)$$

and the order with order number m in the track direction (tangential direction) and order number n in the perpendicular (radial) direction is given by

$$R_{m,n} = [\exp(i\phi) - 1] \frac{\beta}{p} \frac{\gamma}{q} \operatorname{sinc}\left(\frac{\pi m \beta}{p}\right) \operatorname{sinc}\left(\frac{\pi n \gamma}{q}\right) \qquad (2.52)$$

where the sinc(x) function is defined by $\sin(x)/x$. The phase difference ψ_{10}

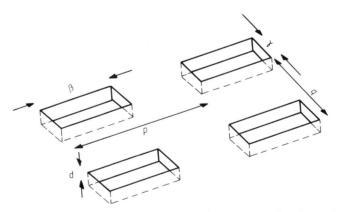

Figure 2.19 A simple disc model based on rectangular depressions with vertical walls and uniform depth. For an analysis of the read-out of optical discs according to this model the reader is referred to Korpel (1978).

between, for example, the first radial order $R_{0,1}$ and the zeroth order $R_{0,0}$ is

$$\psi_{10} = \arg(R_{0,1}) - \arg(R_{0,0})$$

and this is evaluated to be equal to

$$\psi_{10} = \pi - \tan^{-1}\left(\frac{\cot(\phi/2)}{1 - 2\beta\gamma/pq}\right). \qquad (2.53)$$

In figure 2.20 the value of ψ_{10} is depicted as a function of the phase depth ϕ of the depressions. The parameter S given by

$$S = \frac{\beta}{p}\frac{\gamma}{q}$$

and equal to the relative modulated area of the disc, is 0.167, 0.333 and 0.500. The first value applies to a pit structure with a tangential duty cycle β/p of 0.5 and a radial duty cycle of 0.33. The second situation could apply to a continuous track ($\beta/p = 1$) with a value of $\gamma/q = 1/3$ and the last situation to a continuous track with a track width equal to half the track spacing. Note that in this extreme case the angle ψ_{10} is no longer a monotonically increasing function of ϕ but takes on the discrete values $\pi/2$, $3\pi/2$ etc independently of the ϕ value.

A more realistic pit model is depicted in figure 2.18. Calculations with this model have to be carried out numerically. In figure 2.21 the angle ψ_{10} is shown not as a function of the phase depth ϕ but as a function of the

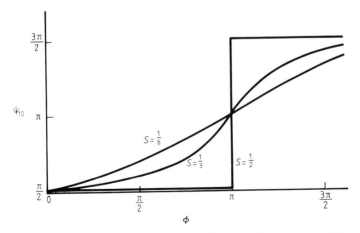

Figure 2.20 The phase difference ψ_{10} between the zeroth and first orders as a function of the phase depth ϕ of the depressions. The parameter S applies to the relative area that is occupied by the depressions on an optical disc.

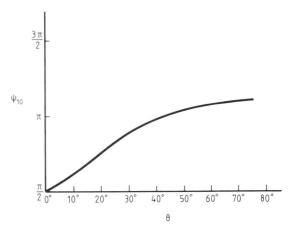

Figure 2.21 The phase difference ψ_{10} between the zeroth and first diffracted orders as a function of the inclination of the pit walls and with a fixed maximum depth of the depressions equal to 130 nm ($\lambda = 633$ nm and the refractive index of the disc substrate is 1.50).

sloping wall angle θ. An increasing effective depth is obtained in the mastering process (see Chapter 5) by making the pit walls steeper. In comparison with figure 2.20, the angle ψ_{10} increases more gradually and finally reaches the limit given by the maximum depth of the pits. In §2.2.3 it was explained how the value of ψ_{10} determines the optimum detection method in the read-out system (PP or CA detection).

2.3.4. Numerical results

In this section some system parameters are varied and their influence on the AC and DC detector signal will be calculated. The DC signal is normalised with respect to the signal obtained from a disc without any modulation on it. For the AC signal we either show its variation over a signal period or we plot the amplitude of its fundamental frequency. This latter quantity is normalised with respect to an arbitrarily chosen standard frequency that delivers a sufficiently sinusoidal signal at read-out. This reference frequency ν_R is chosen 1/6 of the cut-off frequency ν_C of the optical disc system.

For the LaserVision system the typical values of ν_C and ν_R are

$$\nu_C = 2\frac{NA}{\lambda} s = 11.6 \text{ MHz}$$
$$\nu_R = 2 \text{ MHz}$$

(2.54)

where $\lambda = 633$ nm, NA $= 0.40$ and $s = 9.20 \text{ m s}^{-1}$. For the Compact Disc system

$$\nu_C = 2\frac{NA}{\lambda}s = 1.40 \text{ MHz}$$
$$\nu_R = 230 \text{ kHz} \tag{2.55}$$

where $\lambda = 790$ nm, $NA = 0.45$ and $s = 1.25$ ms^{-1}.

The Gaussian aperture factor σ. In equation (2.47) the Gaussian amplitude distribution over the pupil of the objective was specified by a constant σ according to

$$t(r, \phi) = \exp\left(-\frac{\sigma}{2}r^2\right)$$

where r is the normalised pupil radius. The light intensity at the rim is $\exp(-\sigma)$ and it is easily shown that the light power that is lost outside the pupil is also equal to $\exp(-\sigma)$. An appreciable drop-off of light intensity at the pupil rim causes a broadening of the scanning spot (see figure 2.16) and a poor signal transfer at the higher frequency side, but the fraction of the total laser power captured by the objective is larger. The trade-off between these two effects is shown in figures 2.22(a) and 2.22(b). In figure 2.22(a) the signals are normalised with respect to the total laser power and in figure 2.22(b) with respect to the laser power captured by the objective which is the normal procedure. The values plotted in figure 2.22(a) are proportional to the signal amplitude, those in figure 2.22(b) to the modulation depth. The optimum choice is determined by signal-to-noise considerations. A good compromise between signal strength and frequency roll-off has been a σ value of 1.5, which corresponds to an intensity at the pupil rim of 0.22.

The situation described above applies to a HeNe laser used in video-disc players. A semiconductor laser as used in the Compact Disc system has a more complicated radiation profile. In order to get a sufficiently uniform pupil illumination quite a lot of light power gets lost but the required light level in this system is significantly lower than in a video-disc system.

The ideal frequency response. With the 0 dB level given by the response at the reference frequency ν_R, we now plot the frequency response given by an ideal optical system. In the case of a video-disc system the interesting frequency region is situated around the FM carrier (see Chapter 7). This carrier is swept from 7.1 to 7.9 MHz (PAL system). Figure 2.23 shows four situations with different parameter values and rather drastic differences appear. A higher NA improves the frequency response but this implies a somewhat more sensitive optical read-out system. For instance the focal depth of the scanning spot decreases quadratically with the NA of the reading beam. The aberrations of an objective increase with even higher

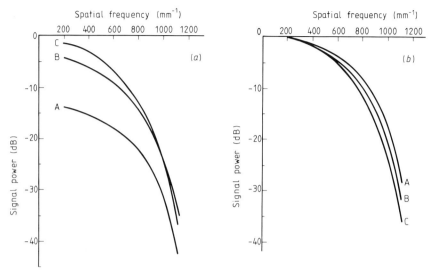

Figure 2.22 The signal power as a function of the average spatial frequency on the disc. The signal power at a certain spatial frequency is obtained by taking the ratio of the signal amplitude at that spatial frequency and the amplitude of the signal at the reference frequency and then squaring this quantity. (*a*) The signal power is normalised with the total available laser power. Curve A applies to a fairly uniform amplitude over the beam cross section ($\sigma = 0.25$) corresponding to an important loss in useful laser power captured by the objective. The values of σ are 1.00 and 2.00 for curves B and C respectively. (*b*) The signal power is now normalised with the signal at a spatial frequency of approximately 200 mm^{-1} (reference frequency). Curve A, $\sigma = 0.25$; Curve B, $\sigma = 1.00$; Curve C, $\sigma = 2.00$.

powers of the NA which means that the manufacturing of these objectives becomes more critical. A more uniform pupil illumination ($\sigma = 0.5$) equally improves the frequency response but at the cost of less signal amplitude and consequently a more complicated detection circuit. It is the trade-off between cost factors, reliability etc that will decide on a certain design.

The non-ideal frequency response.   In a practical situation the scanning spot is more or less degraded by stationary imperfections of the optics (e.g. aberrations of the objective) and by time dependent effects like defocusing, disc tilt and local imperfections of the disc substrate. The degraded spot causes a drop in frequency response. Accompanying effects may be bad functioning of the focus and radial servo systems and this may lead to track jump, for example.

The consequences of spot degradation on the television image may be a smaller signal-to-noise ratio or the appearance of drop-outs due to the smaller modulation depth of the signal. In a Compact Disc player the effect

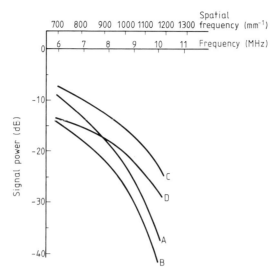

Figure 2.23 The influence of the Gaussian parameter σ and the numerical aperture NA on the frequency response of the optical read-out. The response of curve C at a frequency of 200 mm^{-1} has been chosen as the 0 dB level. The wavelength of the light is 633 nm. In figures 2.24 to 2.30 the numerical aperture of the scanning objective is 0.40. The curve parameters are: A, $\sigma = 1.5$, NA = 0.40, $\nu_C = 11.6$ MHz; B, $\sigma = 0.5$, NA = 0.40, $\nu_C = 11.6$ MHz; C, $\sigma = 1.5$, NA = 0.45, $\nu_C = 13.1$ MHz; D, $\sigma = 0.5$, NA = 0.45, $\nu_C = 13.1$ MHz.

of spot degradation is less reliable discrimination on the 0 and 1 signal levels. This may lead to an increased bit error rate (BER).

Figures 2.24–2.30 show the change in frequency response when typical wavefront errors (aberrations) are present. The meaning of the different aberration coefficients has already been described (p. 30).

In figure 2.24 the wavefront error $W = W_{20}r^2$ yields an axial (in depth) displacement Δz of the scanning spot equal to

$$\Delta z = 2 \frac{W_{20}\lambda}{(\text{NA})^2} \,. \tag{2.56}$$

The focal depth Δz_f is determined by the condition $|W_{20}| = 0.25$ which leads to a scanning spot quality that is 'just' diffraction-limited. In an optical disc system the focal depth is typically 2 μm and the focus servo system should keep the scanning spot at least to within this distance from the disc surface. The lower frequency response due to defocusing is especially apparent at the medium frequencies, halfway to the cut-off frequency of the optical system. The decrease in frequency response is due to a non-uniform interference between zeroth and first diffracted orders. The

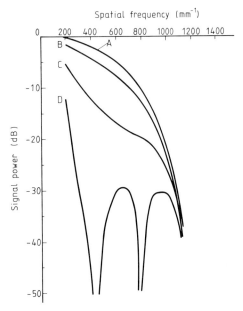

Figure 2.24 The frequency response in the presence of different amounts of defocusing. A: $W_{20} = 0$; RMS OPD $= 0.00\lambda$. B: $W_{20} = 0.25$; RMS OPD $= 0.07\lambda$. C: $W_{20} = 0.50$; RMS OPD $= 0.14\lambda$. D: $W_{20} = 0.75$; RMS OPD $= 0.21\lambda$.

local phase difference between two shifted orders in a defocused situation is deduced from the expressions on p. 20 when the influence of the non-uniform (quadratic) wavefront is added

$$\Delta\phi(x', y', t) = \psi_{10} + 2\pi vt + 2\pi W_{1,0}(x', y') - 2\pi W_{0,0}(x', y')$$
$$= \psi_{10} + 2\pi vt + 2\pi W_{20}[(x' - x_0')^2 + y'^2]$$
$$- 2\pi W_{20}(x'^2 + y'^2)$$
$$= \psi_{10} + 2\pi vt + 2\pi W_{20}x_0'^2 - 4\pi W_{20}x_0'x' \qquad (2.57)$$

and this phase difference is a linear function of the coordinate x'. The maximum variation $\Delta\phi$ over the overlapping region is given by the width $|\Delta x'|$ in the x' direction and equals (figure 2.25)

$$|\Delta\phi_{max}| = 4\pi W_{20}x_0' |\Delta x'|$$
$$= 4\pi W_{20}x_0'(2 - x_0'). \qquad (2.58)$$

The maximum phase excursion is found at the value $x_0' = 1$ which corresponds to half the cut-off frequency. The varying phase difference $\Delta\phi(x', y')$ is the reason for the interference fringes that appear in the overlapping region; these are straight fringes in the case of pure defocusing. A value of $\Delta\phi_{max} = 2\pi$ causes an almost perfect averaging out of the signal in the overlapping region and the substitution of this value in equation (2.58) gives ($x_0' = 1$)

$$\Delta\phi_{max} = 2\pi = 4\pi W_{20}$$

$$W_{20} = 0.50 \tag{2.59}$$

or a defocusing of two focal depths.

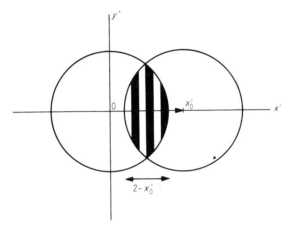

Figure 2.25 The intensity variation (a pattern of straight lines) in a region of overlap on the detector in the case of a defocused scanning spot.

The fringe pattern behaves as a travelling wave (see equation (2.57)) and the direction of motion in the detector plane is reversed when the defocusing changes sign.

In figure 2.26 spherical aberration of the scanning spot is either due to the objective (thicknesses, spacings or refractive indices of the lenses are not correct) or due to the disc when its thickness does not have the nominal value.

The spherical aberration introduced by a plane parallel plate that is traversed by a converging beam with a numerical aperture NA is given by

$$W_{40} = \frac{(n^2 - 1)}{8n^3} d(\text{NA})^4 \tag{2.60}$$

where d is the thickness of the plate and n its refractive index. In an optical disc system the far from negligible spherical aberration introduced by the disc substrate is cancelled by the objective that has been designed to

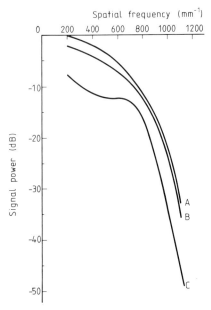

Figure 2.26 The frequency response in the presence of different amounts of spherical aberration of the scanning spot. In each situation the best focus position has been chosen by a defocusing $W_{20} = -W_{40}$. A: $W_{40} = 0.0$; RMS OPD $= 0.00\ \lambda$. B: $W_{40} = 1.0$; RMS OPD $= 0.07\ \lambda$. C: $W_{40} = 2.0$; RMS OPD $= 0.14\ \lambda$.

introduce the same amount of spherical aberration with opposite sign. In practice problems arise when the disc thickness deviates from its standardised value (Δd). A numerical example shows the steep influence of the NA value of the optics.

	d(mm)	n	$\lambda(\mu m)$	NA	W_{40}	RMS OPD(λ)
Laser Vision	0.1	1.50	0.63	0.40	0.18	0.013
Compact Disc	0.1	1.56	0.78	0.45	0.24	0.017
Data Disc	0.1	1.51	0.78	0.55	0.54	0.038

The table shows that an increase of 30% in the numerical aperture yields tolerances that are three times tighter for the disc thickness. For a more professional application like the optical data disc this is acceptable.

In figure 2.27 coma may be due to the objective (decentred or tilted lenses) but it can also be introduced by a tilted disc at read-out. The expression for W_{31} due to disc tilt is

$$W_{31} = \frac{(n^2 - 1)}{2n^3} d(\text{NA})^3 \alpha \qquad (2.61)$$

where α is the disc tilt in radians and d the disc thickness. When $d = 1.2$ mm, $\lambda = 633$ nm and NA is 0.40 (LaserVision), the value of W_{31} is 0.2 for a disc tilt of 0.5 degrees. In figure 2.27 the comatic error is oriented in the track direction (curve D) and perpendicular to it (curve C). In the first case the influence on the frequency response is clearly visible but in the second case its influence is hardly noticeable. The coma lobe of the scanning spot (see figure 2.17) is now directed towards the neighbouring tracks and generates cross-talk. This phenomenon will be treated in §2.4.

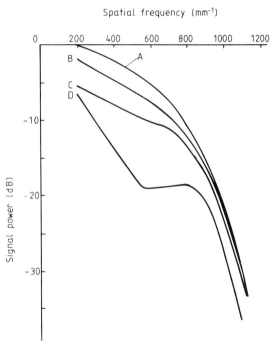

Figure 2.27 The frequency response in the presence of different amounts of coma of the scanning spot. The coma lobe precedes the scanning spot in the track direction. A: $W_{31} = 0.00$; RMS OPD $= 0.00\,\lambda$. B: $W_{31} = 0.63$; RMS OPD $= 0.07\,\lambda$. C and D: $W_{31} = 1.26$; RMS OPD $= 0.14\,\lambda$.

An astigmatic focused wave shows two axially displaced focal lines whose directions are perpendicular to each other. In between these two focal lines the 'best focus' or 'circle of least confusion' is situated. Astigmatism can be made inoffensive when reading one-dimensional structures by focusing the focal line parallel to the structure. On optical discs we are dealing with two-dimensional structures and an optimum read-out of both main directions is not possible in the presence of astigmatism. In figure 2.28, curves

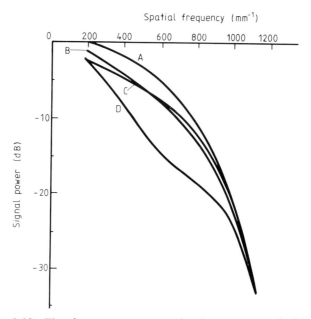

Figure 2.28 The frequency response in the presence of different amounts of astigmatism of the scanning spot. The effect of astigmatism is not very harmful when the best focus position is chosen or when the astigmatic line is perpendicular to the track (curves B and C). When the astigmatic line parallel to the tracks is focused on the disc (curve D) a very serious degradation of the response is observed. $W_{22} = 0.35$, RMS OPD = 0.07 λ.

B and C correspond to the best focus position and to the situation with the focal line perpendicular to the tracks. In this case the tracks are best resolved by the scanning spot.

A realistic mixture of aberrations that may occur during play-back of a disc is shown in the table below.

	Origin	λ	RMS OPD(λ)
W_{40}	Objective	0.30	0.020
W_{40}	Disc $\Delta d = 0.05$ mm	0.24	0.017
W_{31}	Disc tilt $\alpha = 0.5°$	0.20	0.022
W_{22}	Laser residual astigmatism	0.05	0.008
W_{22}	Objective field astigmatism	0.15	0.025
		Best focus	0.058

The frequency response with this scanning spot quality is shown in figure 2.29 (curve B). During play-back of the disc a defocusing Δz of the order of 2 μm may occur ($W_{20} = 0.25$) and curve C shows the frequency response in this defocused situation. Compared with curve C of figure 2.24 ($W_{20} = 0.5$), they are almost identical in the higher frequency region. This means that the presence of aberrations tightens the tolerance on defocusing during play-back and in the example considered here, this tolerance is reduced by one focal depth. In practice, one aims at an aberration level of 0.05 λ RMS OPD at most in the beam that converges to the disc. Disc imperfections and small defocusing yield a total OPD of 0.07 to 0.10 λ, which corresponds to the 'just' diffraction-limited situation. A remedy against larger defocusing or other defects is then found by electronic manipulations of the signal (drop-out correction in video signals or error correction in digital signals).

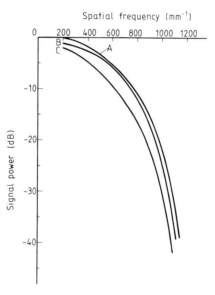

Figure 2.29 The frequency response in the presence of several residual aberrations of the incident wave (curve B). In curve C an extra defocusing of one focal depth has been added, a situation that can occur accidentally in practice.

We conclude this discussion with a graph of the DC content of the signal for various tracking errors v_0. The DC content of the detector signal is proportional to the average light level that is reflected by the disc and is obtained by low-pass filtering the detector signal. The variation of the DC content as a function of tracking is often used for deriving a tracking error signal. In figure 2.30 the top–top variation of the DC content of the signal is shown as a function of the track spacing. The standard track spacing is approximately 1.6 μm (equal to a spatial frequency of 600 mm^{-1}) and this value is close to half the cut-off frequency of the optical system. Much closer packing of tracks (e.g. 1.2 μm) gives an unreliable tracking error signal due to the small modulation depth and also tightens disc fabrication tolerances. Cross-talk becomes equally unacceptable when the radial density is pushed that far.

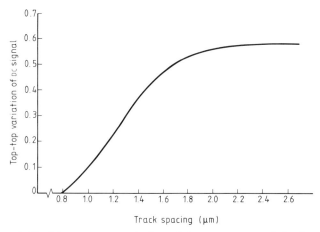

Figure 2.30   The top–top variation of the DC content of the detector signal when the scanning spot is crossing the information tracks.

2.4   Signal quality

In this section we consider the signal-to-noise ratio and three other effects that determine the signal quality.

Firstly the amplitude of cross-talk is calculated as a function of parameters such as scanning spot quality, track spacing, amplitude or phase structures etc. It is on video discs that cross-talk is most harmful. A second phenomenon typical of video discs is the generation of intermodulation products between the main carrier of the signal and the sound sub-carriers. These products may be generated when recording and development of the master disc are off-optimum (see Chapter 5). The final read-out step introduces additional non-linearity. It will be indicated which pit geometry and read-out conditions are likely to generate a minimum of intermodulation.

Finally a phenomenon is treated which is typical for the read-out of digital signals, intersymbol interference (ISI). ISI is due to a not infinitely small (spatial) impulse response of a system. For an optical system, the impulse response (the scanning spot) is not point-like but finite because of diffraction. Moreover, there is the non-linearity of the optical system inherent to the squaring operation of the detector (complex amplitude → intensity). Both effects are taken into account for the calculation of the location of the transitions in a digital signal.

2.4.1 Cross-talk

From the light intensity distribution of the scanning spot (figure 2.17) it can be seen that a small amount of light impinges on neighbouring tracks and will pick up spurious, unwanted signals from these tracks (cross-talk). The amplitude distribution of the scanning spot (see, for example, figure 2.16) is more adequate to describe cross-talk because the spurious signal is generated by the interference of the light amplitude incident on the neighbouring track with the main zeroth order of the light. This interference effect greatly enhances the cross-talk.

When two images (or video pictures) are mixed the effect is hardly noticeable to the eye if the intensity of one image is less than 1% of the intensity of the other. The cross-talk level in a (demodulated) analog video signal should thus be − 40 dB with respect to the maximum intensity white level of that signal. Translated to the modulated signal on the video disc, this leads to an acceptable cross-talk level of − 34 dB with respect to the main carrier of the FM modulated signal. With a diffraction-limited scanning spot it is easy to remain below this cross-talk limit (at the standard track spacing of 1.7 μm), but an aberrated scanning spot immediately causes an increase in cross-talk. A comatic spot with the coma flare directed towards a neighbouring track is the worst case. The coma may be introduced by a tilt of the optical disc with respect to the optical axis of the objective. Cross-talk becomes visible on the television screen as moiré patterns that incessantly move and change their orientation. No simple disc model exists for calculations that give reliable quantitative results for cross-talk, which is why Hopkins's analysis is extended to treat the cross-talk problem (Hopkins 1979).

A sequence of five tracks is chosen, each of which contains a different frequency. This sequence then is formally repeated over the disc in order to generate a periodicity in the radial direction (figure 2.31). Each track contains a different spatial frequency and one calculates the frequency content of the detector signal for various radial positions of the scanning spot. On a video disc the frequencies in neighbouring tracks are close together and are situated within the sweep range of the main FM carrier. The greatest difference arises when a track portion containing a line synchronisation pulse is adjacent to a track portion carrying a white picture line, a situation that may occur on video discs which are scanned with constant linear velocity (see Chapter 7). The FM carrier frequencies then equal $\nu_1 = 6.9$ MHz and $\nu_2 = 7.9$ MHz which correspond to spatial frequencies of 800 and 920 mm^{-1} respectively at a scanning velocity of 8.6 m s^{-1}.

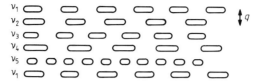

Figure 2.31 The disc model that is used for cross-talk calculations. Each track contains a different spatial frequency (ν_1 to ν_5) and this sequence of five tracks is repeated in the radial direction. The signal power at a certain frequency ν_1 is virtually uninfluenced by the tracks with an identical frequency that are five track distances away.

In figure 2.32(a) the detected power at the frequencies ν_1 and ν_2 is shown for a varying radial position ν_0 of the scanning spot. The ideal aberration-free scanning spot yields cross-talk levels that are very low (<40 dB). In practice residual aberrations of the objective and also disc tilt, that

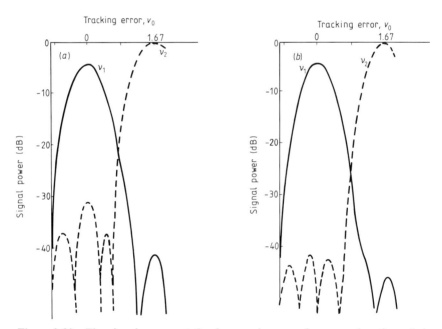

Figure 2.32 The signal power at the frequencies ν_1 and ν_2 as a function of the radial position ν_0. Cross-talk is defined as the ratio of the signal power at a spurious frequency (generated by a neighbouring track) and the signal power at the frequency that is originated by the scanned track. In order to obtain a practical value the tracking error ν_0 is not taken exactly equal to 0 but a residual error of 0.2 μm is accounted for. The aberrations of the scanning spot are those from figure 2.29 with a defocusing of 2 μm added to them. (a) NA $= 0.40$; (b) NA $= 0.45$.

introduces coma, are encountered. A value for the comatic coefficient W_{31} of 0.2 seems a reasonable value, yielding an RMS OPD of the comatic wave-front equal to 0.022 λ. The other aberrations are those from figure 2.29 with a small defocusing of half a focal depth ($W_{20} = 1/8$) superimposed on them. The track spacing equals 1.67 μm and the numerical aperture is 0.40. The cross-talk should be a function of the scanning spot dimensions and in figure 2.32(b) the numerical aperture has been raised to 0.45.

The width of the depressions on a video disc usually lie between 0.5 and 0.7 μm because pits that are too narrow or too wide would significantly lower the AC signal. However, on a digital data disc with burnt holes (or other pure 'amplitude' effects), the width (or radius) of the holes should preferably be as large as the scanning spot itself in order to obtain a maximum signal. Together with the hole diameter the cross-talk is likely to increase and this is illustrated in figure 2.33(a) and 2.33(b) where the recorded holes (spaced 2 μm apart) have diameters of 1.0 and 1.5 μm and the track spacing is 1.67 μm.

Cross-talk levels also depend on the average spatial frequency of the information and have a tendency to increase with spatial frequency. This

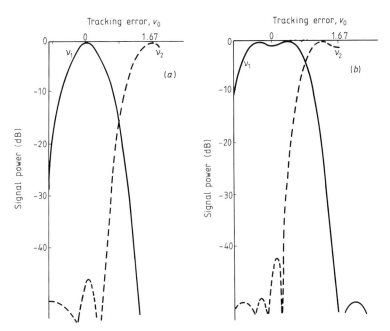

Figure 2.33 The signal power at the frequencies ν_1 and ν_2 when the disc pattern consists of burnt holes (amplitude pattern). The numerical aperture is 0.45. (a) The hole diameter is 1.0 μm; (b) the hole diameter is 1.5 μm.

is understood by noticing that at high spatial frequencies the overlapping region of zeroth and first orders becomes narrower first in the tangential direction, which of course explains the signal drop. However, at high spatial frequencies a significant narrowing of the overlapping region occurs, also in the radial direction, and this means that the effective detector area is becoming smaller in the radial direction. As was shown in §2.2.2, a small detection area is equivalent to a more coherent read-out of the information and, as a consequence, small signals interfering with a strong coherent background become more pronounced.

In figure 2.34 the calculated cross-talk level is shown as a function of the track spacing for two different scanning velocities (8.6 and 9.5 m s^{-1}) The calculations have been carried out supposing a worst case disc tilt of 1°. Depending on the required cross-talk level one chooses that combination of track spacing and scanning velocity that yields the smallest product and thus the largest spatial density and playing time. For relatively small track spacings it is useful to increase the scanning velocity in order to obtain a net gain in playing time. When a cross-talk level of, for example, -30 dB is permitted it is advantageous to choose a scanning velocity of 9.5 m s^{-1} and a track spacing equal to 1.4 μm instead of 8.6 m s^{-1} combined with 1.65 μm track spacing. Apart from a small gain in playing time this choice offers a better signal transfer owing to the lower spatial frequencies involved. When the cross-talk requirements are severe (< -35 dB) a large track spacing is necessary and the scanning speed is no longer a sensitive parameter.

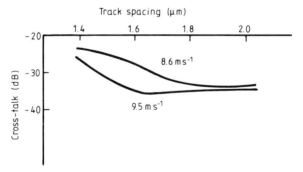

Figure 2.34 The cross-talk level as a function of the track spacing at different scanning velocities, *s*.

All the calculations described above have been verified experimentally and theory and experiment generally were in very good agreement.

Methods have been proposed for decreasing the track spacing while still having acceptable cross-talk levels. By alternating the depth of neighbouring tracks, it is possible to vary the angle ψ_{10} from track to track by approximately $90°$ (figure 2.35(a)). Each track now is read in its optimum way, e.g. either in CA or PP and the neighbouring track is hardly 'seen' in this way because its phase angle ψ_{10} is $90°$ out of phase (Braat 1983a). Central aperture and push–pull readings have a rather different frequency response (see figure 2.12) and a refinement of the method consists in not applying $0°$ (CA) or $180°$ (PP) phaseshifts between the two detector halves but values of $+90°$ and $-90°$. In this way the suppression of cross-talk is equally effective while the frequency responses of the two read-out modes are now equalised. Experiments have revealed that a reduction of the track spacing by a factor of almost two (1.67 μm to 0.90 μm) is feasible in this way.

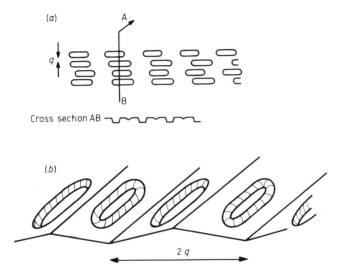

Figure 2.35 Two methods that aim at a reduction of the cross-talk between tracks or at a track spacing reduction at constant cross-talk level. (a) The average depth of the pits is changed from track to track. (b) The information is written on the slopes of a V-grooved substrate.

Another proposal is to record the information on both slopes of a V-grooved spiral track (figure 2.35(b)) with the normal track spacing (Nagashima 1983). The method is effective when the detector aperture is somewhat larger than the aperture of the scanning objective and when the proper detector sections are used for reading the positive or negative slope of the V-grooved substrate.

2.4.2. *Intermodulation*
The main part of the spectral band of a video signal is occupied by the luminance signal. The colour and sound signals are situated in the upper

part of the band. In the FM modulated signal that is recorded on the disc, the colour band is not separated from the luminance signal. However, the two audio channels are first stripped from the video signal, modulated on special sub-carriers and then added to the FM modulated main carrier. In figure 2.36(a) the time variation of this composite signal (Vaanholt 1982) is shown. After a clipping operation the signal at a frequency ν_1 (main carrier) shows pulse-length modulation owing to the relatively slow amplitude variation of the sub-carriers (average frequency ν_2). De Haan and Velzel (1977) have treated the effect of a clipping operation on the sum of two sinusoidal frequencies. The mixing of two frequencies ν_1 and ν_2 via a limiter yields pulses of varying length (pulse length modulation) and the spectrum of such a limited signal contains intermodulation products. The frequencies $\nu_1 \pm 2\nu_2$ are inevitably present in the spectrum while the frequencies $\nu_1 \pm \nu_2$ are only there when the clipping level of the limiter is not equal to the average (DC) level of the signal. In this case an asymmetry of the read-out signal is observed, equivalent to a duty-cycle not equal to 0.50.

The optical read-out step is certainly not comparable with a clipping operation but non-linearities are likely to occur because of the squaring action of the detector. However, the occurrence of intermodulation pro-

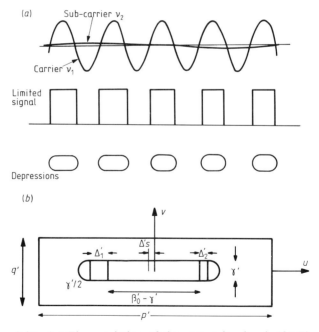

Figure 2.36 (a) Time variation of the composite signal. (b) The pit model is a case of a duty-cycle modulation of the signal. An asymmetrical lengthening (or contraction) of the pits is observed.

ducts at the frequencies $\nu_1 \pm \nu_2$ cannot be easily associated with the notion of asymmetry or duty-cycle of the depressions along the information track because the average geometrical duty-cycle of two-dimensional depressions is not well defined. In addition to this uncertainty, the optical edge response is shifted in position with respect to the geometrical edge as was shown in §2.2.2 for a black and white step as an object.

The approach adopted here is to calculate the position and shape of a general (mth) depression in the track of a master disc (on the final pressed disc the shape of the pits may be somewhat different but generally one observes just a small overall change of the average length of the pits). A Fourier transform of the disc reflection function, that is given by the sum of all different length-modulated depressions, yields the diffracted orders of the disc. In principle, sum and difference frequencies $\nu_1 \pm \nu_2$ will be present in the spectrum of diffracted orders (Hopkins 1979).

In the mastering process the modulation in the recording energy is derived from an electronic signal which can be represented by a constant plus a time dependent function which, converted into space coordinates, is given by

$$E(u) \propto \cos\left(\frac{2\pi u}{p_1'}\right) + \varepsilon \cos\left(\frac{2\pi u}{p_2'}\right) + \varepsilon_0 \qquad (2.62)$$

where p_1' is the period of the pits and p_2' the period corresponding to the length modulation of the pits (sub-carrier). The value of p_2' is supposed to be much larger than p_1'. A typical value of the factor ε, the relative strength of the sub-carrier, is 0.10 (-20 dB level).

The term ε_0 denotes an unwanted off-set of the recording signal and determines the average length of the length-modulated pits. The average pit length is β_0' and its value is obtained by neglecting the slowly varying term $\varepsilon \cos(2\pi u/p_2')$ in equation (2.62) and putting $E(u) = 0$. The position of the pit wall in the tangential direction is now given by the expression

$$\cos\left(\frac{\pi \beta_0'}{p_1'}\right) = -\varepsilon_0. \qquad (2.63)$$

With $\varepsilon_0 = 0$ the ratio β_0'/p_1' (duty-cycle) equals 0.5. The pit walls of the mth pit (with its centre close to $u = mp_1'$) are given by

$$\cos\left(\frac{2\pi[mp_1' + (\beta_0'/2) + \Delta_1']}{p_1'}\right) + \varepsilon \cos\left(\frac{2\pi[mp_1' + (\beta_0'/2) + \Delta_1']}{p_2'}\right) = -\varepsilon_0 \qquad (2.64a)$$

and

$$\cos\left(\frac{2\pi[mp_1' - (\beta_0'/2) - \Delta_2']}{p_1'}\right) + \varepsilon \cos\left(\frac{2\pi[mp_1' - (\beta_0'/2) - \Delta_2']}{p_2'}\right) = -\varepsilon_0 \qquad (2.64b)$$

where Δ_1' and Δ_2' are as shown in figure 2.36(b).

An approximate solution of equation (2.64) for small values of the arguments is

$$\Delta_1' = -\frac{\varepsilon}{2\pi} p_1' \cos\left(\frac{2\pi[mp_1' + (\beta_0'/2)]}{p_2'}\right)$$

$$\Delta_2' = -\frac{\varepsilon}{2\pi} p_1' \cos\left(\frac{2\pi[mp_1' - (\beta_0'/2)]}{p_2'}\right) \qquad (2.65)$$

where we have supposed that $\varepsilon \ll 1$ and $\Delta' \ll \beta'$ which is correct for small amplitudes of the length modulation ($\varepsilon \ll 1$). The shift of the centre of the mth pit is given by

$$\Delta's = \frac{\Delta_1' - \Delta_2'}{2} = \varepsilon\frac{p_1'}{p_2'}\beta_0' \sin\left(2\pi m\frac{p_1'}{p_2'}\right) \qquad (2.66)$$

and the length increment of the mth pit equals

$$\Delta\beta' = \Delta_1' + \Delta_2' = -\frac{\varepsilon}{\pi} p_1' \cos\left(2\pi m\frac{p_1'}{p_2'}\right). \qquad (2.67)$$

With these values for the position and the length of a general mth depression on the disc, it is possible to calculate the diffracted orders and finally the frequency content of the detector signal. In practice, a shift in the average length β_0' of the depressions is not obtained without affecting the width of the depressions and the slope of the walls (see Chapter 5).

Figure 2.37 plots the so-called asymmetry components of the calculated signals that correspond to several recording levels at the mastering stage of a video disc. The level changes from 0.7 to 1.3 of its central value. The calculated values are in very good agreement with the measured values. It

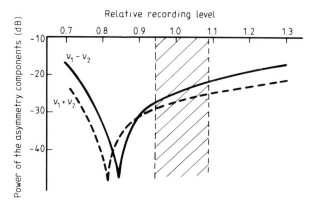

Figure 2.37 The asymmetry components $IP_{\nu_1-\nu_2}$ and $IP_{\nu_1+\nu_2}$ as a function of the recording level at the mastering stage. The shaded range has proven to be the best one for minimum visibility of intermodulation on the television screen.

is seen that the minimum of intermodulation occurs at different recording levels for the frequencies $(\nu_1 - \nu_2)$ and $(\nu_1 + \nu_2)$. Because of the frequency response of the optics one would expect that the power at frequency $(\nu_1 - \nu_2)$ would be larger than the power of the component at $(\nu_1 + \nu_2)$. There is a region where the situation is reversed. The electronic correction of the optical frequency response that emphasises $(\nu_1 + \nu_2)$ with respect to $(\nu_1 - \nu_2)$ makes their power difference still larger, for which FM demodulation in particular is sensitive. The visibility of intermodulation on the television screen is then large. The suppression of intermodulation is most successful when the intermodulation products are not minimum but have the proper power differences expected on the basis of the optical frequency response (hatched region in figure 2.37).

A plausible explanation of the foregoing results is possible with the aid of figure 2.38, which shows the diffracted orders R_0, R_{ν_1}, $R_{\nu_1-\nu_2}$, $R_{\nu_1+\nu_2}$, R_{ν_2} and $R_{-\nu_2}$ and their overlapping regions on, for example, the right-hand side of the detector. The intermodulation products IP at frequencies $\nu_1 \pm \nu_2$ are due to interference between the diffracted orders

$$
\begin{array}{llll}
\text{IP}_{\nu_1-\nu_2} & R_0\,R_{\nu_1-\nu_2} & A+B+C+D & \\
& R_{\nu_1}\,R_{\nu_2} & A+C+D & \\
\text{IP}_{\nu_1+\nu_2} & R_0\,R_{\nu_1+\nu_2} & A+D & (2.68)\\
& R_{\nu_1}\,R_{-\nu_2} & A+C. &
\end{array}
$$

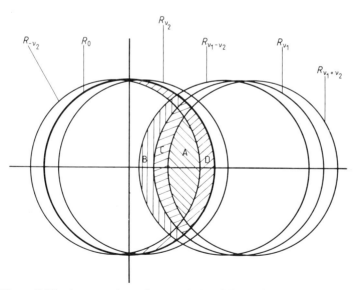

Figure 2.38 An overview of part of the diffracted orders that contribute to the power of the intermodulation products $\text{IP}_{\nu_1-\nu_2}$ and $\text{IP}_{\nu_1+\nu_2}$.

(The picture will be simplified by supposing that the diffracted orders are real and that the phase difference between the zeroth order and higher orders is exactly π.)

The asymmetry orders $R_{\nu_1-\nu_2}$ and $R_{\nu_1+\nu_2}$ are zero when the geometrical duty-cycle of the depressions, as they are 'seen' by the scanning light spot, equals 50%. The optical non-linearity caused by the interference of R_{ν_1} and R_{ν_2} or R_{ν_1} and $R_{-\nu_2}$ ensures that the intermodulation products will not be zero.

Small values of intermodulation are obtained when the asymmetry of the depressions is balanced by the optical non-linearity. When the signals due to the interference of orders are weighted with their overlapping regions according to equation (2.68) one finds

$$
\begin{aligned}
\text{IP}_{\nu_1-\nu_2} &= -R_0\,R_{\nu_1-\nu_2} & (A+B+C+D) \\
&+ R_{\nu_1}\,R_{\nu_2} & (A+C+D) \\
\text{IP}_{\nu_1+\nu_2} &= -R_0\,R_{\nu_1+\nu_2} & (A+D) \\
&+ R_{\nu_1}\,R_{-\nu_2} & (A+C).
\end{aligned}
\tag{2.69}
$$

The orders $R_{\nu_1-\nu_2}$ and $R_{\nu_1+\nu_2}$ having equal amplitude as well as R_{ν_2} and $R_{-\nu_2}$ the intermodulation products disappear when, according to equation (2.69)

$$
\begin{aligned}
\text{IP}_{\nu_1-\nu_2} = 0 \quad &\text{when} \quad R_{\nu_1\pm\nu_2} = \frac{(A+C+D)}{(A+B+C+D)}\,\frac{R_{\nu_1}R_{\nu_2}}{R_0} \\[2mm]
\text{IP}_{\nu_1+\nu_2} = 0 \quad &\text{when} \quad R_{\nu_1\pm\nu_2} = \frac{(A+C)}{(A+D)}\,\frac{R_{\nu_1}R_{\nu_2}}{R_{\nu_0}}.
\end{aligned}
\tag{2.70}
$$

Equation (2.70) shows that the intermodulation products $\text{IP}_{\nu_1-\nu_2}$ and $\text{IP}_{\nu_1+\nu_2}$ are cancelled at different values of the amplitude of the orders $R_{\nu_1\pm\nu_2}$. These orders are associated with the average length of the depressions implying that a simultaneous cancelling of the intermodulation products is impossible. It is also clear that the exact cancelling is a function of the frequency ratio ν_2/ν_1 that determines the sizes of the overlapping regions.

In practice it is possible to keep the intermodulation products down to the -40 dB level which makes them virtually invisible on the television screen. The cancelling of the cross products is increasingly difficult when the average frequency on the disc approaches the optical cut-off frequency. The limit of 70% of the cut-off frequency should not be exceeded in practice for the FM carrier frequency.

2.4.3 Intersymbol interference

In §2.4.1 the influence of cross-talk on an analog signal like a video signal was discussed. A digital (binary) signal is not very sensitive to small amplitude variations as introduced by cross-talk when the level is smaller than -25 dB. But the position of the transitions in the digital signal needs to be determined with great precision. In the modulation scheme EFM used for the Compact Disc system (see Chapter 7) the optically detected position of a transition should deviate by not more than ± 0.5 of a clock pulse length from its true position. The position tolerance $\Delta\xi$ in the tangential direction thus equals

$$\Delta\xi = \pm 0.5\, sT_{\text{clock}} = \pm 0.5\, \frac{1.25}{4.32 \times 10^6} = \pm 0.6\ \mu\text{m} \qquad (2.71)$$

where s is the scanning velocity and T_{clock} the clock period. A transition that for some reason is shifted outside its proper clock window introduces an error. Off-sets in the transition moments are mainly due to the finite extent of the scanning spot in the track direction. The position of a detected transition in a data stream thus depends on the digital data that precede and follow the actual signal. This phenomenon is named intersymbol interference but one could equally well call it cross-talk in the track direction.

Intersymbol interference (ISI) causes a narrowing of the digital eye and thus a greater probability that errors will be detected. Some knowledge about the contribution of the optics to the ISI and next to the bit error rate (BER) would require the calculation of the optical signal for a large number of different data sequences on the disc. From these data one could derive the RMS value of the transition jitter due to the optical read-out. When the 'optical' jitter is added to other noise sources, a bit error rate can be predicted. Calculation time is prohibitive for such a Monte Carlo-like procedure.

One can get an impression of the shape of the digital eye by plotting some optically detected data sequences one on top of the other, a picture that also becomes visible on the oscilloscope when one triggers the digital signal to the clock frequency.

In figure 2.39(a) such a digital eye is shown when the optical read-out is perfect and just introduces a drop-off in frequency response according to the ideal optical modulation transfer function (see, for example, curve A in figure 2.24). The limited optical bandwidth yields a maximum possible slope of the detector current according to (Maréchal and Françon 1970)

$$\frac{\mathrm{d}i}{\mathrm{d}\xi} = 1.6\, i_{\max} \frac{\text{NA}}{\lambda} \qquad (2.72)$$

where ξ is the spatial coordinate and $i_{\max}$ is the maximum variation in the detector current between the 0 and 100% reflection level. The NA of the Compact Disc system is typically 0.45 and the wavelength of the AlGaAs laser is 0.80 μm.

Serious deterioration of the eye pattern is observed when aberrations are present that elongate the scanning spot in the track direction and thus increases the ISI. In figure 2.39(b) the information track is read with an

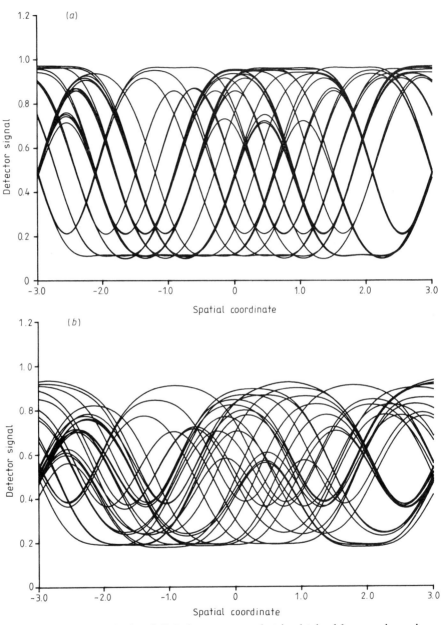

Figure 2.39   The calculated digital eye pattern that is obtained by superimposing the detector signals generated by a certain number of different pit sequences on the disc. These sequences all obey the EFM modulation scheme that has been adopted for the Compact Disc system. The distance between two transients (the eye width) is 0.3 μm. The unit along the horizontal scale is 1 μm. (*a*) For a perfect optical readout system. (*b*) The scanning spot is astigmatic.

astigmatic light spot whose focal line parallel to the track is in focus on the disc (the astigmatic coefficient W_{22} is 0.35). The eye pattern is rather disturbed now and the experiment shows that an unacceptable bit error rate is detected. The eye narrowing and the increased eye jitter are due to a more elongated scanning spot and a corresponding smoother slope or edge response of the optical system. As in video-disc systems where a correction of the optical MTF is currently being done by electronic means, one has tried to steepen the edge response in a Compact Disc player by means of a so-called equalising filter. The shape of this filter (its modulus) is shown in figure 2.40. The middle frequencies are multiplied by a factor of 2 with respect to the low and high frequencies. The edge responses in the ideal case ($W = 0$) and in the case of a scanning astigmatic focal line ($W_{22} = 0.35$) are shown in figure 2.41 with (a) and without (b) the equalising filter. With equalisation the ideal edge response becomes steeper but at the same time one observes more fringing which predicts an increased ISI. Figures 2.42(a) and 2.42(b) show the eye patterns from figure 2.39(a) and 2.39(b) with the equalising filter incorporated. The transition jitter is larger in the case of an ideal scanning spot but it is greatly reduced when scanning the disc with an astigmatic focal line.

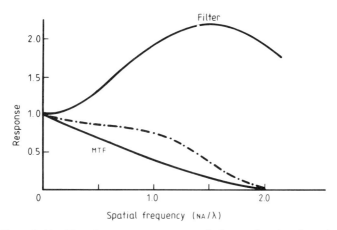

Figure 2.40 The frequency response of the optics (MTF) and the equalising filter. The final frequency response of the system is given by the chain curve.

Finally figures 2.43(a) and 2.43(b) represent a situation where the digital eye of the detector signal has completely disappeared with or without the equalising filter. The defocusing of the (non-aberrated) scanning spot here equals two focal depths ($W_{20} = 0.50$, $\Delta z = 4$ μm). Now it is only with the aid of the error correction capability of the digital signal that an error-free reconstruction can be achieved.

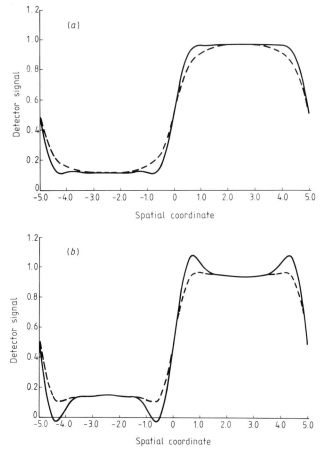

Figure 2.41 The edge response of the optical read-out system for an ideal scanning spot and for the astigmatic scanning line ($W_{22} = 0.35$). (*a*) The pure optical response. (*b*) The response with the electronic filter incorporated.

2.4.4 Signal-to-noise ratio

The total noise power in the detector signal of an optical disc system is the sum of a number of contributions with different physical origin such as

(*a*) dark current noise of the detector

(*b*) photon shot noise

(*c*) noise of the electronic amplifier

(*d*) noise due to microroughness of the optical disc (also present in non-recorded regions)

(*e*) noise due to irregularities of the recorded effects (depressions in a video or audio disc or magnetic domains in an optical data disc).

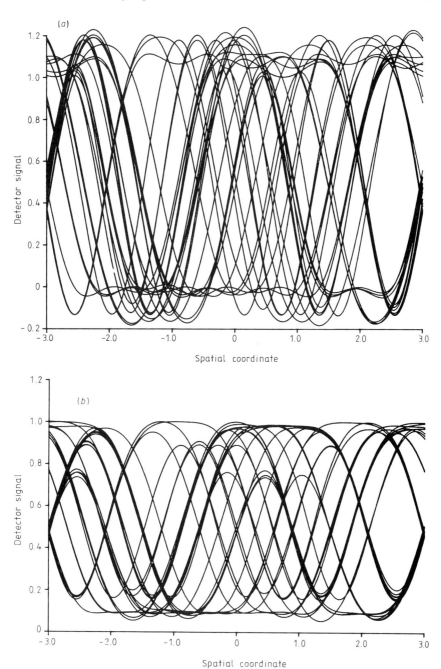

Figure 2.42 The same legend applies as for figure 2.39 but now with the equalising filter added to the detection circuit. (*a*) The ideal scanning spot. (*b*) The astigmatic line.

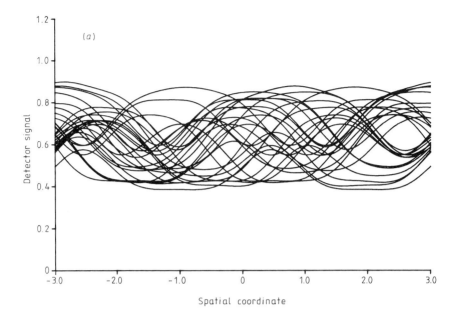

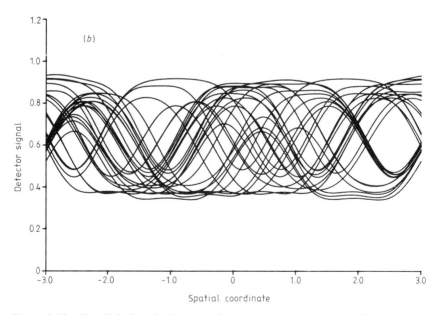

Figure 2.43   The digital eye in the case of a scanning spot that is heavily defocused (4 μm). (*a*) Without the equalising filter. (*b*) With the equalising filter. Although some improvement in response is observed in (*b*), the position jitter of the transients is such that only an electronic error correction yields a perfect reconstruction of the digital signal.

A physical limitation is set by the photon shot noise while a technological limitation is set by, for example, the microroughness of a disc substrate. The dominating noise source is generally (e) especially when the recording of the signal is done with non-professional equipment (e.g. home recording of digital data). When considering pre-recorded analog video discs, the noise sources (b) and (d) are the most important and these will be considered more closely in the following paragraphs. The signal-to-noise ratio on discs with digital data is generally no limitation for their final performance.

Photon shot noise. When a light flux with average power P_D is incident on a detector, the photons generate electrons with a certain quantum efficiency η_Q (generally close to unity). The photons are not incident at regular intervals on the detector but their moments of arrival obey Poisson statistics. The detector current has an average value given by

$$i_{av} = \eta_Q \frac{P_D}{h\nu} e = Ne \qquad (2.73)$$

where N is the number of useful electrons per second, e the electronic charge and $h\nu$ the energy of an individual photon.

When we limit our observation time to τ the number of events equals

$$N' = N\tau. \qquad (2.74)$$

The standard deviation of a Poisson statistical process is equal to the square root of the number of events (counts) over the period of time considered. The standard deviation of the detector current is thus given by

$$\sigma_i = \sqrt{N\tau} \, \frac{e}{\tau}$$

and the variance of the detector current equals

$$\overline{i_n^2} = \sigma_i^2 = N\tau \frac{e^2}{\tau^2} = \frac{ei_{av}}{\tau}. \qquad (2.75)$$

A measuring bandwidth B is associated with an observation time τ according to $B = (1/2\tau)$ (Bennett 1960) resulting in a detector current variance

$$\overline{i_n^2} = 2Bei_{av}. \qquad (2.76)$$

When the modulation depth of the signal is m, the signal power of a sinusoidal carrier frequency is proportional to $1/2 \, m^2 i_{av}^2$ and the carrier-to-noise ratio CNR is given by

$$\text{CNR} = \frac{m^2 i_{av}}{4Be}. \qquad (2.77)$$

The signal-to-noise ratio is obtained by integrating the signal and the noise power over the effective bandwidth and then taking the quotient.

For a video-disc system the photon noise power should be at least 65 dB (3×10^6 times) down with respect to the carrier power if the (normalised) measuring bandwidth B is 30 kHz (Heemskerk 1978). When the modulation depth is 0.10 and the quantum efficiency 0.8, the light power on the detector must be according to equations (2.73) and (2.77)

$$P_D \geqslant \frac{4B(h\nu)\mathrm{CNR}}{\eta_Q m^2} \qquad (2.78)$$

and this yields the numerical value ($\lambda = 633$ nm)

$$P_D \geqslant 15 \ \mu\mathrm{W}.$$

Assuming the total transmission from the source via the disc to the detector to be 10%, a useful light power of the source equal to

$$P_S \geqslant 150 \ \mu\mathrm{W} \qquad (2.79)$$

is required. According to the laws of photometry the light power P concentrated in a coherent scanning spot equals

$$P = L\Omega S \qquad (2.80)$$

where L is the luminance of the source, Ω the solid angle of the converging wave and S the area of the scanning spot. The product ΩS is of the order of λ^2 (Heemskerk 1978). Combining equation (2.80) with the condition of equation (2.79), the minimum luminance of the source must be

$$L \geqslant \frac{150 \times 10^{-6}}{(0.633 \times 10^{-4})^2} = 40\,000 \ \mathrm{W\,cm}^{-2}\,\mathrm{sr}^{-1}. \qquad (2.81)$$

This value is so large that classical light sources are inadequate for the readout of video discs.

The CNR value that is desired when reading out digital (e.g. Compact) discs is approximately 45 dB measured over the same bandwidth of 30 kHz. A luminance value of 400 W cm^{-2} sr^{-1} is sufficient now. Even then alternatives such as a mercury lamp or a CRT flying spot are marginal and technically not very attractive. The HeNe or AlGaAs lasers are the only light sources so far that easily fulfil the power (or luminance) requirements of an optical disc system.

Microroughness of the substrate.   There are several methods to characterise the microroughness of a surface. Scanning of the surface with a very sensitive mechanical stylus (skate) yields information on its roughness albeit mainly in one direction. With an interferometric measurement accurate data on surface rugosity can also be gathered. However, a directional measurement of the intensity scattered by a surface is the most complete method to get data on the two-dimensional roughness of a surface. When scanning an optical disc, part of the light amplitude scattered by the information carrying surface is due to this roughness and interferes coherently with the light amplitude scattered by the pits. This results in a noise background superimposed on the desired signal. In order to analyse the noise in the signal one considers the effect of a phase grating with a very small height amplitude. For a reflective disc substrate with a shallow phase grating present on it, the spatially varying reflection coefficient $A(\xi, \eta)$ is equal to

$$A(\xi, \eta) = \exp\left[\frac{i4\pi nd}{\lambda} \cos\left(\frac{2\pi\xi}{p_\xi}\right)\right]$$

$$\approx 1 + \frac{i4\pi nd}{\lambda} \cos\left(\frac{2\pi\xi}{p_\xi}\right) - 8\pi^2 n^2 \frac{d^2}{\lambda^2} \cos\left(\frac{4\pi\xi}{p_\xi}\right) \tag{2.82}$$

where d is the amplitude of the phase grating, p_ξ its period in the ξ direction and λ/n the wavelength of the light within the substrate. The diffracted orders of such a grating have an amplitude of

$$R_0 = 1$$

$$R_{\pm 1} = i\,\frac{2\pi nd}{\lambda} \tag{2.83}$$

$$R_{\pm 2} = -\frac{4\pi^2 n^2 d^2}{\lambda^2}.$$

The read-out of such a shallow phase grating with CA detection (see equations (2.19) to (2.21)) in a first approximation does not yield any response because the phase angle ψ_{10} has a value of exactly $\pi/2$. A second-order approximation that also takes into account mutual interference between first orders and between zeroth and second orders gives the time dependent response

$$i_{CA}(t) = \frac{8\pi^2 n^2 d^2}{\lambda^2}\, \mathrm{MTF}(2\nu) \cos(4\pi\nu t) \tag{2.84}$$

where ν is the time frequency associated with the spatial period p_ξ. The response thus introduces a frequency doubling of the grating pattern.

The read-out with push–pull detection yields a response in the small signal approximation according to equation (2.24): PP detection was devised to enhance the signal in the case of shallow phase patterns. With the angle ψ_{10} equal to $\pi/2$, equation (2.24) is written

$$i_{PP}(t) = \frac{8\pi nd}{\lambda}\,(\mathrm{MTF}(\nu) - \mathrm{MTF}(2\nu)) \sin(2\pi\nu t). \tag{2.85}$$

Going over to a surface with two-dimensional random microroughness, one would like to calculate the noise power contained within a certain bandwidth in the case of CA or PP reading. Rough surfaces can be analysed by measuring the scattered light power as a function of the scattering angle (Church 1977). Figure 2.44 shows such a 'scatterogram' where the scattered intensity is shown normalised with the specular reflection. The general scattering direction (θ, ϕ) is related to a spatial frequency component (f_ξ, f_η) on the random surface by the expression

$$f_\xi = \frac{\sin\theta\cos\phi}{\lambda} \qquad f_\eta = \frac{\sin\theta\sin\phi}{\lambda} \qquad (2.86)$$

and the scattered intensity $I(\theta, \phi)$ in a direction given by the angles (θ, ϕ) is proportional to the noise power spectrum $S(f_\xi, f_\eta)$ according to

$$S(f_\xi, f_\eta) = \frac{I(\theta, \phi)}{\lambda^2 \Delta f_\xi \Delta f_\eta I_R} \qquad (2.87)$$

where I_R is the specularly reflected power and the quantity

$$\lambda^2 \Delta f_\xi \Delta f_\eta = d\Omega \qquad (2.88)$$

defines the solid angle subtended by the detector during the scattering experiment. The increment in spatial bandwidth Δf_ξ is related to the increment in temporal bandwidth B via the scanning velocity s by

$$B = s\Delta f_\xi. \qquad (2.89)$$

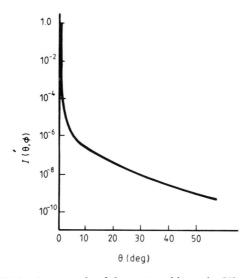

Figure 2.44   An example of the scattered intensity $I(\theta, \phi)$ of a polished metallised surface as a function of the scattering angle θ. $\phi = 0$, $d\Omega = 2 \times 10^{-5}$ sr.

In one-dimensional scanning (in the x direction) of a surface with two-dimensional random roughness the total scattered power within a frequency band Δf_ξ contributes to the noise power. In figures 2.45 and 2.46 the domain of integration is shown with weighting due to the optical transfer function MTF.

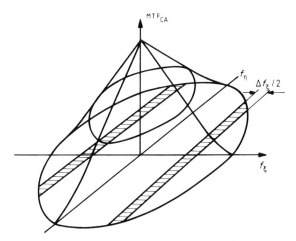

Figure 2.45 The area of integration in the domain of spatial frequencies that has to be considered when calculating the noise in the signal due to surface roughness of the disc. The rim of the circle in the (f_ξ, f_η) plane corresponds to a spatial frequency of $2\mathrm{NA}/\lambda$. The area of integration is weighted with the modulation transfer function in the case of central aperture (CA) detection.

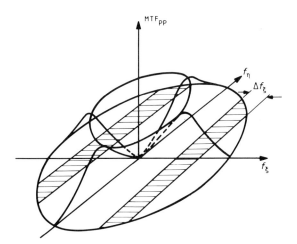

Figure 2.46 Same legend as for figure 2.45 with a weighting factor according to the push–pull (PP) modulation transfer function.

In the case of CA detection, the noise power $\overline{i_{CA}^2}$ at a certain temporal frequency ν with bandwidth B is approximated from the scattered intensity squared at the spatial frequency $f_\xi/2$ with a bandwidth $\Delta f_\xi/2$. In the case of PP detection, the noise power $\overline{i_{PP}^2}$ is given by the scattered intensity itself at the frequency f_ξ and with a bandwidth Δf_ξ. Although PP read-out basically is more sensitive to surface noise, the noise power in the detected signal at higher spatial frequencies is still acceptable while in this region the intensity scattered by a microrough surface is much less than in the low frequency region. Measurements have shown that at a scanning velocity of $10 \, \mathrm{m \, s^{-1}}$, a CNR value of 64 dB measured over 30 kHz bandwidth is possible with CA read-out. This value corresponds with an RMS roughness of 3 nm of the substrate. The PP detection method then yields a CNR of the order of 55 dB. It should be noted that different amounts of spatial noise can be 'housed' in the same temporal bandwidth by simply changing the scanning velocity s (equation (2.89)).

The total amount of captured spatial noise is determined by the numerical aperture of the scanning objective. The spread-out of this spatial noise over the temporal frequencies is a function of the scanning velocity that should always be mentioned when CNR values due to surface noise are given.

2.5   Optical error signals

The read-out of optical discs cannot be imagined without the servosystems that assure radial and vertical tracking of the information. The scanning velocity is high (from 1.25 up to $25 \, \mathrm{m \, s^{-1}}$) and the scanning spot must be maintained in focus and on track with sub-micron precision. The apparatus should also be fairly insensitive to vibration and shocks. Early experiments with video-disc systems used a mechanical focus stabilisation of a foil-like disc by running it through a narrow air gap. The focus tolerance of the optical read-out system is of the order of 1 μm and focusing within this limit is not easily achieved with such a passive mechanical stabilisation. Actual optical disc systems all use servo systems in order to obtain a correct scanning of the information track.

Servo systems preferably need as input a bipolar error signal that carries the sign of the corrective action to be taken. These error signals are generally derived by optical means and many methods have been proposed for the generation of radial and focus error signals. The next two sections will describe the type of radial and focus error signals that are most commonly used and will mention briefly alternatives which have been patented or have been proposed in literature.

2.5.1   Radial error signals

In most cases when error signals have to be generated one is not interested in the high frequency content of the detector signal. The light distribution is detected with a low-pass filter such that the high frequency variations due to the pits or holes are suppressed. Optically one could say that the pits are rushing along so fast that we are only able to see a track due to its average grey level and individual pits or holes are no longer visible.

Twin-spot method. The DC content of the detector signal contains information on the position of the scanning spot with respect to the information track, the value being lowest when the the spot is on track (figure 2.47). In order to get an adequate error signal two additional scanning spots are projected onto the disc with an off-set v_0'. Approximating the variation of the DC content with a cosine function according to

$$S_{DC}(v_0) = a + b \cos\left(2\pi \frac{v_0}{q}\right) \qquad (2.90)$$

the two satellite spots captured on two separate detectors yield the signals

$$S_1(v_0 + v_0') = a + b \cos\left(\frac{2\pi(v_0 + v_0')}{q}\right)$$

$$S_2(v_0 - v_0') = a + b \cos\left(\frac{2\pi(v_0 - v_0')}{q}\right) \qquad (2.91)$$

where q is the track spacing and v_0 the position of the main scanning spot. The dependence of the quantity b on the track spacing q was shown in figure 2.30.

The difference signal of S_1 and S_2 equals

$$S_{rad}(v_0) = -2b \sin\left(\frac{2\pi v_0'}{q}\right) \sin\left(\frac{2\pi v_0}{q}\right) \qquad (2.92)$$

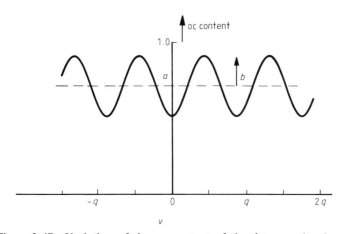

Figure 2.47 Variation of the DC content of the detector signal as a function of the radial position of the scanning spot. The track spacing equals q and when $v = nq$ the spot is supposed to be centred on a track

which now is an uneven function of the radial position v_0. The amplitude (and slope) of $S_{rad}(v_0)$ is maximum when $\sin(2\pi v_0'/q) = 1$ or when $v_0' = q/4$.

In figure 2.48 the satellite spots are generated by means of a (phase) grating that is imaged onto the objective stop. The off-set of the satellite spots is $q/4$ in the radial direction. The off-set in the track direction is much larger (typically 20 μm). By adjusting the angular position of the grating the off-set v_0' is varied and the error signal S_{rad} is optimised. The set-up is relatively simple and very stable.

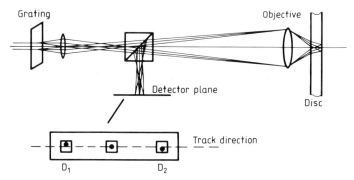

Figure 2.48   The generation of the two satellite spots with the aid of a grating.

Radial push–pull method.   Using the twin spot method one measures the total light flux per spot in a conjugate plane of the disc where the individual spots are again well separated. Any variation in light intensity over the cross section of the reflected beams is of no importance for this method. The radial push–pull tracking method purposely detects these variations in order to obtain directly a radial tracking signal by separating the light flux through the pupil of the objective in two parts. Figure 2.49 shows the light distribution in the pupil and it is composed of a zeroth order and of diffracted first orders that are due to the tracks on the disc. The considerations of §2.2.3 where expressions for the high frequency signal were derived can be applied also to the DC variations of the signal when the scanning spot moves from track to track. The time factor in the signal is replaced by a tracking error v_0 and the radial push–pull signal then becomes

$$S_{rad}(v_0) \propto \sin(\psi_{10})\sin\left(\frac{2\pi v_0}{q}\right) \tag{2.93}$$

according to equation (2.24) where the MTF value now has to be taken at the spatial frequency $(1/q)$ with q equal to the track spacing. The track spacing generally is a constant over the whole disc and approximately equal to half of the cut-off frequency of the optical system. The push–pull MTF function (see figure 2.12) is maximum here. Equation (2.93) contains a factor $\sin(\psi_{10})$ that depends on the average depth of the pits. Pits with an average depth close to a quarter of a wavelength and amplitude (black and white) structures have a value of ψ_{10} close to π and yield a very small push–pull signal. During the mastering process the pits should be optimised far enough away from this forbidden region.

The radial push–pull method is optically very easy to implement. Possible off-sets in DC level between the two detector halves that might introduce a tracking error are cancelled by always checking for the optimum read-out of the high frequency signal.

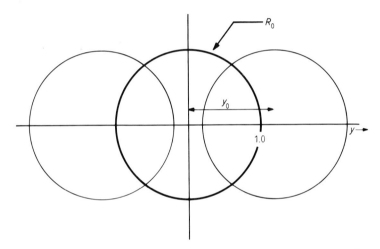

Figure 2.49 The diffraction pattern on the detector due to the regular track structure on the disc (the track period is q). Intensity fluctuations due to off-track movements of the scanning spot are present in the overlapping areas of zeroth and first orders. $y_0 = \lambda/q\mathrm{NA}$.

Radial wobble method. When an extra movement is given to the scanning spot relative to the tracks, it is possible to extract a radial error signal from the intensity fluctuations on the detector that are caused by this extra movement. Using equation (2.90) for the DC level on the detector we obtain with a sinusoidal movement $w\sin(2\pi\nu_0 t)$ superimposed on the tracking error v_0

$$S(v_0) = a + b\cos\left(2\pi\frac{v_0}{q} + \frac{2\pi w}{q}\sin(2\pi\nu_0 t)\right). \tag{2.94}$$

The time variation of the tracking error v_0 is assumed to be much slower than the frequency ν_0 of the wobble movement. The phase of the detected signal at the frequency ν_0 is a function of the tracking error v_0 (see figure 2.50) and changes over π radians when crossing a track.

With the aid of synchronous detection of the detector signal and the wobble signal itself (e.g. the drive current of a pivoting mirror that forces the scanning spot to wobble) one can detect this phase change and derive a tracking error signal. By writing equation (2.94) as

$$S(v_0) = a + b \cos\left(\frac{2\pi v_0}{q}\right) - \frac{2\pi w}{q} b \sin\left(\frac{2\pi v_0}{q}\right) \sin(2\pi \nu_0 t) \qquad (2.95)$$

where the wobble amplitude w is assumed to be small and by multiplying this signal (after band-pass filtering at the frequency ν_0) with the drive signal $\sin(2\pi \nu_0 t)$ one obtains

$$S_{\mathrm{rad}}(v_0) \propto \frac{\pi b w}{q} \sin\left(\frac{2\pi v_0}{q}\right) [1 - \cos(4\pi \nu_0 t)]. \qquad (2.96)$$

After the suppression of the frequency component $2\nu_0$ one has an error signal that is bipolar with respect to the tracking error v_0. The amplitude of the error signal is proportional to the wobble amplitude w. An upper

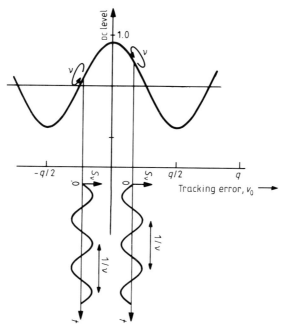

Figure 2.50 Small variations of the radial position of the scanning spot (frequency ν) induce an AC signal on the detector that changes its phase over 180° when the scanning spot crosses a track. In the figure the DC level on-track is larger than off-track. Such a situation can occur, e.g. on recordable data discs.

limit to the value of w is set by the amount of cross-talk that is permitted and also by the more difficult filtering operations that are necessary when the ratio w/q is pushed too far. In practice a wobble amplitude of 5 to 10% of the halfwidth of the scanning spot (0.05 to 0.10 μm) is used. The wobble frequency is approximately ten times the bandwidth of the servo system (15 to 30 kHz).

Instead of wobbling the scanning spot in the read-out unit one could equally well introduce a track wobble on the disc itself. Although this solution is quite attractive it has so far not been adopted because of standardisation agreements.

Another proposal for deriving a radial tracking error signal asks for two extra tracks containing particular frequencies such that the correct tracking of the information track is obtained when equal amounts of the 'guiding' frequencies are detected. A more complicated mastering process and a loss of radial density do not favour this method.

A futher method uses a quadrant detector over the cross section of the returning beam and extracts a radial error signal by comparing the phases of the high frequency signals on the four quadrants (Braat and Bouwhuis 1978). A necessary condition is that the average spatial frequency in the information track is not too low because of the push–pull like transfer function of this method. On video discs with constant angular velocity this causes problems on the outer side of the disc.

2.5.2 *Focus error signals*
Most of the methods that yield focus error signals rely on the fact that the laser beam reflected by the disc is imaged back onto itself when the scanning spot is perfectly in focus on the disc. By introducing some asymmetry in the light path on the way back to the laser it is possible to detect deviations from optimum focus on the disc. The disc does not have to carry any information on it.

The Foucault knife-edge method. In figure 2.51 the method used by Foucault for the testing of the sphericity of astronomical mirrors is reproduced. In the diagram (2.51(a)) the mirror is supposed to be perfect but the knife is out of focus and this causes an unequal illumination on the screen. In the direct neighbourhood of optimum focus the light distribution is rather complicated (Linfoot 1950) but further away a more geometrical picture is permitted and a defocusing is seen to enhance the illumination of one part of the screen with respect to the other. Putting two detectors in the plane of the screen a focus error signal is obtained by the subtraction of the two detector signals. The focus error signal changes from its maximum negative to its maximum positive value over a distance of approximately four focal depths (figure 2.51(b)) and does not drop to zero very quickly. The distance measured at the detector and translated to the disc corresponds to two focal depths because of the reflective system. A rapid variation in the neighbourhood of focus means a large sensitivity to focus errors. The long range of defocusing over which the signal can be well discerned from zero involves a large acquisition range of the servo system. An acquisition range which too is small may give rise to parasitic zero crossings during the start-up of the servo system. The position of the knife-edge determines the balance of the light fluxes to the two detectors when the scanning spot is in focus and a small displacement of the edge from its middle position will be interpreted as a defocusing and subsequently 'corrected' by the servo system. In order to decrease the positional sensitivity of the method, a prism is used instead of a knife edge (figure 2.51(c)). With four detectors D_1 to D_4 one extracts the focus error signal by coupling them according to the

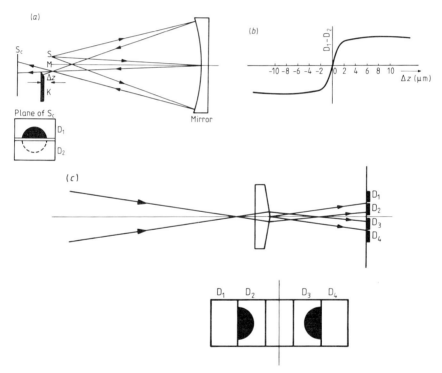

Figure 2.51 (a) A schematic drawing of the set-up used by Foucault for testing mirrors. S is the light source that is positioned close to the centre of curvature M of the mirror. The knife edge K is defocused over a small distance Δz and the illumination on the screen S_c is asymmetrical. (b) The difference signal of the two detectors D_1 and D_2 as a function of the defocusing Δz. The full change from minimum to maximum of this difference signal is observed over a range of a few focal depths. (c) A more stable version of the Foucault method where the knife edge has been replaced by a prism.

scheme $D_1 - D_2 - D_3 + D_4$. A displacement of the prism edge will increase the light flux on, for example, the detectors D_1 and D_2 but this does not introduce an off-set of the focus error signal but merely decreases the steepness of the signal. The detector signal $D_1 + D_2 - D_3 - D_4$ might be used as a position error signal for the prism.

Pupil obscuration method. In figure 2.52 a method is shown that closely resembles the Foucault knife-edge experiment. The edge now is placed far away from the focal point of the returning beam and a split detector is positioned exactly in focus. Geometrical optics immediately show that the difference signal of the split detector yields an appropriate focus error signal. Close to the optimum focus diffraction effects have to be taken into account in order to find the steepness of the error signal around focus (§2.6.3). Instead of an obstructing edge it is useful to adopt a prism and to use two split detectors instead of one (figure 2.52(*b*)). The parameter that is very senstive to a displacement is the position of the split detector and the double arrangement with a prism substantially relaxes this tolerance.

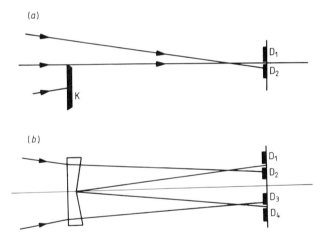

Figure 2.52 (*a*) The pupil obscuration method with a knife edge, K, far away from focus. (*b*) The same method with the knife edge replaced by a prism.

In figure 2.53(*a*) the intensity distribution in the detector plane is shown. The line separating a pair of detectors is represented by $x = 0$. The beam is correctly focused on the detectors and the intensity distribution is symmetrical. In figure 2.53(*b*) the scanning spot is 2 μm out of focus on the disc (one focal depth) and most of the light now is captured by one detector. Figure 2.54 depicts the focus error signal derived with this method.

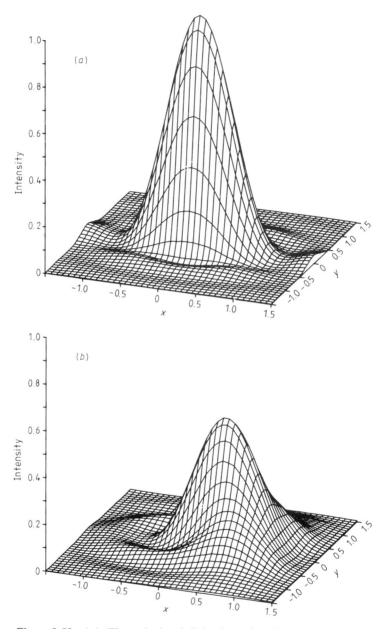

Figure 2.53 (*a*) The calculated light intensity distribution on the
detector in the case of the half obscured focused beam (see figure 2.52).
The beam returning from the disc is assumed to be free of aberrations.
The unit of length is λ/NA (where NA is 0.10 at the detector side) and
this yields a value of 8 μm. (*b*) The same as (*a*) but now the scanning
spot is 2 μm (one focal depth) out of focus on the disc.

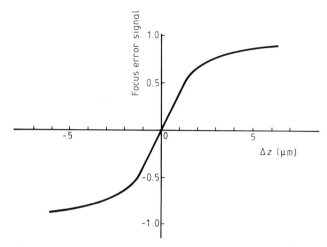

Figure 2.54 The focus error signal obtained with the beam obscuration method. Along the horizontal axis the defocusing of the scanning spot on the optical disc has been plotted. Due to the read-out in reflection the defocusing in the detector plane is twice as large.

Astigmatic method. This method was devised by Bricot *et al* (1976). An asymmetry in the axial direction around focus is present in an astigmatic beam that on each side of 'best' focus shows either a horizontally or a vertically oriented astigmatic line. In figure 2.55 the astigmatic lines are caused by a cylindrical lens that is positioned in the returning beam and a quadrant detector with its separating lines at $45°$ and connected according to the scheme $D_1 - D_2 + D_3 - D_4$ will deliver a useful focus error signal.

The cylindrical power of the lens determines the axial distance between the astigmatic lines and the steepness of the error signal around focus. A trade-off between acquisition range and sensitivity is possible here. In practice a value of W_{22}, the astigmatic wavefront aberration, equal to 3 or 4 is

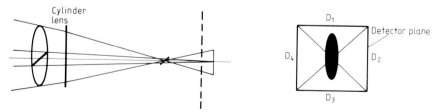

Figure 2.55 An astigmatic pencil with two astigmatic lines in the focal region. The light distribution on the detector is shown schematically for the case of a detector position close to the vertical focal line.

a good compromise. When operating in focus, the light distribution on the quadrant detector is that corresponding to the 'best' focus or 'circle of least confusion'. Light intensity variations over the beam cross section are smoothed in this astigmatic focal point and a doubling of the arrangement is not vital for reliable operation of this set-up.

Critical angle method. The critical angle determines up to what angle of incidence light is transmitted at an interface when going from a dense to a less dense medium (e.g. from glass to air). Beyond the critical angle the light is totally reflected. In figure 2.56 a parallel bundle is returning from the disc and reflected by the prism. When the angle of incidence on the prism hypotenuse is adjusted to be close to the critical angle the split detector will receive a uniform light flux. A defocusing of the disc makes the returning beam divergent or convergent and there will be an imbalance on the split detector which after subtraction of the two detector signals results in a useful focus error signal.

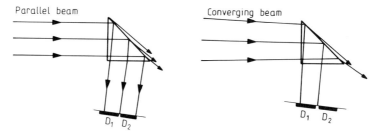

Figure 2.56   The critical angle method based on total internal reflection in a prism.

Defocusing fringes. Methods have been proposed that make use of the diffraction of the light by the information on the disc. Their major advantage is that in principle the optimum focus is found while in the methods described above a (time varying) off-set is always possible. On the other hand the acquisition range is small so that the start-up of the focus servo system may be problematic. These methods might be useful when they are used together with some other means to increase the acquisition range.

On p. 42 it was shown that in the overlapping regions of zeroth and first orders fringes appear as soon as the information is out of focus. The fringes move at the frequency of the signal and the direction of motion is reversed when the defocusing changes sign. With a proper detector configuration (Braat and Bouwhuis 1978) a focus error signal is obtained but the experiment shows that an acquisition range of approximately 10 μm is the maximum attainable.

2.6 The optical read-out system

It was pointed out on p. 66 that the light source in an optical disc system should be a laser in order to get a sufficiently high signal-to-noise ratio. The early experiments with optical discs all relied on HeNe gas lasers because this was the only relatively low cost and commercially available continuous laser source at that time. Since then the AlGaAs semiconductor laser has undergone very rapid development with respect to available power and lifetime. In the future disc systems will be exclusively based on the semi-conductor laser. This leads to an important miniaturisation of the optical read-out system. The entire optical pick-up with all optical functions incorporated in it will fit into a cylinder some 30 mm high and 10 mm in diameter. In the following sections such a small size optical pick-up that mainly consists of the laser light source, the scanning objective and the detectors that yield the high frequency signal and the focus and radial error signals (figure 2.57) will be described.

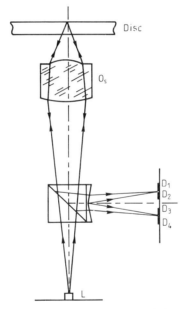

Figure 2.57 A schematic drawing of the small size optical pick-up. L is the semiconductor laser source, O_s the scanning objective and D_1 to D_4 are the detectors. The beam splitting cube carries two small angle prisms that deviate the light to the four detectors.

2.6.1 The semiconductor laser

The physical properties and the lasing action of the aluminium gallium arsenide (AlGaAs) laser have been described by Thomson (1980). The optically active region is confined to a stripe of approximately 5 μm in length and 0.3 μm in width. The total output power (typically 3 to 5 mW) is radiated in a elliptical cone of light. The angular half widths are respectively $\pm 5°$ in the direction parallel to the stripe and $\pm 20°$ in the direction perpendicular to the stripe. In order to get an illuminating beam that is sufficiently uniform in amplitude and phase over its circular cross section the useful angular extent of the laser beam is of the order of $5°$. This corresponds to a useful numerical aperture of the laser beam equal to 0.10. The fraction of emitted power that is contained within this NA of 0.10 is approximately 20% (coupling efficiency). At larger values of the NA a compensation of the astigmatism of the laser beam with a cylindrical lens is to be recommended.

The wavelength λ of the actual AlGaAs laser is situated in the near infrared (800 nm) and can be varied by changing the chemical composition of the laser. A shorter wavelength is advantageous with respect to the information density that can be achieved on an optical disc. However semiconductor lasers operating in the visible region of the spectrum ($\lambda < 700$ nm) at present suffer from rapid degradation and do not meet the lifetime specifications (> 5000 hours) of an optical disc pick-up.

The spread in wavelength ($\Delta\lambda$) of the laser is less than 0.1 nm and the emitted spectrum generally consists of one single mode. The coherence length of the laser is at least some centimetres. The emitted light that reaches the laser after reflection at the disc is still coherent and causes feedback effects resulting in rapid time variations of the output. In practice a decrease in signal-to-noise ratio is detectable, especially when the optical pathlength from source to disc is of the order of the laser coherence length.

2.6.2 The scanning objective
The trend to small size has guided the optical design work in this field. Apart from the development of miniaturised microscope objectives new techniques are also applied in lenses with aspherical surfaces or gradient-index lenses.

A conventional scanning objective.   The objective collects the useful cone of light emitted by the laser and focuses it on the back of the disc where the information is present.

The main parameters of the objective are its numerical aperture and useful image field. Due to the high information density on optical discs the NA should be of the order of 0.4 to 0.5 (a Compact Disc player is equipped with an NA = 0.45 objective). The required image field diameter depends strongly on the mode of operation of the servo systems. When the entire optical system (laser, objective, diodes) is translated both in the radial and vertical direction the image field can be small and the design is simplified. The field angle is limited to less than $\pm 1°$ or to a field diameter of less than 200 μm. In systems with a random access or an instant jump feature (see Chapter 4) the image field must be substantially larger (up to a diameter

·of 1000 μm). Over this entire field the quality should be at least 'just diffraction-limited'.

A classical objective design for an optical pick-up is shown in figure 2.58(a). The objective is split up in a collimating part that may consist of a simple plano-convex lens and the proper objective that consists of four lenses. For focusing the objective is moved with respect to the collimator. This differs from a microscope objective in the absence of colour correction so a single glass type may be used an no cemented doublets are necessary. High-index glass is used ($n = 1.75$ to 1.80) in order to obtain a good quality with a small number of elements. The following table shows the characteristics of a typical objective.

Focal distance	8 mm
NA	0.45
Field diameter	1.0 mm (OPD at 400 μm from the centre is 0.052 λ)
Field curvature	6 μm at the rim
Diameter	7.5 mm
Length	11 mm
Weight	<2 g (mount included)

A scanning objective with aspherical surfaces. For reasons of cost and weight alternatives to the classical microscope objective have been sought. One alternative is the single lens with aspherical surfaces (Haisma *et al* 1979). The diameter of the useful field of such a lens can become very large (some field curvature is generally admitted because of the active focusing in an optical disc player). There is a large variety of possible designs for such aspherical lenses, all with large field diameters (Braat 1983b). Selection of a design is mainly decided by its manufacturing tolerances (e.g. minimum asphericity of the surfaces). The moulds for the aspherical surfaces are machined on a precision lathe and the single lens objectives are obtained by hot pressing of glass, by applying a small aspherical plastic layer on a lens with spherical surfaces or by injection moulding of plastic lenses with the required shape. The characteristics of a large field aspherical lens are shown in the table below (see also figure 2.58(b)).

Focal distance	8 mm
NA	0.45
Field diameter	2.0 mm (OPD at 800 μm from the centre is 0.047 λ)
Field curvature	24 μm at the rim
Asphericity (S$_1$)	± 25 μm (with respect to the best fit sphere)
Asphericity (S$_2$)	± 2 μm
Diameter	7.5 mm
Thickness	8.5 mm
Weight	<2 g (mount included)

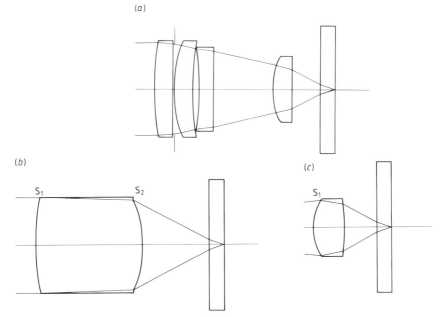

Figure 2.58 (*a*) A scanning objective consisting of four lens elements with spherical surfaces. The collimating part of the light path has been omitted. (*b*) A single lens with two aspherical surfaces (S_1 and S_2) yielding an extremely large image field. (*c*) A single lens with one aspherical surface (S_1) that combines the collimator and objective function. The useful image field is limited to 200 μm.

Another type of aspherical lens is found when a large field is no longer required (diameter < 200 μm). In this case it is even possible to aspherise only one surface of the lens. In figure 2.58(*c*) such a lens is shown for use in a Compact Disc player. The lens combines the function of both the collimator and the objective. The characteristics of a small field aspherical lens are shown in the table below.

Focal distance	3.7 mm
NA (object side)	0.10
NA (image side)	0.45
Field diameter	0.2 mm (OPD at 80 μm from the centre is 0.045 λ)
Field curvature	2 μm at the rim
Asphericity (S_1)	±11 μm (with respect to the best fit sphere)
Diameter	4.1 mm
Thickness	3.2 mm
Optical throw	26.0 mm
Weight	<0.25 g (mount included)

A gradient-index scanning objective. A second solution that leads to a single lens with the required specifications is the use of gradient-index glass material. The effect of the index gradient is mainly to correct the spherical aberration of the single lens and diffraction-limited operation up to an NA of 0.40 has been reported (Yamamoto 1982). The image field is rather limited but this not very important when the entire optical system is actuated.

2.6.3 The substrate of the optical disc

On its way to the information layer the light passes through the plastic disc with its standardised thickness of 1.2 mm. The principle of read-out of the information through the disc has been adopted because it offers a very simple and effective means to protect the information layer from the top surface. On the back surface the disc is aluminised and covered with a non-transparent layer. The diameter of the light beam on the top surface of the disc is typically 0.7 mm. Formally the disc is a plane parallel plastic plate that is part of the light path and has to be of optical quality. By optical quality it is meant that the extra aberrations added to the wavefront on its passage through the disc are so small that their influence on the frequency response of the optical read-out system is negligible. The extra aberrations may be due either to local imperfections of the disc or to an incorrect thickness or orientation (tilt) of the disc. The tolerances on the latter two parameters are ± 0.1 mm and $\pm 0.5°$. The problem that can be caused by the top surface of the disc is an unreliable operation of the radial servo system when, for example, scratches in the tangential direction are present. Careful handling of the disc is always to be recommended.

2.6.4 The detector

The light reflected by the disc is captured again by the objective and guided to the detection unit by the beam splitting cube. On the detector side of the cube a prism is applied (see figure 2.57) such that its apex line is parallel to the tracks on the disc. The prism has a twofold function.

(*a*) The light beam is split in two parts according to a line parallel to the tracks. The light captured by the detectors D_1 and D_2 on one side and by D_3 and D_4 on the other side of this tangential line can be used to obtain a radial push–pull error signal (see §2.5.1) with the detectors connected according to $D_1 + D_2 - D_3 - D_4$.

(*b*) The light deviated by one half of the prism is guided to two detectors that will receive equal fluxes when the reflected beam is focused exactly in the detector plane. Out of focus an imbalance between the two detectors is present as described in §2.5.2 (the pupil obscuration method). The other half of the prism yields the complementary signal and the focus error signal is obtained from the detectors by connecting them according to the scheme

$D_1 - D_2 - D_3 + D_4$. The intensity distribution in the detector plane and the focus error signal of this set-up were illustrated in figure 2.53.

The final operation is the addition of the signals from the four detectors and this yields the high frequency signal.

References

Bennett W R 1960 *Electrical Noise* (New York: McGraw-Hill) p. 15

Bouwhuis G and Braat J J M 1978 Video disk player optics *Appl. Opt.* **17** 1993

—— 1983 Recording and reading of information on optical disks in *Applied Optics and Optical Engineering* ed R Shannon (New York: Academic)

Braat J J M 1983a Optically read disks with increased information density *Appl. Opt.* **22** 2196

—— 1983b Aspherical lenses in optical scanning systems *Proc. SPIE* **399** 294

Braat J J M and Bouwhuis G 1978 Position sensing in video disk read-out *Appl. Opt.* **17** 2013

Bricot C, Lehureau J C, Puech C and le Carvennec F 1976 Optical readout of videodisc *IEEE Trans. Consum. Electron.* **CE-22** 304

Broussaud G, Spitz E, Tinet C and le Carvennec F 1974 A video disc optical design suitable for the consumer market *IEEE Trans. Broadcast Telev. Receivers* **BTR-20** 332

Dekkers N and de Lang H 1974 Differential phase contrast in a STEM *Optik* **41** 452

Goodman J W 1968 *Introduction to Fourier Optics* (San Francisco: McGraw-Hill) pp. 37–42, 48–53, 63–5

de Haan M R and Velzel C H F 1977 Intermodulation and moiré effects in optical video recording *Philips Res. Rep.* **32** 436

Haisma J, Hugues E and Babolat C 1979 Realization of a bi-aspherical objective lens for the Philips Video Long Play System *Opt. Lett.* **4** 70

Heemskerk J P J 1978 Noise in a video disk system: experiments with an (AlGa) As laser *Appl. Opt.* **17** 2007

Hopkins H H 1953 On the diffraction theory of optical images *Proc. R. Soc.* A **217** 408

—— 1979 Diffraction theory of laser read-out systems for optical video discs *J. Opt. Soc. Am.* **69** 4

Korpel A 1978 Simplified diffraction theory of the video disk *Appl. Opt.* **17** 2037

Linfoot E H 1950 The Foucault test in *Recent Advances in Optics* (Oxford: Clarendon) pp. 128–74

Maréchal A 1947 Etude des effets combinés de la diffraction et des aberrations géometriques sur l'image d'un point lumineux *Rev. Opt. Theor. Instrum.* **26** 257

Maréchal A and Françon M 1970 in *Diffraction, Structures des Images* (Paris: Masson et Cie) p. 62

Nagashima M 1983 High density optical disk with V-shaped grooves *Appl. Phys. Lett.* **42**(2) 144

Thomson G H B 1980 *Physics of Semiconductor Laser Devices* (New York: Wiley) pp. 287–307

Vaanholt H 1982 The coding format for composite PAL video signals and stereo sound in LaserVision optical video disc systems *4th Int. Conf. on Video and Data Recording, Southampton* (London: IERE) pp. 351–65

Velzel C H F 1978 Laser beam reading of video records *Appl. Opt.* **17** 2029

Welford W T 1960 Length measurement at the optical resolution limit by scanning microscopy in *Optics in Metrology* ed P Mollet (Oxford: Pergamon) pp. 85–91

Yamamoto N 1982 Selfoc microlens with a spherical surface *Appl. Opt.* **21** 1021

Zernike F 1934 Beugungstheorie des Schneidenverfahrens und seiner verbesserten Form, der Phasenkontrastmethode *Physica* **1** 689

———1938 The concept of degree of coherence and its applications to optical problems *Physica* **5** 794

3 Vector Theory of Diffraction

J Pasman

3.1 Introduction

In the previous chapter the diffraction of light by the information-carrying structure on optical discs was treated on a scalar basis. In the scalar model light is considered to propagate as waves of scalar amplitude $U(r, t)$. When such a wave is diffracted by an obstacle the diffracted light is calculated by assuming that at the surface of the obstacle the phase of the wave is modified in accordance with the obstacle's height profile. The amplitude of the reflected or transmitted light at the surface is taken as the amplitude of the incident field multiplied by the Fresnel reflection or transmission coefficient for normal incidence. In practice, in the case where the information is stored as depressions rather than as changes in reflection, this amplitude is taken as a constant over the surface, irrespective of the variations in the local slope of the surface.

This approach is valid only as long as the wavelength of the incident light is small compared with characteristic transverse dimensions of the scattering structure. In physical terms this means that on a local scale the incident light basically sees plane interfaces. On optical discs however the information density is so large that the dimensions of the depressions carrying the information are of the order of the wavelength of the light. In that case the vectorial electromagnetic character of light becomes of interest (Ping Sheng 1978, Dil and Jacobs 1979). As a consequence the light wave needs to be considered as an electromagnetic wave with certain polarisation properties specified by the vector fields $E(r, t)$ and $H(r, t)$ in accordance with Maxwell's equations. At an interface between two media, where there is optical contrast, the diffraction is governed by the boundary conditions imposed on the local electromagnetic fields $E(r, t)$ and $H(r, t)$. As a result the diffraction depends on the state of polarisation of the incident light and the optical contrast.

Although the scalar theory, having the great advantage of being relatively simple, still gives satisfactory results in this regime of small dimensions it is clear that this theory is fundamentally unable to describe such polarisation effects and one has to resort to a more elaborate vectorial theory to obtain a more complete description of diffraction by optical disc structures. Usually these structures are regarded as regular depressions in a dielectric or metallic substrate, periodic in one dimension (i.e. continuous grooves) or two dimensions (i.e. pits). The scalar approach is to regard these structures as uniaxial or biaxial phase gratings. As shall be seen from the results of vectorial calculations this concept has to be extended and the structure must be considered as a more general combined amplitude and phase grating.

In 1907 Lord Rayleigh proposed a method to solve the problem of diffraction of a plane electromagnetic wave by a grating. In his analysis the diffracted far field is seen to consist of a linear combination of transmitted and reflected plane waves and evanescent waves propagating along the grating surface. The propagating plane waves are usually called diffraction orders, the directions of which satisfy the well known grating formula

$$\sin(\theta_d) = \sin(\theta_i) + m\lambda/p$$

where θ_d and θ_i are the angles of diffraction and of incidence, with respect to the normal to the grating surface, λ is the wavelength of the light, p is the period of the grating and m is the order number.

The basic problem of electromagnetic grating theory now is to answer the question of how the electromagnetic energy of the incident field is distributed over the diffracted waves. In other words, what are the relative intensities of the diffracted orders. Rayleigh's method was based on the assumption, now known as the Rayleigh hypothesis, that the total electromagnetic field, even the field very near the grating and in the grooves, is fully specified by the same combination of diffracted waves that composes the far field, thus neglecting any secondary waves in the groove region. In that case a set of equations can be derived from the boundary conditions from which the amplitudes of the diffracted orders can be calculated. The range of validity of this hypothesis has been the subject of much discussion (Lippmann 1953, Meecham 1956, Millar 1969, Yasuura 1971, van den Berg 1981) and Rayleigh's method shall not be used here. Only in the last two decades has it become possible to rigorously solve the diffraction problem for periodic structures of arbitrary geometry and arbitrary electromagnetic contrast (see Petit 1980). These methods formulate the diffraction problem in terms of differential or integral equations.

The next section will give an outline of the integral representation technique that is used in calculations on diffraction by optical disc structures. When dealing with optical discs various diffraction situations are encountered in which the vectorial theory can be applied. The most obvious case is at read-out of pits on video and audio discs and pregrooves on data discs. In the manufacturing process of the master disc (see Chapter 5) diffraction experiments are used to control and inspect the dimensions of the pits or grooves (Roach *et al* 1978, Dil and Wesdorp 1979, Olijhoek *et al* 1981, Pasman 1983). In §3.3 some of the results of these calculations are presented.

3.2   Mathematical analysis

It is outside the scope of this book to give a detailed account of all steps that lead from Maxwell's equations to the differential integral equations describing the diffraction problem. For this analysis we refer to de Hoop (1977). Instead we will give a brief outline in order to give a general idea of the origin of terms in these equations. The reader who is more interested in the results of the theory than in the mathematics is referred to §3.3.

Maxwell's equations describe the local behaviour in and around a point r of the electromagnetic field which depends both on time and space. When we consider only time harmonic fields of a single angular frequency ω (monochromatic approximation) we may drop the time dependency. This means that we consider only one frequency component of the temporal Fourier spectrum of the electromagnetic quantities. In this case in Maxwell's equations the time derivatives are replaced by the multiplicative factor $-i\omega$. Thus the equations describe only the spatial distribution of the fields, which in our case is the main interest. The space dependency of the fields is analysed by applying Fourier theory, where spatial Fourier transforms are now taken rather than the previously mentioned temporal transform. By doing so integral equations can be derived which represent the electromagnetic fields in a point in space in terms of superposition integrals over a boundary around that point. This 'influence at a distance' replaces the local character of Maxwell's equations. This transformation of Maxwell's equations into the integral representation can be illustrated by considering the general case of a monochromatic field present in a subdomain $V(r)$ in space (figure 3.1). The theory will then be applied to the case of diffraction where there are two such regions in space: one where the radiation is incident and one where the scattering or diffracting medium is present. The integral equations of both regions are coupled by the boundary conditions imposed on the electromagnetic fields.

First we shall consider the case of a monochromatic field of angular frequency ω present in an homogeneous isotropic subdomain $V(r)$ bounded by a closed surface $S(r = r_s)$ (figure 3.1). This surface may be either a physical or a virtual boundary. When there are no sources present inside $V(r)$ the field has to satisfy Maxwell's equations

$$\nabla \times H(r) = J(r) - i\omega D(r)$$
$$\nabla \times E(r) = i\omega B(r)$$
$$\nabla \cdot D(r) = \varrho(r) \tag{3.1}$$
$$\nabla \cdot B(r) = 0$$

where the electromagnetic quantities $H(r)$, $E(r)$, $B(r)$, $D(r)$, $J(r)$ and $\varrho(r)$ have their usual meanings. In our analysis we omit the time dependent factor $\exp(-i\omega t)$.

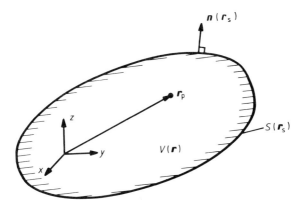

Figure 3.1 Definition of the general geometry.

We can define the spatial Fourier transform $\tilde{A}(k)$ of a vector field $A(r)$ by

$$\tilde{A}(k) = \iiint_{V(r)} \exp(-ik \cdot r) A(r) \, dr. \tag{3.2}$$

The vector k of amplitude $2\pi/p$ is the wavevector associated with a periodicity in the field distribution of spatial frequency $1/p$. Unlike conventional Fourier integrals where the integration is taken over all space, here the integration is only over $V(r)$, which is equivalent to taking conventional Fourier transforms of functions which are considered to be zero outside $V(r)$, even though they in fact need not be zero there. The inverse Fourier transform is then defined by

$$(1/2\pi)^3 \iiint_{\text{all } k} \exp(ik \cdot r) \tilde{A}(k) \, dk = \begin{cases} A(r) & \text{when } r \in V & (3.3a) \\ \tfrac{1}{2}A(r) & \text{when } r \in S & (3.3b) \\ 0 & \text{elsewhere} & (3.3c) \end{cases}$$

where three different values in the right-hand side arise from the decision
to integrate only over $V(r)$.

In order to transform Maxwell's equations (equation 3.1) we need to
know the transform of terms of the form $\nabla \times A(r)$

$$\iiint_{V(r)} \exp(-i k \cdot r) \, \nabla \times \dot{A}(r) \, dr = \iiint_{V(r)} \nabla \times \exp(-i k \cdot r) A(r) \, dr$$

$$- \iiint_{V(r)} A(r) \times \nabla \, \exp(-i k \cdot r) \, dr \qquad (3.4)$$

$$= \oiint_{S(r_s)} \exp(-i k \cdot r) \, n \times A(r) \, dr_s + i k \times \tilde{A}(k)$$

where we have used Gauss's theorem to obtain the surface integral. Here
n denotes the outward normal to $S(r_s)$.

It should be noted that since the domain of integration $V(r)$ is bounded,
a surface integral appears with the vector $n(r_s) \times A(r_s)$ as integrand. This
vector is directed perpendicular to $A(r_s)$ and $n(r_s)$ and has an amplitude
equal to the component of $A(r_s)$ tangential to the boundary $S(r_s)$. Equation
(3.1) can now be transformed into

$$i k \times \tilde{H}(k) - \tilde{J}(k) + i\omega \tilde{D}(k) = \tilde{J}^e_s(k)/i\omega\mu \qquad (3.5a)$$

$$i k \times \tilde{E}(k) \qquad - i\omega \tilde{B}(k) = - \tilde{J}^m_s(k) \qquad (3.5b)$$

where the electric surface current $J^e_s(r_s)$ and analogously the magnetic
surface current $J^m_s(r_s)$ are defined by

$$J^e_s(r_s) = - i\omega\mu \, n \times H(r_s) \qquad (3.6a)$$

$$J^m_s(r_s) = \qquad n \times E(r_s) \qquad (3.6b)$$

at the surface $S(r_s)$ and $J^e_s = J^m_s = 0$ elsewhere. After substituting the
constitutive relations $J(r) = \sigma E(r)$, $B(r) = \mu H(r)$, $D(r) = \varepsilon E(r)$ and some
manipulations with equation (3.5a) and (3.5b) we arrive at

$$\tilde{E}(k) = [k \cdot k - (\sigma - i\omega\varepsilon)i\omega\mu]^{-1} \cdot \left(\tilde{J}^e_s(k) + \frac{(i k \cdot \tilde{J}^e_s(k))i k}{(\sigma - i\omega\varepsilon)i\omega\mu} - i k \times \tilde{J}^m_s(k) \right)$$

$$(3.7)$$

showing that the field component $\tilde{E}(k)$ is completely specified by the values
of the surface currents $\tilde{J}^e_s$ and $\tilde{J}^m_s$. The field $E(r)$ then follows when the
inverse Fourier transform of equation (3.7) is taken according to equation
(3.3). The right-hand side of equation (3.7) is seen to be a product of two
terms, meaning that the inverse Fourier transform can be written as a
convolution integral of the two inverse transforms of both terms. The
inverse transform of the second term is straightforward. The first term can
be shown to be the Fourier transform of a function well known in electro-

magnetic theory called the Green function $G(R)$ given by

$$G(R) = \exp{(ikR)}/4\pi R \tag{3.8a}$$

with

$$k = [(\sigma - i\omega\epsilon)i\omega\mu]^{1/2} = (n + i\varkappa)2\pi/\lambda. \tag{3.8b}$$

This function describes the propagation of a spherical wave of wavenumber k in a medium of refractive index n and index of extinction $\varkappa$ at a distance R from a local point source of unit strength. The electric field in a point r_p in $V(r)$ then follows from

$$\oiint_S G(|r_p - r_s|) \cdot J_s^e(r_s)\, dr_s + (1/k^2)\ \nabla_p \nabla_p \cdot \oiint_S G(|r_p - r_s|) \cdot J_s^e(r_s)\, dr_s$$

$$- \nabla_p \times \oiint_S G(|r_p - r_s|) \cdot J_s^m(r_s)\, dr_s = \begin{cases} E(r_p) & \text{when } r_p \in V \\ \tfrac{1}{2}E(r_p) & \text{when } r_p \in S \\ 0 & \text{elsewhere.} \end{cases} \tag{3.9}$$

We see that is possible to write the field E in r_p in terms of the fields at the boundary $S(r_s)$ of a closed domain around r_p. In other words, once we know the fields at the boundary we can calculate the field amplitude at each point r_p within that bounded domain. This is a rigorous restatement of Huygens' principle. The integrals in equation (3.9) can be considered to be superposition integrals where the tangential components of the magnetic and electric fields at the surface $J_s^e(r_s)$ and $J_s^m(r_s)$ act as oscillator strengths and the Green function forms an impulse response describing the transfer from r_s to r_p.

The preceding discussion treated the general case of a wave in an homogeneous medium $V(r)$. When dealing with diffraction we must take into account two regions $V_0(r)$ and $V_1(r)$, the first being the region of incidence of the wave and the latter being the scatterer (figure 3.2). The optical contrast between the two media is defined by the, generally complex, indices of refraction of the media in regions V_0 and V_1: n_0 and $n_1 + i\varkappa_1$, $\varkappa_1$ being the extinction coefficient. This means that the scattering medium may be dielectric ($\varkappa = 0$), metallic ($\varkappa > 0$) or even infinitely conducting ($\varkappa \gg 0$). The electric fields $E_0(r)$ and $E_1(r)$ in regions V_0 and V_1 are written as

$$E_{0,1} = E_{0,1}^i + E_{0,1}^s$$

where $E_{0,1}^i$ is the incident field which would be present in all space in absence of optical contrast and $E_{0,1}^s$ is the scattered field, i.e. the difference between the actual field and the incident field.

The fields in the two subdomains V_0 and V_1 are coupled by the boundary conditions, stating that the tangential components of $E(r)$ and $H(r)$ are

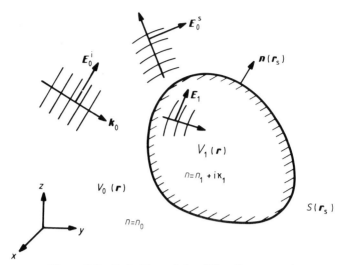

Figure 3.2 Definition of the diffraction geometry.

continuous across the boundary

$$n \times E_0(r_s) = n \times E_1(r_s)$$

$$n \times H_0(r_s) = n \times H_1(r_s).$$

(3.10)

Following de Hoop we can apply the foregoing analysis to the two sub-domains to get the equations for medium 0 and medium 1.

For medium 0

$$\left(1 + \frac{\nabla_p \nabla_p}{k_0^2}\right) \cdot \oiint_S G_0(|r_p - r_s|) J_s^e(r_s)\, dS(r_s) - \nabla_p \times \oiint_S G_0(|r_p - r_s|) J_s^m(r_s)\, dS(r_s)$$

$$= \begin{cases} -E^s(r_p) & \text{when } r_p \in V_0(r) & (3.11a) \\ -\frac{1}{2} E^s(r_p) + \frac{1}{2} E^i(r_p) & \text{when } r_p \in S(r_s) & (3.11b) \\ E^i(r_p) & \text{when } r_p \in V_1(r). & (3.11c) \end{cases}$$

For medium 1

$$\left(1 + \frac{\nabla_p \nabla_p}{k_1^2}\right) \cdot \oiint_S G_1(|r_p - r_s|) J_s^e(r_s)\, dS(r_s) - \nabla_p \times \oiint_S G_1(|r_p - r_s|) J_s^m(r_s)\, dS(r_s)$$

$$= \begin{cases} E_1(r_p) & \text{when } r_p \in V_1(r) & (3.12a) \\ \frac{1}{2} E_1(r_p) & \text{when } r_p \in S(r_s) & (3.12b) \\ 0 & \text{when } r_p \in V_0(r) & (3.12c) \end{cases}$$

where the (complex) wavenumbers k_0 and k_1 are defined by

$$k_0 = k n_0 \qquad k_1 = k(n_1 + i\varkappa_1)$$

k being the free-space wavenumber. Analogous expressions hold for the magnetic fields.

These integral expressions can be considered in two different ways.

(*a*) The first way is to consider only the equations (3.11b) and (3.12b). They form integral equations which implicitly give the unknowns $E^s(r_s)$, $E_1(r_s)$, $H^s(r_s)$ and $H_1(r_s)$ at the boundary. For a numerical evaluation of the integral equations two methods can be used. First, in the moment method, the integrals are approximated by summations of sub-integrals over sub-areas in which $J_s^e(r_s)$ and $J_s^m(r_s)$ are assumed to be constant. We then arrive at a matrix equation where the fields in all these sub-areas are the unknowns. Solving this equation gives the fields at the boundary. A disadvantage of this method is in general the large number of sub-areas and hence the large rank of the matrix. The second method, particularly suited for periodic structures, is to expand the surface currents in a (limited) number of Fourier components. These components can be taken outside the integrals and again a matrix equation is obtained, now with the Fourier components as unknowns.

(*b*) A second way is to consider expressions (3.11a), (3.12a), (3.11c) and (3.12c) to be integral representations, rather than implicit equations, of the fields $E(r_p)$ and $H(r_p)$ outside the boundary $S(r_s)$ in terms of the fields $E(r_s)$ and $H(r_s)$ at the boundary. In that case the surface currents can be calculated in a relatively simple way by using equations (3.11c) and (3.12c), since in these equations the right-hand sides are known. Once the currents are known, they can be inserted into equations (3.11a) and (3.12a) to give the diffracted fields in a point of observation r_p. As an example this method, proposed by Wirgin (1979), is now treated in more detail for the case of a plane wave diffracted by a uniaxial grating. We consider for instance a polygonal height profile, the geometry of which is defined in figure 3.3.

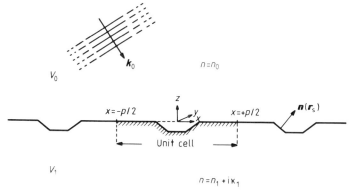

Figure 3.3 Diffraction geometry in the case of a uniaxial periodic polygonal height profile.

The interface $S(r_s)$ between the scattering medium in V_1 and the free space V_0 is periodic in the x direction with period p and is of infinite extent in the x and y directions.

When this periodic structure is illuminated by a normally incident plane wave, the diffraction problem is periodic and hence the surface currents and the diffracted fields must show the same periodicity, meaning that they can be expanded in Fourier series. When the wave is not normally incident, the phase of the wave changes over the interface and by introducing inverse phase factors in the analysis the periodicity is restored. In this case we speak of quasiperiodic currents, fields etc.

Omitting the time harmonic factor $\exp(-i\omega t)$ the incident field may be written as

$$E^i(r_p) = \hat{e}_i \exp(i\alpha_0 x_p + i\beta_0 y_p - i\gamma_0 z_p) \tag{3.13}$$

where α_0, β_0, γ_0 are the components of the incident wavevector k_0 in the x, y and z directions respectively. The complex amplitude vector of the electric field $\hat{e}_i$ is usually taken of unit amplitude. The direction of $\hat{e}_i$ specifies the state of polarisation. When we restrict our analysis to the case where the incident light propagates in the x–z plane (i.e. $\beta_0 = 0$) at an angle θ_i with the normal (i.e. $\alpha_0 = k_0 \sin\theta_i$), it appears that the diffraction problem decomposes into two independent polarisation eigenstates, one in which the electric vector is linearly polarised parallel to the grooves and one in which the magnetic vector is parallel to the grooves. The first case is called parallel, E, TE or P polarisation, the second perpendicular, H, TM or S polarisation. This means that there is no cross-talk between these polarisation eigenstates and diffraction of light of any polarisation can be treated by solving the diffraction problem of both orthogonal eigenstates separately. Thus we may write (figure 3.4)

$$E^{i,\parallel} = (0,1,0) \qquad \exp[ik_0(x_p \sin\theta_i - z_p \cos\theta_i)] \qquad \text{for E pol} \tag{3.14a}$$

$$E^{i,\perp} = (\cos\theta_i, 0, \sin\theta_i) \quad \exp[ik_0(x_p \sin\theta_i - z_p \cos\theta_i)] \qquad \text{for H pol.} \tag{3.14b}$$

Since $J(r_s)\cdot\exp(-i\alpha_0 x)$ is periodic the quasiperiodic surface currents may be expanded in the Fourier series

$$J_s^{e,m}(r_s) = \exp(i\alpha_0 x)\sum_{l=-\infty}^{+\infty} j_l^{e,m}\exp(2\pi i l x_s/p) = \sum_{l=-\infty}^{+\infty} j_l^{e,m}\exp(i\alpha_l x_s) \tag{3.15}$$

with

$$\alpha_l = \alpha_0 + 2\pi l/p. \tag{3.16}$$

Since the vector $j_l^{e,m}$ lies in the surface, it has only two independent components, one in the y direction and the other perpendicular to y, pointing along the surface.

We choose an alternative, quasiperiodic representation of the Green functions $G_{0,1}(|r_p - r_s|)$ in media 0 and 1 in terms of plane waves (Petit 1967)

$$G_{0,1}(|r_p - r_s|) = \sum_{m=-\infty}^{+\infty} \frac{i}{2\gamma_m^{0,1}p} \exp[i\alpha_m(x_p - x_s) + i\gamma_m^{0,1}(|z_p - z_s|)] \quad (3.17)$$

where $\gamma_m^{0,1}$ is defined by

$$\gamma_m^{0,1} = (k_{0,1}^2 - \alpha_m^2)^{1/2}. \quad (3.18)$$

In the derivation of equation (3.17) the integration in the y direction in equations (3.11) and (3.12) has already been performed.

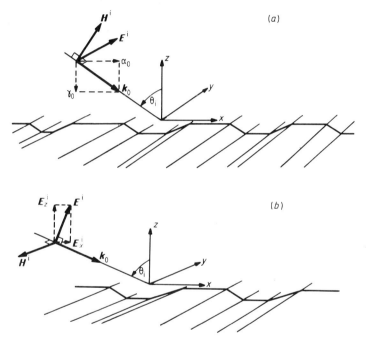

Figure 3.4 Two linearly independent polarisation states: either (a) the electric (E polarisation) or (b) the magnetic (H Polarisation) vector of the incident light is polarised parallel to the grooves.

Now equations (3.15) and (3.17) are substituted in equations (3.11c) and (3.12c). The Fourier components $j_l^{e,m}$ can be taken outside the integral and when the height profile $z_s(x_s)$ is known the integration over x_s along the surface of the unit cell $-p/2 < x_s < p/2$ can be performed. Then the spatial derivatives ∇_p are taken and we arrive at two equations with double summations over m and l. In the right-hand sides of equations (3.11c) and

(3.12c) we have terms $\exp(i\alpha_0 x_p)$ from equation (3.13) and in the left-hand sides the term $\exp(i\alpha_m x_p)$ from equation (3.17). Since such terms of different m are mutually orthogonal, we may decompose the two equations with summations over m and l into a set of equations, one for each m, with summations over l only. This means that we end with a matrix with rows characterised by the index m of the Green functions and columns characterised by the index l of the surface current components. The unknown vector is formed by the components $j_{l,y}^e$ and $j_{l,xz}^m$ for the E polarisation case and $j_{l,xz}^e$ and $j_{l,y}^m$ for the H polarisation case. The components of the right-hand vector in this matrix equation are known, they are all zero except for one component where $m = 0$ which equals $\hat{e}_i$ according to equations (3.13) and (3.14). This matrix equation can be solved in standard ways, for instance with the lower–upper decomposition technique. Once the surface currents are known they can be inserted into equations (3.11a) and (3.12a) to obtain the Fourier components of the transmitted and reflected fields. From these the amplitudes, phases and intensities of the diffracted orders are easily calculated.

An accuracy of about 1% is obtained when 12 Fourier components of the surface currents are included, resulting in a matrix of rank 50.

3.3   Results

3.3.1   Deviations from scalar theory
Some results of the vectorial theory for various diffraction geometries will be given and compared with scalar predictions.

Rectangular pit.   First we consider the diffraction by one rectangular depression with vertical walls in an aluminum substrate (Dil and Jacobs 1978). The geometry is defined in figure 3.5.
The parameters are taken to be

$L = 765$ nm	$n_0 = 1.0$
$W = 525$ nm	$n_1 = 1.5$
$D = 110$ nm	$\varkappa_1 = 6.0.$
$\lambda = 633$ nm	

The normally incident radiation is linearly polarised with the E vector parallel to the long side of the pit. Using the moment method the local fields in the surface at the bottom of the pit are calculated. The scalar prediction would be that the difference in phase of the fields at the top and at the bottom is $2\pi D/\lambda = 0.35\pi$. Also the amplitudes of the electric and magnetic

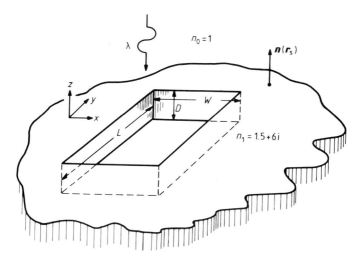

Figure 3.5 Scattering geometry of one rectangular depression in a metallic substrate.

fields, being sums of incident and reflected amplitudes, would be

$$|E_y| = \left| \frac{2}{n_1 + 1 + i\varkappa_1} \right| |E^i| \qquad = 0.3\,|E^i|$$

$$|H_x| = \left| \frac{2(n_1 + i\varkappa_1)}{n_1 + 1 + i\varkappa_1} \right| \left| \frac{k}{\omega\mu} E^i \right| \qquad = 1.9\,\frac{k}{\omega\mu}\,|E^i|\,.$$

Figure 3.6 shows the vectorially calculated phase and amplitude distribution of the equivalent electric surface current J_e at the bottom of the pit. The shaded surfaces represent the scalar predictions.

It is clear that there are large differences between scalar and vectorial results. At the bottom of the pit near the walls perpendicular to the incident E vector the amplitude is large compared with the scalar value, whereas close to the two walls parallel to E the amplitude is small. Also the phase is largest near the walls perpendicular to E.

These results can be explained by comparing them with Sommerfeld's solution to the diffraction by a narrow slit in a perfectly conducting screen (Sommerfeld 1964). Here the incident light induces surface currents which reflect the energy. Again we can consider two polarisation states. When the incident E vector points parallel to the slit, large surface currents are induced near the slit, which even diverge at the edges. Hence much of the light is reflected by the edges which act as line sources and only a little light is transmitted through the slit. An equivalent way of reasoning is based on

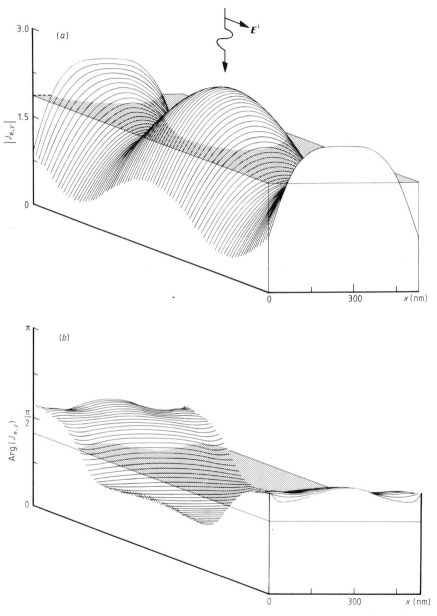

Figure 3.6   Distributions of the amplitude (*a*) and phase (*b*) of the electric surface current $J_{e,y}$ (in units kE^i) at the bottom of a depression in aluminium. The shaded planes represent the predictions of scalar theory.

the consequences of the boundary conditions. Since the screen is a perfect conductor the electric field must be zero inside the screen. The boundary condition also states that the tangential component of the electric field directly outside the conductor must be zero. With the *E* vector polarised parallel to the slit also in the slit near the edges the electric field must be small, meaning that at a distance behind the screen the slit appears to be narrower.

In the other polarisation case the induced electric currents are directed normal to the slit and at the edges of the slit they must be zero, since the currents cannot leave the material. As a consequence the edges will not radiate and the light easily flows through the slit. As to the boundary conditions, at the edge the electric field vector is normal to the surface and hence the field need not be zero. So the light incident near the slit is only little affected by the edges and most is transmitted. Although in this case aluminum is not really a perfect conductor at optical frequencies, the observed polarisation effects may be understood in a qualitative way. When the incident *E* vector is parallel to the walls it is everywhere tangential to the conducting surface. Therefore much light is reflected by the edges and the walls resulting in small fields at the bottom near the walls. This also means that the average phase of the reflected light is smaller than the scalar theory predicts and the pit appears to be shallower. When the *E* vector is normal to the walls little light is reflected by the edges and the electric field being discontinuous across the boundary at the walls may reach the bottom with a relatively large amplitude and is then reflected. The phase is therefore larger in this case.

These polarisation effects become clearer when we consider diffraction by a uniaxial structure, i.e. an array of grooves, when there are no cross-effects near the corners of two walls.

Grooves with vertical walls. Two pure states of polarisation may be distinguished. The scattering geometry is defined in figure 3.7. The width of the lower and upper horizontal parts is taken to be 0.8 λ and the depth is 0.24 λ. The normally incident light illuminates the aluminium substrate of refractive index $n_1 = 1.5 + 6i$.

The calculated electric surface currents at the top and bottom parts are shown in figure 3.8 for both polarisation directions of the incident light. The scalar values are given by the horizontal lines. In the parallel polarisation case the incident electric field is everywhere tangential to the surface. We note that the current at the top oscillates around the scalar value but near the edge the current increases. On the bottom of the groove the current approaches zero amplitude near the walls since the incident field is blocked by the edges and the walls. Also the phase difference of the fields on the lower and upper sides is less than scalar theory would predict.

In the complementary case of perpendicular polarisation the currents on

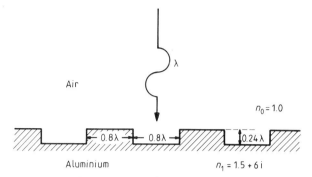

Figure 3.7   Scattering geometry of rectangular grooves in aluminium.

the top surface decrease near the edges and little light is reflected. Instead the electric field easily flows in the groove and large values are attained at the bottom. The phase difference is also large and the groove appears to be deeper than the geometrical depth.

It is clear now that not only the phases but also the field amplitudes at the surface are modulated by the presence of the grooves and as a consequence the structure acts as a combined phase and amplitude grating.

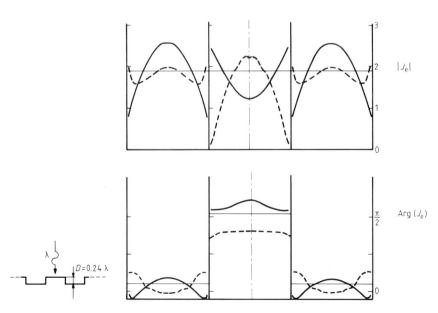

Figure 3.8   Amplitudes and phases of the electric surface currents at the top and bottom parts of rectangular grooves. E polarisation is represented by the broken curves, H polarisation by the full curves. Scalar values are given by the horizontal lines.

The phase depth of the grooves can be defined as the difference in phase in a plane just above the grooves of the fields reflected at the top and at the bottom of the grooves. This phase depth represents the effective depth of the groove as seen by the incident light, which apparently depends on the state of polarisation with respect to the groove direction. This phase depth is of particular interest at read-out of the information on optical discs.

There now follows a more detailed consideration of how the polarisation effects depend on the geometry of the grooves.

In figure 3.9 the average amplitudes and phases of the electric surface currents at the bottom are plotted as a function of the groove width W when the groove depth $D = 0.24\,\lambda$ and as a function of the geometrical depth D for $W = 0.64\,\lambda$. We may draw two conclusions from these graphs. First the apparent size of the groove is always larger in perpendicular polarisation than in parallel polarisation. Second, the deviation from what the scalar approach predicts is large for values of W smaller than λ. For increasing widths this deviation decreases. The depth D is seen to have little effect on the relative deviation even when D approaches zero. Hence it is the

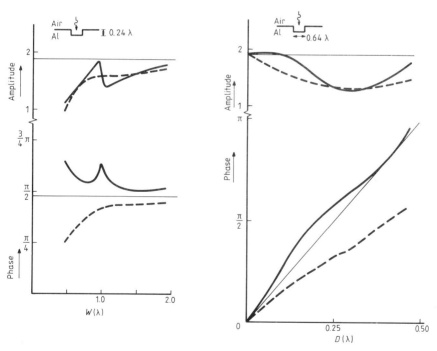

Figure 3.9 Average amplitudes and phases of the electric surface currents at the bottom of a rectangular groove as a function of groove width W and groove depth D. The broken and bold full curves indicate respectively the E and H polarisation cases. Scalar values are indicated by the light full lines.

transverse dimension that determines the validity of the scalar theory, as was stated in the introduction.

It should be noted that these rules of thumb are derived for grooves in a highly conducting metallic surface where there is high optical contrast. In that case the internal electric fields approach zero value and the boundary conditions have radical consequences for the scattered fields. When the optical contrast is less, as is the case with a dielectric grating, the polarisation effects are smaller as will be seen later.

Up to this point we have only considered field distributions in pits and grooves with vertical walls to illustrate the polarisation effects. In practice however we are more interested in diffraction-order amplitudes, rather than surface currents, produced by more realistic structures with non-vertical walls of various optical contrasts. The vectorial diffraction theory, as described in §3.2, will now be applied to two extremes in diffraction problems as encountered in the disc manufacturing process. In both cases grooves only are considered, the optical contrast being very low in the first case and extremely high in the second.

Development of grooves.   As will be explained in more detail in Chapter 5, the pit structure is recorded on a master disc by exposing a thin layer of photosensitive material (resist) by a modulated focused laser spot. The pit structure appears when the photoresist is developed. To compensate for small variations in exposure and development parameters the development has to be monitored in order to stop the development at the moment when the average pit volume has attained its desired value. For this purpose a special test band is recorded on each master where during development the light from a HeNe laser beam is diffracted by the evolving pit or groove structure. The intensities of the transmitted diffraction orders are detected to indicate the stage of the development.

To calculate the diffracted intensities during development we approximate the actual cross section of the grooves by straight line segments resulting in a polygonal height profile (figure 3.10). We also assume that during development the slope of the groove walls increases while the width W at the top of the groove remains unchanged. This means that in this model the opening groove has a triangular cross section until the resist–glass interface is reached and the height profile becomes trapezoidal. The geometrical and optical parameters specifying the diffraction problem are more or less determined by the standard mastering process. The grating period $Q = 1670$ nm, the layer thickness D is about 120 to 130 nm, the groove width W is around 600 nm and the slope angle θ is taken as a variable. The optical contrast is defined by the refractive indices of the glass and resist $n_0 = 1.6$ and of the developer $n_1 = 1.33$, resulting in a reflection of less than 1%. Since these two indices are real and differ only slightly the boundary conditions do not have very different consequences for the two

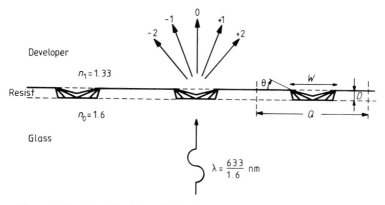

Figure 3.10 Model of the diffraction geometry in the resist development process.

polarisation directions. The field amplitudes at the interface are modulated only slightly and we expect small polarisation effects. Figure 3.11(*a*) and (*b*) plots the diffracted intensities of the first and second transmission orders $I_1^{\|, \perp}$ and $I_2^{\|, \perp}$ for the two cases of polarisation as a function of the slope angle θ for two values of W. The scalar values are also indicated. As was expected the polarisation effects are not very drastic. In particular the first order depends little on the polarisation and it should be noted that in this case the scalar values correspond rather well with the vectorial results. The polarisation direction has more effect on the second order and here we see that the scalar curve lies between the two vectorial curves. The intensities I_1 and I_2 rapidly increase when θ and hence the volume of the grooves increase until the glass substrate is reached. At this stage, indicated in the graphs by an arrow on the bottom axes, the rate at which the volume increases with θ decreases due to the truncating effect of the substrate, resulting in points of inflection in the curves. Also we note that the second-order intensity goes through a maximum when W is larger than some 500 nm. This can be understood by recalling that a grating where the width of the groove is half the period has no even diffracted orders. So, when the average width of the groove increases to values larger than $Q/4$ the second-order intensity reduces.

For geometries such as those appearing at the development of standard masters we may conclude that the first-order intensity depends almost entirely on the volume of the grooves, whereas the second order also strongly depends on the width as compared with the period. These statements are in agreement with scalar predictions and to control and understand the development process we may apply scalar theory with good results. Figure 5.11 shows a measured curve rather than a calculated curve.

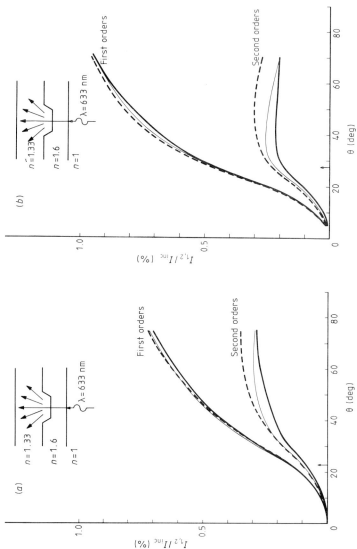

Figure 3.11 Calculated intensities of the first and second diffracted orders during development as a function of the opening angle θ for grooves 500 nm (a) and 600 nm (b) wide in 130 nm thick photoresist. The light full curves give the results predicted by scalar theory. The angle at which the cross section of the groove changes from a triangular shape into a trapezoidal shape is indicated by an arrow on the horizontal axis. The bold full curves are results for H polarisation and the broken curves for E polarisation.

Grooves in silver. We will now consider the case of high electromagnetic contrast. In the mastering process a developed master is coated by evaporation with a thin layer of silver after which diffraction measurements may be performed for diagnostic purposes (see §5.2.4, p. 203). The geometry of the scattering structure on the interface, which is assumed to be unaltered by the evaporated silver layer, is defined in figure 3.12. It is basically the same polygonal structure but now the light of wavelength $\lambda = 633$ nm is incident in air on a highly reflecting metallic surface of complex index of refraction $n_1 = 0.08 + 4.1i$, resulting in a reflection of 98%.

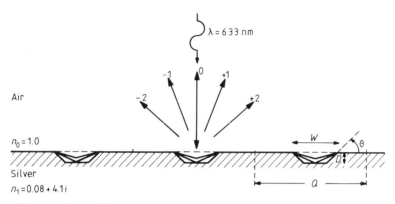

Figure 3.12 Diffraction geometry of grooves of polygonal cross section in silver.

Again we apply the vectorial analysis of §3.2 to calculate the amplitudes of the diffracted reflection orders. From these not only the intensities but also the phases of the orders are derived. As was explained in §2.2.3 (p. 21) the amplitude of the read-out signal at playback is to a large degree determined by the difference in phase of the zero and first orders. This phase difference is related to the phase depth of the groove and it is therefore also a function of the geometry. Measurement of this phase difference is a valuable tool in the inspection and evaluation of master discs and replicas (see §5.2.4). In the phase measurement equipment however the incident beam of light is not normally incident but at such an angle that the direction of the first order coincides with the incoming beam (Littrow mount). For a grating of period $Q = 1670$ nm this means an angle of incidence, θ_i, of $10.9°$. In our calculations we also consider this case to predict phase differences as measured.

Figure 3.13 shows some calculated curves of the intensities (top graphs, $\theta_i = 0$) and phase difference (bottom graphs, $\theta_i = 0$ and $\theta_i = 10.9$) of the diffracted orders as a function of the slope angle θ. The scalar predictions

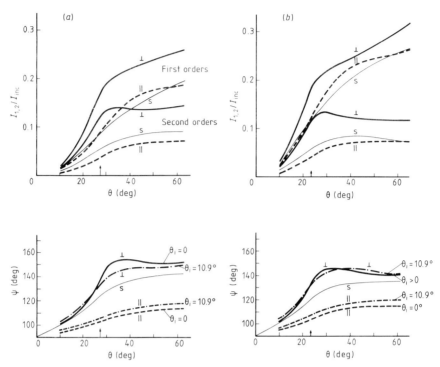

Figure 3.13 Diffraction order intensities (top graphs) and phase differences (bottom graphs) as a function of the slope angle θ for 130 nm deep grooves of width $W = 500$ nm (*a*) and $W = 600$ nm (*b*). E polarisation (broken and chain curves), H polarisation (full bold curves) and scalar (full light curves) curves are calculated for normal incidence. In the bottom graphs the vectorial phase differences are included for incidence at an angle of $10.9°$.

are also included. We note large polarisation effects, both in the order intensities and in the phase difference. For values of W smaller than 575 nm and $\theta \leqslant 30°$ the second order $I_2^\perp$ in H polarisation becomes even larger than the first order in E polarisation! Again we see that the effects of the polarisation direction of the incident light become smaller for larger values of W. In particular this is true for the first order. The second-order intensities and the phase difference ψ always show larger differences between the two polarisation cases, even when the grooves become wider. This is in accordance with the behaviour of the orders in the low contrast case. Again the apparent size of the groove is largest in H polarisation. Although the curves of the scalar theory are qualitatively similar to the vectorial curves, it is clear that they deviate too much to be used successfully in a quantitative analysis of the results of diffraction measurements as performed on grooves on silvered masters. This application is considered in the next section.

3.3.2 Determination of groove geometries by diffraction measurements

In the evaluation of the mastering process and its products, the master discs, it is important to know what geometries are produced on masters and how these geometries depend on various process parameters. Since the dimensions of the structures on masters are so small, standard measurement techniques fail to give accurate results. Optical microscopy can be used for the analysis of larger defects like dust particles, but detailed information on the shape of the pits or grooves is beyond the classical limit set by the resolving power. Techniques which may be used with some success, however, are destructive, and even then, with electron microscopy or Talystep measurements, it is difficult to extract accurate information on the width, depth and slope of depressions only some 0.1 μm deep (figure 3.14).

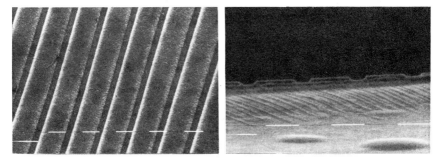

Figure 3.14 Scanning electron micrographs of continuous grooves: left, top view and right, cross section. Each horizontal white bar indicates one micron.

As shown in the last example of §3.3.1. the diffraction of light depends strongly on the scattering geometry and this suggests using these diffraction properties to determine the geometry. For this reason annular areas of grooves (test bands) can be recorded on masters where in each band some recording parameter, such as the intensity or the width of the recording spot, is varied. The groove profile will vary correspondingly and this produces different intensities and phases of the diffracted orders when such test bands are illuminated by the beam of a HeNe laser. By comparing these measured quantities with vectorially calculated intensities and phases the groove geometry may be estimated. For our calculations we again approximate the height profile by straight line segments giving triangular or trapezoidal grooves in a plane interface. Then the geometry is defined by the four parameters D, the thickness of the photoresist layer, W, the width at the top of the groove, the groove period Q, which we take here as a constant value of 1670 nm, and the slope angle θ. The case of normal incidence is considered in the calculation of the intensities, but the phase difference is calculated for light incident at an angle of $10.9°$ to adapt to the scattering geometry in the phase meter. In all cases the wavelength of the light is 633 nm.

Figure 3.15 shows the effect of the groove width W. For very narrow grooves ($W = 450$ nm) we observe very strong polarisation effects. In H polarisation both first- and second-order intensities are about twice as large as the corresponding orders in E polarisation and again the second order in H polarisation is even larger than the first order in E polarisation. Also the phase difference ψ is much larger in H polarisation. When we increase W the largest effects are seen in E polarisation. Compared with the first H polarisation order the first E polarisation order drastically increases. When in graphs of increasing widths we compare points of equal depths, for instance the points indicated by an arrow where the groove reaches the bottom, in E polarisation the second order and the phase difference increase, whereas in H polarisation they both decrease, the phase difference especially at steeper slopes. Of course these effects are caused by the different effects of the boundary conditions in both polarisations. In the E polarisation case the field can hardly penetrate the groove and the groove appears so narrow and shallow that any increase of W has the effect of increasing both the apparent width and depth and as a result the apparent volume and consequently $I_1^{\parallel}$ rapidly increase. For the second E polarisation order the apparent depth increases and the width still appears to be smaller than $Q/4$ and so $I_2^{\parallel}$ also increases for increasing W. In H polarisation however the groove appears to be much larger than $Q/4$ and for larger W the groove width approaches $Q/2$ and hence $I_2^{\perp}$ falls off. This is also the reason why ψ decreases for wider grooves. In scalar theory it can be shown that ψ must be $90°$ when the structure has a duty cycle of $\frac{1}{2}$, i.e. when the effective groove width is half the period.

In the standard mastering process the groove width W usually lies in the region of 500 to 600 nm and in this region we can take advantage of the different polarisation properties occurring when W varies around λ.

The effect of the photoresist layer thickness D is shown in figure 3.16 for the case when $W = 600$ nm. Both graphs are identical for smaller slope angles, when the bottom of the resist layer has not yet been reached, and the curves diverge only for steeper slopes. As expected, larger intensities are calculated for deeper grooves. The polarisation effects remain roughly

---

Figure 3.15 Calculated diffraction order intensities (top graphs) and phase differences (bottom graphs) as a function of the slope angle θ for 125 nm deep grooves of width $W = 450$ nm (a), 500 nm (b), 550 nm (c) and 600 nm (d). E polarisation (broken curves) and H polarisation (full curves) are calculated for normal incidence. In the bottom graphs the phase differences are included for incidence at an angle of $10.9°$. The arrows on the horizontal axes indicate the points where the groove shape changes from triangular to trapezoidal.

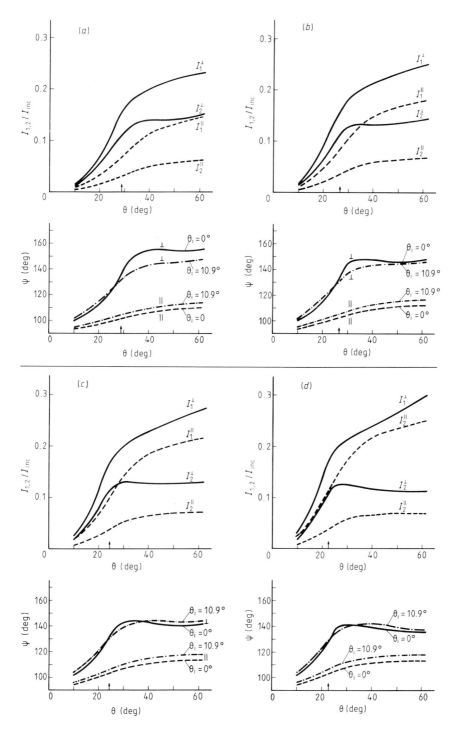

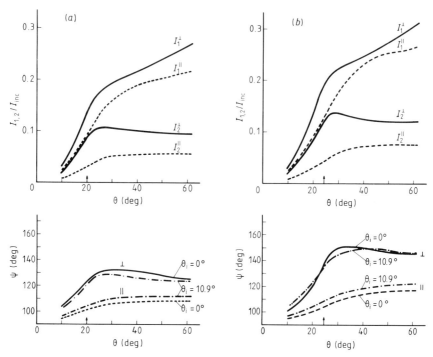

Figure 3.16 Calculated diffraction order intensities (top graphs) and phase differences (bottom graphs) as a function of the slope angle θ for 600 nm wide grooves of depth $D = 110$ nm (*a*) and 135 nm (*b*). E polarisation (broken curves) and H polarisation (full curves) are calculated for normal incidence. In the bottom graphs the phase differences are included for incidence at an angle of $10.9°$. The arrows on the horizontal axes indicate the points where the groove shape changes from triangular to trapezoidal.

the same. The largest effect of the depth is seen in the phase difference. Here deeper grooves mean larger phase depths and hence larger phase differences.

To illustrate the application of this method figure 3.17 shows an example of experimental values measured on a silvered master where test bands were recorded by a light spot of different intensities. The numerical aperture of the recording lens, determining the width of the light spot, was 0.65 in all bands. We see that these experimental values show good correspondence with the theoretical curves of the case where $W = 575$ nm and $D = 122.5$ nm. Also we note that the effect of increasing the recording intensity is to increase the slope of the groove walls whereas the width W remains nearly constant and only for larger intensities tends to larger values.

In this way it is possible to determine groove shapes in a non-destructive way with a resolution of about 25 nm in W, 3 nm in D and $3°$ in θ.

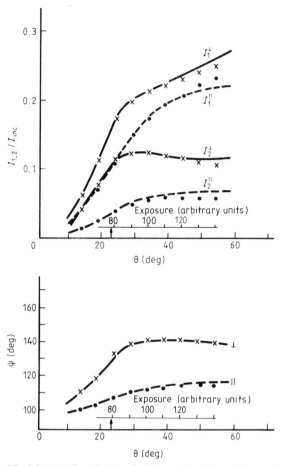

Figure 3.17 Measured values of the order intensities and phase differences for E polarisation (dots) and H polarisation (crosses) as a function of the recording exposure level. The measured values are compared with calculated vectorial curves for the case $W = 575$ nm and $D = 122.5$ nm.

3.3.3 Calculation of read-out signals

Pregrooves. On data storage discs the users write their information in preformatted tracks (see Chapter 6). Such a track consists of a relatively short heading of pits, containing the address etc, followed by a pregroove where user information can be written. This pregroove guides the light spot during write, search and read actions. When the light spot moves over the tracks the light is diffracted in various directions giving rise to different read-out signals as described in Chapter 2. For pregrooves two read-out signals are of particular interest.

The first, the central aperture (CA) signal, is obtained by collecting all the diffracted light which passes through the read-out lens. This signal is used to read the heading pits and the user information which has been written as a modulation of the local reflection. This signal is always positive but it has minimum amplitude when the radial position of the read-out spot is in the centre of a groove.

The second signal, called the radial push–pull (PP) signal is used as a servo signal for keeping the spot on the track (see Chapter 4). It is a difference signal, obtained by subtracting the read-out signals of two detector halves of a radially split diode (figure 3.18). The CA signal then is the sum signal of both halves. When the radial position x of the light spot is at the centre of a groove or in the middle between two grooves, the diffraction problem is symmetric in the radial direction: just as much light energy is diffracted to the right as to the left. In these cases the radial PP signal is zero. In all other positions the PP signal is non-zero, either negative or positive. Both the CA and PP amplitudes are determined by the amplitudes and phases of the diffracted orders (see Chapter 2), which in their turn depend on the groove geometry. It is therefore obvious to use the vectorial theory to calculate these signals as a function of the groove geometry.

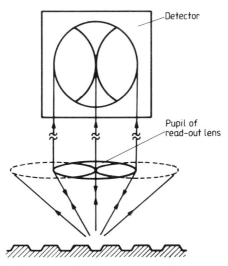

Figure 3.18 Schematic diagram of the read-out arrangement.

Figure 3.19 shows the distribution of the diffracted orders at the detector surface for the case when the plus first and minus first orders just touch. This occurs when the radial spatial frequency is half the cut-off frequency of the read-out lens, i.e. when the track pitch Q equals λ/NA, where NA denotes the numerical aperture of the lens. In that case we only need consider first and zero radial orders. On both detector halves we have two areas of different character. In region I of area S_I only the zero order of amplitude A_0 is present, producing an electrical signal $S_I|A_0|^2$. In region II of area S_{II} the first and zero order overlap and the electrical signal is determined by the interference of both orders

$$S_{II}[\,|A_0 + A_1 \exp(i\psi + i\,2\pi x/Q)|^2\,].$$

The phase difference between first and zero order is ψ when the spot is centred on the groove and it changes linearly with the radial displacement x.

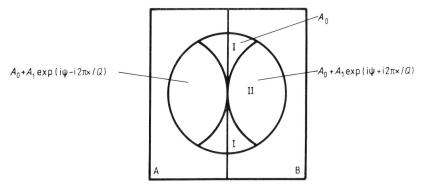

Figure 3.19 Distribution of diffraction orders in the detector plane.

The signals of both detector halves are given by

$$I_A(x) = S_I A_0^2 + S_{II}\{A_0^2 + A_1^2 + 2A_0A_1[\cos\psi\,\cos(2\pi x/Q) + \sin\psi\,\sin(2\pi x/Q)]\}$$
(3.19a)

$$I_B(x) = S_I A_0^2 + S_{II}\{A_0^2 + A_1^2 + 2A_0A_1[\cos\psi\,\cos(2\pi x/Q) - \sin\psi\,\sin(2\pi x/Q)]\}$$
(3.19b)

By adding and subtracting these signals we obtain the CA and PP signals

$$I_{CA}(x) = 2S_I|A_0|^2 + 2S_{II}[A_0^2 + A_1^2 + 2A_0A_1\cos\psi\,\cos(2\pi x/Q)] \quad (3.20a)$$

$$I_{PP}(x) = 4S_{II}A_0A_1\sin\psi\,\sin(2\pi x/Q). \quad (3.20b)$$

These signals must then be normalised by dividing the signals by the signal obtained by reflection at a plane interface. Figure 3.20 shows the general behaviour of the CA and PP signals as a function of the radial displacement.

Two quantities are of special importance namely the maximum normalised amplitude I_{PP} of the PP signal, i.e. when $x = Q/4$, and the normalised CA amplitude I_{CA} in the centre of the groove, i.e. when $x = 0$. This CA amplitude determines the signal space available to the user, since larger values of I_{CA} give better contrast in local changes of reflectivity, for instance produced by the burning of holes in a reflective layer (see Chapter 6).

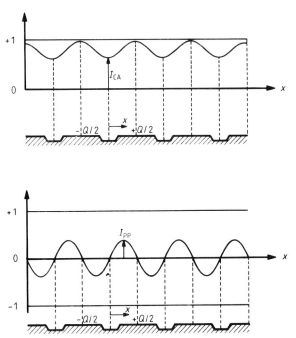

Figure 3.20 CA and PP read-out signals as a function of the radial position x of the spot.

For optimum read-out both PP and CA amplitudes must be as large as possible and we will look at how they depend on the groove geometry. From previous examples we know that very shallow grooves produce a phase difference ψ somewhat larger than $90°$ resulting in a large $\sin\psi$ term in the PP amplitude. In that case however the groove volume and hence A_1 are small. So the groove must be deeper, giving, however, larger values of ψ. As a result we expect an optimum when we plot I_{PP} as a function of the effective groove depth. This optimum value is largest when we take wide grooves, since as we have seen in §3.2.2 this has the effect of both reducing ψ and increasing A_1. Large values of I_{CA} however are only produced by very shallow grooves when ψ is close to $90°$, and in general a compromise must be made between I_{CA} and I_{PP}. This compromise works best for wider grooves since then $\cos\psi$ is smallest.

For a quantitative vectorial investigation of these qualitative ideas the diffraction problem must first be defined. We consider the read-out parameters of the standard data disc system. Here the light of an AlGaAs laser diode of wavelength $\lambda = 820$ nm is focused by a lens of numerical aperture NA $= 0.52$ through a glass substrate of refractive index $n_0 = 1.5$ onto a Te-based layer of refractive index $n_1 = 5.3 + 1.8i$. The track pitch $Q = 1600$ nm. The effect of the read-out through the glass substrate is to scale down the effective wavelength by a factor 1.5 and to reduce the optical contrast. The reflection of the glass–Te interface is now 36%. As compared with the diffraction of the HeNe laser beam by the silver layer, both the effective wavelength and the optical contrast are smaller and for equal geometries the polarisation effects are now expected to be less pronounced. Figures 3.21 (*a*) and (*b*) show the order intensities and phases as calculated

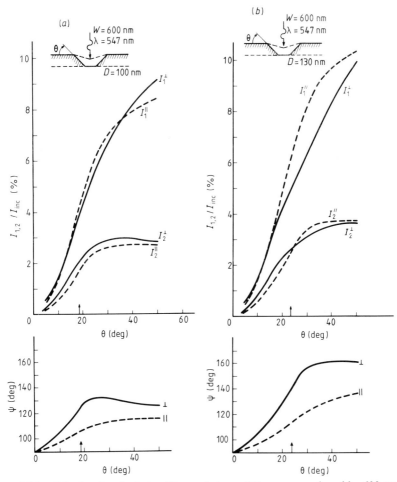

Figure 3.21   Calculated order intensities and phase differences produced by 600 nm wide grooves in a Te compound. The maximum depth is taken to be (*a*) 100 and (*b*) 130 nm. The effective wavelength in the substrate is 547 nm and the reduced refractive index of the Te layer is $n_1 = 3.55 + 1.18i$.

for the case $W = 600$ nm and $D = 100$ and 130 nm. Such computed amplitudes, rather than intensities, and phases are substituted in equations like equations (3.20), where the second orders are also included. By doing so, however, we approximate the diffraction of the incident spherical wave by the diffraction of one normally incident plane wave. In our case, in the glass substrate, the marginal ray only makes an angle of 20° with the normal and we expect the approximation to be a good one. A second approximation is made in equations (3.19) by assuming the incident light to be uniformly distributed over the entrance pupil of the read-out lens. In general this is not the case and one has to integrate the local intensities over the detector surface, rather then just multiply the intensity by the appropriate area S_I or S_{II}. When we consider Gaussian beams, however, the error is very small as long as the intensity at the rim of the entrance pupil is larger than 25% of the intensity at the pupil centre.

The maximum possible PP amplitude amounts to 56%, a value which is reached when $\psi = 90°$ and the reflected light is equally divided over the zeroth order and the two first orders.

Figure 3.22 shows calculated CA and PP amplitudes as a function of θ, when $W = 600$ nm and $D = 130$ nm. The qualitative character of these curves is indeed as expected. The differences observed in both polarisation cases are mainly due to the different phase differences $\psi^{\parallel}$ and $\psi^{\perp}$. In parallel polarisation ψ is much closer to 90°, whereas the amplitudes $A_1^{\parallel}$

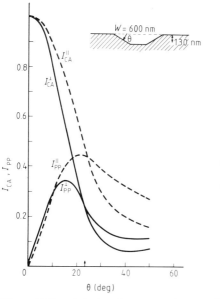

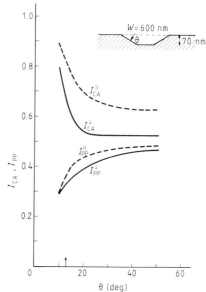

Figure 3.22 Calculated CA and PP amplitudes for both polarisation directions as a function of the slope angle θ when $W = 600$ nm and $D = 130$ nm.

Figure 3.23 Calculated CA and PP amplitudes for both polarisation directions produced by 600 nm wide grooves of depth $D = 70$ nm.

and $A_{\mathrm{I}}^{\perp}$ only differ by at most 15%. As a consequence both the maximum PP amplitudes and CA amplitudes are largest in parallel polarisation.

When we reduce the maximum groove depth to 70 nm (figure 3.23) we observe larger PP and CA amplitudes since ψ cannot now differ much from 90°. The effect of the maximum groove depth D is shown in figure 3.24 where we plot the signal amplitudes obtained when a triangular groove with a slope angle of 30° is truncated at different depths. Again an optimum in the PP signals is observed. When we take the PP signal averaged over the two polarisation states, the maximum value is obtained when D is about 70 nm, close to the scalar prediction of $D = \lambda/8 = 68$ nm. This optimum depth is also found when we take other slope angles.

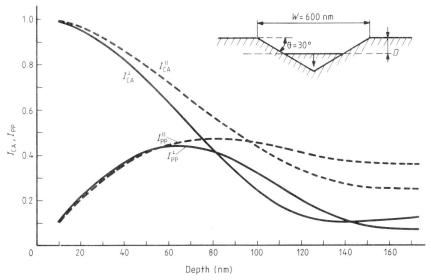

Figure 3.24 Calculated CA and PP amplitudes for both polarisation directions produced by 600 nm wide grooves of slope $\theta = 30°$ as a function of the depth at which the grooves are truncated.

The effect of the groove width W is shown in figure 3.25. The geometrical groove parameters are $\theta = 20°$ and 30° and $D = 60$ nm. Clearly better signals are obtained when the groove becomes wider. This aspect has been considered in more detail in Pasman *et al* (1985).

To conclude this section figure 3.26 shows the PP and CA amplitudes when the groove width is about half the period ($W = 900$ nm). The maximum depth is 160 nm to permit good read-out of heading pits. In this case it is possible to obtain PP amplitudes of 50% with corresponding CA amplitudes greater than 60%.

LaserVision pits. This last section deals with the calculation of the read-out signals produced by pits on video or audio discs. The solution of this diffraction problem combines all the principles of this chapter.

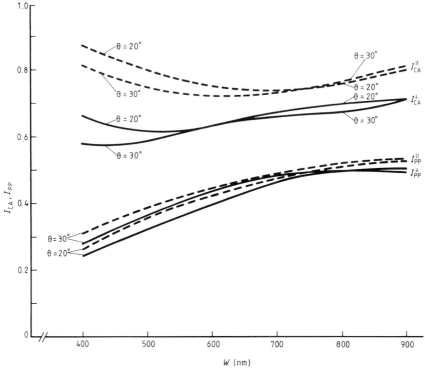

Figure 3.25 Calculated CA and PP amplitudes for both polarisation directions produced by 60 nm deep grooves of slope $\theta = 20°$ and $30°$ as a function of the width W.

Since the diffraction geometry is now a function of both x and y, the problem is not separable into the two linearly independent cases of H and E polarisations. Instead the diffraction problem should be solved for each polarisation of the incident light and, for obvious reasons, parallel and perpendicular polarisation are chosen as examples.

Since we consider the height profile to be periodic in two directions we may decompose the surface currents and electromagnetic fields into double Fourier sums. We also use a Green function, periodic in two directions. We thus obtain equations from which the radial and tangential Fourier components of the surface currents and the fields can be solved in a way analogous to that described in §3.2. From the radially and tangentially diffracted orders the read-out signals can be calculated in the standard way.

In our model the geometry of the pits is defined by six parameters (figure 3.27), the width of the pit at the top W, the depth D, the slope angle θ, the length L of the rectangular part of the pit, the tangential period P and the radial period Q. The ends of the pits are taken to be of semicircular shape resulting in a total pit length $L + W$. The effective pit length however is less.

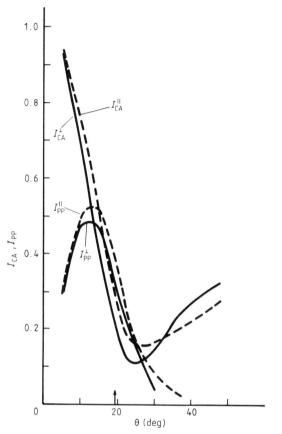

Figure 3.26 Calculated CA and PP amplitudes for both polarisation directions produced by 900 nm wide grooves 160 nm deep as a function of the slope angle θ.

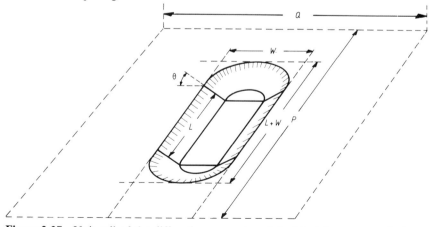

Figure 3.27 Unit cell of the diffraction geometry of the biaxial structure of pits.

The tangential duty cycle DC is here defined as the total length $L + W$ divided by the tangential period P. As a consequence pits of duty cycle greater than 50% are produced by a symmetric recording signal of temporal duty cycle 50%. Other parameters are the wavelength of the read-out light $\lambda = 633$ nm, the numerical aperture NA = 0.45, the refractive index of the substrate $n_0 = 1.5$ and the complex index of refraction of the reflector

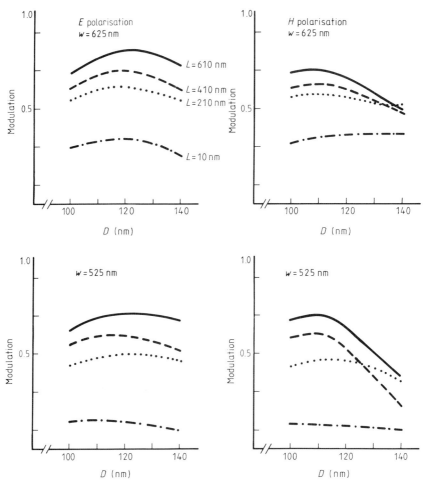

Figure 3.28 Modulation in the read-out signal as a function of the pit depth for two states of polarisation parallel (left-hand graphs) and perpendicular (right-hand graphs) to the track direction. Values of the pit width W are 625 nm (top graphs) and 525 nm (bottom graphs). The length L of the rectangular part of the pit is varied from 10 nm (chain curve) to 610 nm (full curve) via 210 nm (dotted curve) and 410 nm (broken curve). The subsequent pit period follows from $(L + W)/\mathrm{DC}$, where DC is 60% in all cases. The slope angle θ is 45°.

$n_1 = 0.08 + 4.1i$. The effective wavelength in the substrate is now 422 nm which is for most applications smaller than the width and the length of the pits.

The quantity of main interest in the read-out of pits is the modulation depth M of the CA signal defined by

$$M = (I_{max} - I_{min})/(I_{max} + I_{min})$$

where I_{max} and I_{min} are the maximum and minimum values of the CA read-out signal when the spot moves, ideally centred, over the track. Figure 3.28 shows the calculated modulation depth plotted as a function of the pit depth D for some values of L. Two polarisation states of E parallel and perpendicular to the track are considered. The constant parameters are in this case $Q = 1670$ nm, $\theta = 45°$ and DC = 60%. We note that the modulation reaches optimum values at different values of D for the two polarisation directions and again the pits appear to be deepest when the incident light is polarised perpendicular to the long side of the pits. When the pit depth lies between 115 and 130 nm high signal values are obtained for all pit lengths and differences due to polarisation are relatively small.

In conclusion we can say that vectorial diffraction theory, as opposed to scalar theory, is most successfully applied to diffracting obstacles of which the transverse dimensions are close to the wavelength of the light. In that case polarisation effects are most prominent and such effects can therefore be used to determine the scattering geometry. Read-out of optical discs is always performed through a substrate which reduces the effective wavelength by roughly a factor of 1.5. Because of this factor and the observation that the chosen pit geometries produce relatively small polarisation effects, scalar theory may also be applied to give satisfactory results. This is especially true for calculations on complex structures such as cross-talk and intermodulation calculations. In the case of a biaxial structure with an extra periodicity the vectorial calculations, though still possible in principle, become so complex and elaborate that the work is hardly balanced by the differences in results obtained when the simple scalar theory is used.

References

van den Berg P M 1981 Reflection by a grating: Rayleigh methods *J. Opt. Soc. Am.* **71** 1224–9

Dil J G and Jacobs B A J 1979 Apparent size of reflecting polygonal obstacles of the order of one wavelength *J. Opt. Soc. Am.* **69** 950–60

Dil J G and Wesdorp C A 1979 Control of pit geometry on video discs *Appl. Opt.* **18** 3198–202

de Hoop A T 1977 *Modern Topics in Electromagnetics and Antennas* PPL Conference Publication 13 (Stevenage, Herts: Peter Peregrinus) Ch 6

Lippmann B A 1953 Note on the theory of gratings *J. Opt. Soc. Am.* **43** 408

Lord Rayleigh (J W Strutt) 1907 On the dynamical theory of gratings *Proc. R. Soc.* A **79** 399–416

Meecham W C 1956 Variational method for the calculation of the distribution of energy reflected from a periodic surface *J. Appl. Phys.* **27** 361–7

Millar R F 1969 On the Rayleigh assumption in scattering by a periodic surface *Proc. Camb. Phil. Soc.* **65** 773–91

Olijhoek J F, Peek T H and Wesdorp C A 1981 Mastering for Philips optical disc systems, Eur. Conf. on Opt. Syst. and Appl. 1980 *SPIE* **236** 464–6

Pasman J H T 1983 Rigorous diffraction theory applied to video disc geometries Max Born Centenary Conference 1982 *SPIE* **369** 674–80

Pasman J H T, Olijhoek J F and Verkaik W 1985 Third international conference on optical mass data storage 1985, Developments in optical disc mastering *SPIE* **529** 62–8

Petit R 1967 Sur la diffraction d'une onde plane par un reseau infiniment conducteur *C.R. Acad. Sci., Paris* **264** 1441–4

——(ed) 1980 *Electromagnetic Theory of Gratings* (Berlin: Springer)

Ping Sheng 1978 Theoretical considerations of optical diffraction from RCA VideoDisc signals *RCA Rev.* **39** 512–55

Roach W R, Carroll C B, Firester A H, Gorog I and Wagner R W 1978 Diffraction spectrometry for VideoDisc quality control *RCA Rev.* **39** 472–511

Sommerfeld A 1964 *Optics* (New York: Academic) §39

Yasuura K 1971 A view of numerical methods in diffraction problems *Progress in Radio Science 1966–1969* ed. W V Tilston and M Sauzada (Brussels: Union Radio-Scientifique Internationale) pp. 257–70

Wirgin A 1979 Simplified theory of the diffraction of an electromagnetic wave by a perfectly conducting biaxial periodic surface *Opt. Comm.* **28** 275–9

4 Control Mechanics

G van Rosmalen

4.1 Introduction

In contrast to the well known gramophone, where the pick-up needle is mechanically guided by the track, no such guiding mechanism is available in optical disc systems, where the contactless read-out is achieved via a cone of light. Hence the focused spot must be driven by a number of control systems in such a way that the track is followed accurately.

The system most suitable for this purpose is the feedback control system of which figure 4.1 gives a general block diagram. Such a position control follows the moving track within some tenths of a micrometre, even when the track errors are of the order of magnitude of millimetres. The position error denoted in figure 4.1 is the difference between the positions of the track and the spot. Possible errors can be classified according to their causes into disc errors, player errors and external disturbances such as jolts to the player.

The functioning of the optical position detection—the first block in figure 4.1—is described in Chapter 2. For the stability of the feedback system an electronic network—block 2—is required. The control commands are converted into actual spot displacements by means of electromechanical systems (actuators)—the last block.

For tracking with a light spot at least two position controls are necessary, namely one in the vertical and one in the radial direction. These controls are usually called focus and radial controls, respectively. In video-disc systems, moreover, a tangential control is incorporated to compensate for variations in the read-out speed.

Although the tracking systems are similar for the three current optical disc systems, LaserVision (LV), Compact Disc (CD) and Digital Optical

Recording (DOR), there are great differences in design, owing to the various system properties. First we will consider why and how position control systems have evolved.

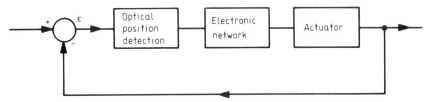

Figure 4.1   Block diagram of the feedback control system.

4.2   History

Early in 1970, after the first tests with a disc with spirally arranged microfilm pictures, it became clear at Philips that this was not the appropriate method of picture storage. Soon the alternative idea was formulated—a spiral track of depressions (pits), the information coded as the length of the pits and the intervals between them (lands), to be read out optically.

The first experiments with a track of pits took place in mid-1971. The first signal recorded in this way was supplied by a checker-board video generator. On playback a checker-board could vaguely be seen through the snow on the screen. An elliptical spot (1 μm in the tangential direction and with a width of 3 μm) was used for the recording and the track-to-track spacing was 6 μm. A very flat glass plate 6 mm thick, used as substrate, was supported on a circular air-bearing at the outer edge of the disc. In this way the glass plate could be rotated to within 5 μm in a level surface, and the surface was always in focus. The eccentricity that occurred after the disc was taken off and replaced on the read/write equipment made it clear that a tracking system was needed.

As a first attempt a piezoelectrically driven tilting mirror was used, resulting in an effective eccentricity reduction by a factor of 50. Thus an eccentricity of 15 μm could be reduced to the maximum acceptable, 0.3 μm. A still better result, a reduction of 500 times at 25 Hz, was obtained with an electromagnetically driven tilting mirror (moving-coil drive). Consequently the 6 μm track-to-track spacing could then be reduced to 2 μm (currently (1984) 1.6 μm) yielding an extension of the playing time.

Now a smaller spot was required, resulting in a smaller depth of focus, which made a focus control necessary. On 5 September 1972 an operating Video Long Play (VLP) system was demonstrated during a press conference: 30 minutes of colour picture with sound on a glass plate; the player was equipped with a tracking and a focusing system (*Philips Technical Review* 1973 **33** 177–93).

The results of experiments with self-stabilising rotating foil replicas were unsatisfactory and they were replaced by thick plastic discs. The use of plastic as substrate material was inspired by the expected advantages as to reproduction because of the similarity to the substrate material for gramophone records. The application of plastic discs with a thickness of about 1.5 mm imposed stronger demands on both control systems.

Another problem was the so-called time error, caused by variations in the local speed. As a possible solution to this problem a second tilting mirror was added with the axis of tilting perpendicular to that of the first. The entire optical system was mounted on a carriage that could move beneath the disc so that the reading spot could be displaced from the innermost to the outermost track. For the drive of the carriage, the so-called 'caterpillar' was introduced. This was an accurate drive with two magnetically anchorable legs with a piezoelectric muscle between them (see figure 4.2).

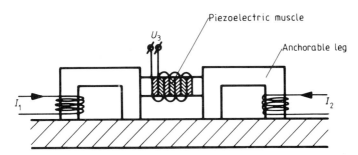

Figure 4.2 Caterpillar concept for the drive of the carriage. The table shows the driving sequence for right-hand movement.

	I_1	U_3	I_2
1	on	pos.	off
2	on	pos.	on
3	off	neg.	on
4	on	neg.	off
5	on	pos.	off
6	on	pos.	on
		etc	

When objectives with larger fields became available, the caterpillar was replaced by a carriage drive with a belt, an electric motor and a reducing gear. The position of the carriage was controlled from the average position of the tilting mirror.

At present the LV player is provided with five control loops, namely:

rotational speed of the disc; tangential tracking; radial tracking; carriage control and focusing control.

After 1975 the work on VLP gained momentum for various reasons. Firstly the confidence in the control systems used began to grow and secondly, the much smaller semiconductor laser seemed to be an alternative for the large gas laser which was in use as light source. The combination of these two facts resulted in a larger range of applications.

Figure 4.3   Light pen.

In industry it became possible to produce the the LV player and in the laboratory three parallel activities were started. The first of these was the development of a composite LV light path with a semiconductor laser. The solution of the optical, electrical and control problems proved to be an elaborate task. After a year this resulted in the so-called light pen (see figure 4.3), which is so compact and light that it can accurately follow the bouncing and wobbling track. A second development resulted in the current Compact Disc. Although the idea seems to be the most natural, many problems had to be faced. For instance, the coding of the signal, the error correction and last but not least, how to produce an economical consumer product. The third development was the implementation of an LV disc as a computer storage medium (Digital Optical Recording (DOR)). A compact, large computer memory became a possibility, especially in combination with a semiconductor laser. The information is stored in the form of holes burnt in a thin metal layer. The possibility of vast amounts of information on the one hand and fast access on the other appeal to the imagination.

4.3 Error spectrum

One is tempted to think that when a flat disc rotates provision is needed only for the accurate following of the outwards spiralling track. It will be apparent, however, that this error in the radial tracking is of minor importance compared with other, less obvious errors.

We formally define the error at a time t as the difference between the desired position and the actual position of the read-out spot, with the control systems switched off. It is usually described in an x,y,z coordinate system. The z axis is chosen perpendicular to the disc surface, the focusing direction, whereas the x axis is chosen in the radial direction. The y axis represents the tangential direction.

This error, the sum of spot and track deviation, is determined by displacements of the light source, free vibrations of tilting mirrors, play in the carriage and guiding mechanism, out-of-roundness and warp of the disc, eccentricity of the hole in the disc, etc.

We distinguish between various mechanisms of excitation. In an LV player, the dominant excitation stems from the mechanical imbalance of the rotating disc. Much smaller sources are external impacts such as jolts to the player and even footsteps on the floor on which the table with the player stands. For a CD player we have a different situation. Here the internal vibrations are much smaller than the external ones because of the much lower rotational speed and the smaller disc. In the following sections we will discuss the errors due to imperfections of the disc, the read-out equipment and external disturbances.

4.3.1. Disc errors

Disc errors are caused by geometrical deviations of the information-carrying relief on the disc, with respect to the master surface. This relief is embedded in a transparent plastic disc that thus forms part of the read-out light path. Local imperfections in the disc, such as gas bubbles and scratches in the layer material (so-called *Pickelschrammen,* see figure 4.4.) cause large errors. Other important disc errors are warp, out-of-roundness and eccentric location of the hole.

By far the largest disturbances are the vertical movements of the rotating track due to warp. In the time domain they can be described as a sequence of height variations, but a more convenient description is in terms of the frequency spectrum. This spectrum can be measured with the set-up shown in figure 4.5.

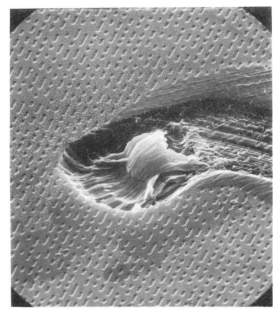

Figure 4.4   Pickelschramm.

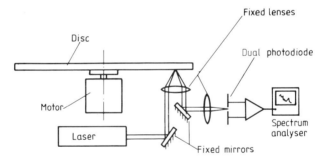

Figure 4.5   Set-up for the measurement of the frequency spectrum.

When the disc rotates at a speed of 25 c s^{-1}, the frequency spectrum of the height variations has a fundamental frequency of 25 Hz. Figure 4.6 shows a frequency spectrum. The radial and tangential error spectra have similar distributions.

4.3.2   Player errors

An optical disc player incorporates a laser, a number of mirrors, an electrically driven objective for the focusing of the spot and a photodiode for the electric detection of the reflected spot. The spot position is a function of the positions of all constituent elements in the light path. In the LV player the light path elements are rigidly attached to a carriage which can move in the radial direction. As the tilting mirrors and carriage have to be flexibly suspended, disturbing forces will result in large spot displacements. The largest disturbing force acting on the positions of the components in an LV player is the imbalance force caused by the rotating disc.

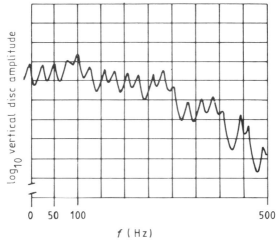

Figure 4.6 Frequency spectrum of the focus signal.

This imbalance force is given by

$$F_c = m\omega^2 r$$

where F_c = imbalance force; m = mass of the disc; ω = angular frequency ($2\pi f$) in rad s^{-1} and r = distance between centre of gravity and rotation axis (for a symmetrical disc this is equal to the eccentricity).

For an LV disc with a mass of 0.2 kg and an eccentricity of 0.1 mm in a PAL/CAV player (constant angular velocity) at playback speed ($f = 25$ Hz), an imbalance force $F_c = 0.5$ N is found.

Owing to this force the carriage will swing between the two extreme positions of its play, resulting in a radial spot displacement of 50 μm or more. Furthermore, bending of the frame and displacements of the various light path elements due to the acceleration forces also lead to spot displacements that can reach 100 μm.

The total radial spot displacement with respect to the information tracks can easily be determined by switching off the radial tracking in an LV player under operation, whereupon the radial error signal can be measured (see §2.5.1.). Figure 4.7 shows such a measured radial error signal. Each period represents one track-to-track spacing. At the points of reversal of the displacement the periods are the largest. By counting the number of periods within the deviation (in figure 4.7 36 periods are found) the total relative spot displacement can be determined by multiplying this number by the track-to-track spacing. Thus in figure 4.7 the total peak-to-peak spot deviation amounts to $36 \times 1.67 \ \mu m = 60 \ \mu m$.

Another important perturbing source in the LV player is the moving objective. When a player is in use the disc surface has to be followed by the read-out objective. The frequency spectrum of the deviation of this mass during read-out is very similar to the disc spectrum depicted in figure 4.6. The reaction forces due to accelerations and decelerations of the objective mass of 10 g can be found everywhere in the player. This disturbance is often very serious because of the excitation of high frequency resonances in construction parts that influence the spot position.

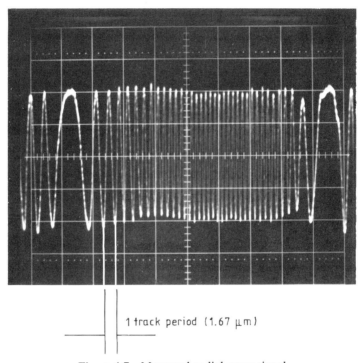

1 track period (1.67 μm)

Figure 4.7   Measured radial error signal.

4.3.3   *External disturbances*

Owing to external forces of acceleration, deviations of the spot position with respect to the information track will be found. For instance, in a room with a wooden floor, footsteps will cause accelerations within the player. Horizontal as well as vertical accelerations can thus be introduced (see figure 4.8).

In an LV player the mechanical disturbance caused by the imbalance of the fast rotating disc is several times higher than that caused by external forces. For this reason external disturbances have never been of importance in the development of LV control systems.

The situation for the CD player is quite different. Owing to the lower rotational speed of the disc (8 revolutions per second at a maximum), its smaller mass and consequently the smaller imbalance for given dimensional tolerances, the imbalance forces are much smaller.

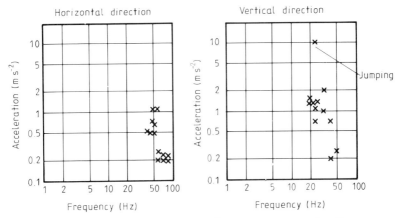

Figure 4.8 Accelerations due to footsteps on a wooden floor.

For a CD disc with a weight of 15 g, an eccentricity of 0.1 mm and $\omega = 2\pi f = 50$ rad s^{-1}, we find an imbalance force

$$F_c = 15 \times 10^{-3} \times 50^2 \times 0.1 \times 10^{-3} = 3.75 \times 10^{-3}\ \text{N}.$$

Compared with the 0.5 N in the LV calculation we can see that in the CD player external disturbances form the main error source. Of course this will cause problems when the player is used in a car instead of in the home.

4.3.4 Error spectra

After we have considered the various error sources, we can specify the maximum errors we may expect when a disc is played. Because of the statistical character of the errors of various origins, such a specification always represents the worst case situation.

The errors are described by their frequency spectra. As an example we show the worst case LV vertical error specification (top curve in figure 4.9). The spectra of other errors in radial and tangential directions for LV, CD etc are qualitatively similar. From figure 4.9 it can be seen that frequency components below 30 Hz can have a maximum amplitude of 1050 μm. Above 1100 Hz, this amplitude should be 2 μm at a maximum. An example of an actual spectrum is shown in the same figure (lower curve).

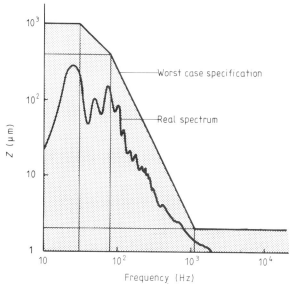

Figure 4.9   Worst case and actual LV vertical disturbances.

After we know what error level to expect, we consider what reduction is necessary to bring the errors to within acceptable limits.

4.4   Reduction

4.4.1   Tracking demands
The allowed spot deviations in all directions are limited by the requirements determined by the optical principles of the read-out (see Chapter 2). Table 4.1 shows the maximum permissible deviations of the spot position for three different read-out systems. In the LV column the numbers are given for a light path with a HeNe gas laser as the light source ($\lambda = 633$ nm) and an AlGaAs semiconductor laser ($\lambda = 780$ nm). The CD numbers are for an AlGaAs laser.

Table 4.1   Maximum allowed tracking error (in μm).

	LV		CD
	HeNe NA = 0.40	AlGaAs NA = 0.50	AlGaAs NA = 0.47
Vertical	± 2	± 1.5	± 2
Radial	± 0.15	± 0.15	± 0.2
Tangential	± 0.15	± 0.15	—

$$y = H(x-y) \qquad \text{or} \qquad y = H\varepsilon \qquad (4.3)$$

which yields

$$\frac{y(\mathrm{i}\omega)}{x(\mathrm{i}\omega)} = \frac{H(\mathrm{i}\omega)}{1 + H(\mathrm{i}\omega)}.$$

Figure 4.15 shows this closed loop transfer function $H/(1 + H)$, which corresponds to the open loop transfer in the same figure. We note that for low frequencies the spot displacement y does indeed equal the track displacement x. Another interesting result from equations (4.2) and (4.3) is the relation

$$\frac{\varepsilon}{x} = \frac{1}{1 + H(\mathrm{i}\omega)}.$$

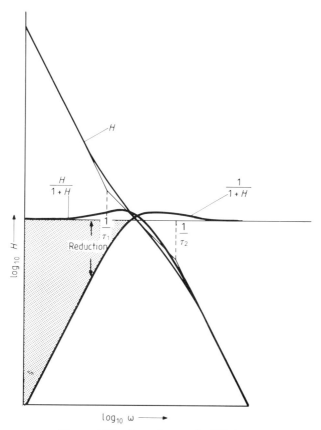

Figure 4.15 Open loop gain H(iω).

This expression gives the fraction of the incoming disturbance x which remains as a residual error ε after feedback. The ratio x/ε, being the reciprocal of this fraction, is defined as the reduction factor $R(i\omega)$

$$R(i\omega) = 1 + H(i\omega).$$

Usually the relative residual error ε/x, rather than the reduction factor R is plotted in the amplitude Bode diagram. An example is shown in figure 4.15. An important point is the intersection of $H/(1 + H)$ and $1/(1 + H)$ where $H = 1$. The corresponding frequency is called the control bandwidth or the bandwidth. In the literature the -3 dB point of the $H/(1 + H)$ transfer is sometimes defined as the bandwidth. In practice the maximum of the $H/(1 + H)$ transfer is a suitable approximation in the absence of the $1/(1 + H)$ transfer.

From figure 4.15 we can conclude that the bandwidth only increases with the open loop gain $H(i\omega)$. For reasons of stability also the break frequencies $1/\tau_1$ and $1/\tau_2$ then have to shift to higher frequencies. A higher bandwidth results in a larger reduction of disturbances (shaded region in figure 4.15).

So far we have considered the objective assembly to be floating. Alternatively, the objective mass may be suspended on leaf springs. In that case the current-to-position transfer is no longer a double integration over the whole frequency scale. Such a leaf-spring suspended objective assembly is an example of the more general class of spring-mass-damper systems. Since such systems exhibit a resonance behaviour which can have various consequences for the control loops under consideration, we will discuss such a spring-mass-damper system in more detail.

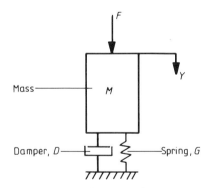

Figure 4.16   Spring-mass-damper system.

Figure 4.16 is a schematic diagram of the principal parts with mass M, spring constant G and damping D, driven by a force F. The equation of motion of the mass is given by

$$M\ddot{y}(t) + D\dot{y}(t) + Gy(t) = F(t).$$

When we consider one frequency component ω in the frequency domain, differentiation with respect to time can be replaced by multiplication by $i\omega$, yielding

$$(-\omega^2 M + i\omega D + G)y \exp(i\omega t) = F \exp(i\omega t)$$

resulting in a transfer function of

$$\frac{y}{F} = \frac{1}{G}\left(-\frac{M\omega^2}{G} + \frac{Di\omega}{G} + 1\right)^{-1} = \frac{1}{G}\left(-\frac{\omega^2}{\omega_0^2} + \frac{2\beta i\omega}{\omega_0} + 1\right)^{-1}. \qquad (4.4)$$

The amplitude Bode diagram of this transfer function is shown in figure 4.17 for various values of the damping constant β

$$\beta = \frac{D}{2\sqrt{MG}}.$$

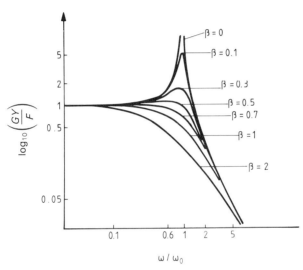

Figure 4.17 Amplitude Bode diagram.

The plot can be directly compared with the original second-order transfer of the floating objective (see figure 4.13(c)). We note that for very high frequencies both transfer functions are identical (compare equation (4.1) with (4.4)). At low frequencies the transfer is dominated by the spring constant G, which limits the gain to a flat level of $1/G$. For intermediate frequencies, we note a resonance behaviour of the transfer function. For low damping constants β, a resonance peak is observed near the frequency ω_0

$$\omega_0 = \sqrt{\frac{G}{M}}. \qquad (4.5)$$

The quality factor Q of the resonance, defined as $1/2\beta$, gives the height of the peak relative to the low frequency level. In optical disc systems Q

values of 10 to 100 are found, depending on the choice of the spring material.

The positive consequence of the resonance peak is that extra gain is introduced in the open loop, thus increasing the disturbance reduction factor R of closed loop control system. At lower frequencies, however, the limited gain reduces the reduction factor. To a certain extent this can be compensated for by inserting an electronic lag network in the loop. This network introduces extra gain for frequencies below the additional break frequency ω (see figure 4.18).

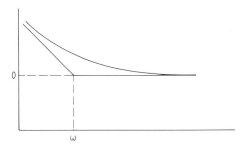

Figure 4.18   Lag network.

4.5.2   Stability

In the preceding section we considered only the amplitude plots of transfer functions. As already mentioned, transfer functions are not only specified by their amplitude but also by their phaseshift. Such phaseshifts are of particular interest for the stability of control systems. When we consider the open loop gain $H(i\omega)$ to be complex variable of modulus $|H(i\omega)|$ and phase $\phi(i\omega) = \arg (H)$ we see that the closed loop transfer $H/(1 + H)$ can approach infinity for values of ω where H is close to -1. This means that a very small disturbance of the disc or even some noise contribution in the closed loop results in an oscillatory movement of the objective with a very large amplitude. Such a system is called unstable. When both the following conditions are fulfilled

$$|H(i\omega)| = 1 \qquad \text{and} \qquad \arg(H(i\omega)) = 180°$$

the system is unstable.

When both conditions are not (nearly) satisfied at the same frequency, stability is secured. When the complex variable $H(i\omega)$ is represented in the complex plane, the instability point, or pole, is located on the negative real axis. The pure double integrator of the previous section produces a phaseshift of 180° over the full frequency scale, which is reflected by the minus sign in equation (4.1). As a result, in figure 4.19, the open loop gain $H(i\omega)$ traverses the negative real axis and there will always be a frequency where

$H(i\omega)$ equals -1, resulting in an unconditionally unstable closed loop (positive feedback). Instability is avoided by including the lead network with the time constants τ_1 and τ_2 chosen around the frequency where $|H|$ crosses the 0 dB baseline of the amplitude Bode diagram shown in figure 4.13(d) ($|H| = 1$). In the frequency range between $1/\tau_1$ and $1/\tau_2$ an extra phaseshift is introduced which may amount to $+90°$ when the slope is $+1$ (see figure 4.13(e)). As a result the total open loop gain avoids the -1 point of figure 4.19.

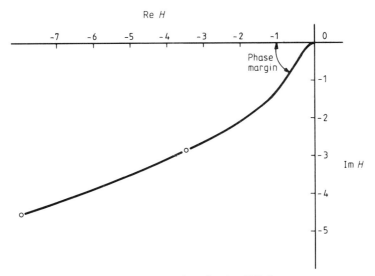

Figure 4.19 Polar plot for $H(i\omega)$.

In this way stability is assured by modifying the second of the two above conditions when the first is fulfilled. The minimum phaseshift necessary for stability is often called the phase margin. Analogously the amplitude margin can be defined as the minimum distance on the negative real axis between $H(i\omega)$ and -1.

The resulting closed loop gain, as in figure 4.15, still shows a trace of the instability point as a little resonance peak with an amplitude greater than 1 near the frequency where $|H| = 1$. The height of the peak depends on the damping of the system as determined by the choice of the parameters τ_1 and τ_2 of the lead network. This peak level determines the shape of the system's response to a step-shared input. A satisfactory compromise between over-shoot level and response duration is made when the peak level amounts to about 3 dB.

At high frequencies electromechanical constructions, like the objective drive, often show parasitic resonances due to unwanted spring-mass-damper effects as described in the previous section. In this case narrow high resonance peaks are superimposed on the low gain part, with slope -2 and phaseshift $180°$ of the open loop gain, which may introduce instability if the quality factor is so high that $|H|$ reaches 1. To be certain that $|H|$ still has an amplitude margin, the frequencies of such resonances are designed to be as high as possible. This implies small masses and high spring stiffnesses (e.g. equation (4.5)). In practice such resonance peaks often have a quality factor of about 100, which implies that the resonance frequency should be at least a factor 10 higher than the frequency where $|H|$ crosses the 0 dB line. In principle one can reduce such resonances by using an electronic band-reject filter, but because of the limited frequency stability of both filter and peak, such filters often provide little help. In some cases, however, these resonances can be used to advantage, as described in §4.9.

4.6   Actuators

The spot displacements necessary for tracking are obtained using an electromechanical device, the actuator. When an actuator can displace the spot in more than one direction it is called a two-dimensional or three-dimensional (2-D or 3-D) actuator.

Before going into closer detail of the current-to-position transfer function of the preceding section we will first define the actuator constant K. Strictly speaking, this factor only holds for that part of the transfer function where the slope is -2. It then follows that $\ddot{x} = KI$. When we specify the actuator by its current-to-acceleration transfer function, we find a transfer constant K, with the dimension $m\ s^{-2}A^{-1}$. K is given usually in $g\ A^{-1}$, where g is the acceleration due to gravity ($g \simeq 10\ m\ s^{-2}$).

For the determination of K for a translation actuator, such as the objective focus drive, it is sufficient to measure the current at which the objective is just lifted. This simple measurement method is also suitable for actuators with which the spot is driven radially as well as tangentially via corresponding translations of the objective. It is, however, only suitable when the acceleration of the spot is equal to that of the driven mass.

The relation between the accelerations of the spot and the driven mass is called the optical position transfer K_{opt} which, together with the drive transfer K_d and the mechanical transfer K_m, forms the total actuator transfer. Figure 4.20 shows the total actuator transfer split up into the three constituent transfers.

In a focusing actuator the optical transfer usually amounts to unity, or nearly unity in the case that the incident beam is not collimated. In the case of a tilting mirror, however, the angular acceleration of the mirror is transferred via the objective to a spot acceleration.

The mechanical transfer is determined by the transfer function of a mass-spring system consisting at least of a drive mass m_d and a driven part of mass m_p, possibly supplemented by a suspension spring.

The function of the drive is the conversion of current to force with the highest efficiency possible. To be able to describe parasitic resonances, which limit the bandwidth, the masses of the drive and the driven part are assumed to be separated. They are connected via a spring and a damper.

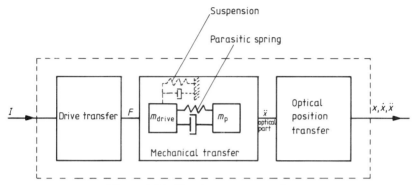

Figure 4.20   Total actuator transfer.

When the suspension consists of a spring element, it will influence the mechanical transfer. If 2-D or 3-D actuators are used, conflicting requirements may have to be imposed on the suspension when it has to guide the driving force.

4.6.1   Drive

An important part of the actuator transfer is formed by the drive transfer depicted in figure 4.21, which in this case is driven from a current source. Although the impedance of the coil (consisting of an inductance L and a resistance R) is of minor importance when the system is driven by current, it may have consequences for the design of the current source and the supply voltage.

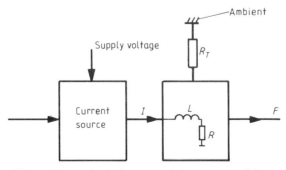

Figure 4.21   Block diagram of the actuator drive.

In order to ensure that too large a supply voltage is not required or that the current source does not bottom at high frequencies, a small electric time constant L/R is required, which implies the use of a minimum amount of iron in the coil.

The average dissipated mechanical energy is negligible compared to the electric energy dissipated in the resistance R of the coil. The dissipated power $P = I_{\text{eff}}^2 R$ causes a rise in temperature over the thermal resistance R_T between coil and ambient

$$\Delta T = T_{\text{coil}} - T_{\text{amb}}. \tag{4.6}$$

For thermal equilibrium

$$\Delta T = PR_T \qquad \text{and} \qquad P = I_{\text{eff}}^2 R$$

so that

$$\Delta T = I_{\text{eff}}^2 RR_T. \tag{4.7}$$

For a current conductor in a magnetic field, the force acting on the conductor is given by

$$F = BIl\sin \alpha \tag{4.8}$$

where F = force exerted on the conductor; B = magnetic induction; I = current; l = length of the conductor in the field; α = angle between current and field direction. The force F acts perpendicular to both current I and magnetic induction B (see figure 4.22).

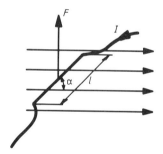

Figure 4.22   Conductor in a magnetic field.

The drive sensitivity K_d, defined as $K_d = F/I$ then equals $K_d = Bl \sin \alpha$.

Besides this sensitivity, the maximum force F_{max} that can be exerted is also important. We distinguish between the peak value $F_{\text{max peak}}$ and the average value $F_{\text{max av}}$ of the maximum force. $F_{\text{max peak}}$ is determined by the maximum current and voltage of the current source, whereas $F_{\text{max av}}$ depends on the maximum allowed temperature in the driving coil. From equations (4.6), (4.7) and (4.8) it follows that

$$F_{\text{max av}} = BIl\sin \alpha \left(\frac{T_{\text{coil}} - T_{\text{amb}}}{RR_T}\right)^{1/2} = K_d \left(\frac{T_{\text{coil}} - T_{\text{amb}}}{RR_T}\right)^{1/2}. \tag{4.9}$$

Table 4.2 Possible driving combinations, the dashes indicate 'no example'

Moving part	Stationary part					
	Coil in air	Permanent magnet and yoke	Coil and iron	Coil and permanent magnet	Permanent magnet in air	Coil, iron permanent magnet
Coil in air	—	Loudspeaker and CD player radial tracking	—	—	Prototype LV objective drive	—
Permanent magnet and yoke	Focusing 2-D actuator for DOR		Brushless DC motor	—		—
Coil and iron	—	Small DC motor	AC motor	—	—	—
Iron	Reed relay		Ordinary relay	—		TAOHS and polar relay
Permanent magnet in air	CD focus actuator		Currently LV tilting mirrors	Prototype 2-D tilting mirror		—

All driving combinations given in table 4.2 are subdivided into a stationary and a moving part. They contain a coil, a permanent magnet and possibly an iron yoke. The open positions in table 4.2 represent non-functioning combinations, whereas positions with 'no example' give functioning combinations that were not applied. The functioning combinations can be divided into two major groups, namely those with a moving coil and those with a moving magnet.

A moving coil construction has a number of advantages and drawbacks. Besides problems with wire breakage of the supply leads, the moving component usually has a bad thermal contact with the environment owing to the movable suspension (high R_T). The heat generated in the moving coil thus results in a temperature increase at the moving part which is undesirable if this part is susceptible to temperature, such as, for instance, the objective ($T_{coil\ max}$ should be low). Both the high R_T and the low $T_{coil\ max}$ result in a decrease of $F_{max\ av}$.

An advantage of the moving coil system is that the stationary magnet system may be larger, so that a stronger magnetic field can be applied (B high).

The opposite argument holds for a moving permanent magnet and a stationary coil. Here the heat removal from the coil poses a smaller problem (R_T low) and the maximum permissible temperature in the coil is higher ($T_{coil\ max}$ high). In this case $F_{max\ av}$ is decreased because of the lower magnetic field (B low) as a smaller magnet is used.

A high K_d value is favourable not only because it results in a high $F_{max\ av}$ value but also because small drive currents can be used. Relatively high currents can cause cross-talk in the photo diode current of the optical position detection circuit, which may be a factor 10^6 smaller. In the closed feedback loop this may lead to instability.

The K_d factor for a given drive varies with the deviation. This results in a variation of the gain of the control loop. To reduce this variation, the length of the magnetic field can be increased so that, at the end of its stroke, the coil stays completely within the magnetic field (see figure 4.23(a)). A more concentrated magnetic field, together with a long coil yields the same result (see figure 4.23(b)), namely a more constant, although low, K_d factor. For this reason the design is usually such that K_d varies at most by about 20%, which is acceptable.

Such a solution is possible when a moving coil is used in a stationary magnetic field from a permanent magnet and an iron yoke. Problems with the choice of a moving magnet and stationary coils, however, arise from the large mass of the magnet–yoke assembly.

An alternative solution consists of a combination of a magnet and a coil, both of them in air. In this way extra, elegant features are possible. To gain an insight into the interplay of forces between coil and magnet, we will use the ribbon-current model. In this model, for modern magnetic materials

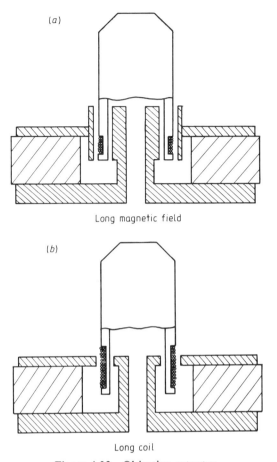

Figure 4.23 Objective actuator.

like ferroxdure and SmCo, with relative permeabilities close to 1, the permanent magnet is represented as a block of air with a current along its surface (see figure 4.24). This current is a function of the kind of magnetic material and is given per unit of height. A characteristic value for a rare earth magnet is 700 A mm^{-1}. This implies that an SmCo magnet of 10 mm in height and magnetised in this direction can be represented as a block of air with a ribbon current of 7000 A. Since currents, depending on their respective directions, mutually attract or repel, the most ingenious magnet–coil combinations can easily be understood and designed in this way.

For the calculation of a magnet–coil combination in air, we use the following expression

$$\mathrm{d}B_p = \frac{\mu I_1 \sin \phi \, \mathrm{d}s}{4\pi r^2}$$

where dB_p = magnetic induction in a point p induced by a current I_1 over a length ds at a distance r. μ denotes the permeability of air $(= 4\pi10^{-7}\,\mathrm{N\,A}^{-2})$. The magnetic induction dB is directed perpendicular to ds and r (see figure 4.25).

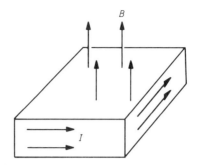

Figure 4.24   Ribbon-current representation of a permanent magnet.

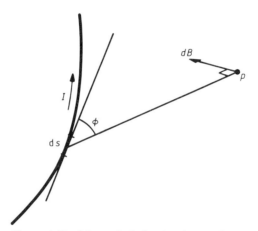

Figure 4.25   Magnetic induction in a point p.

A current-conducting wire through p with a length of dl and a current I_2 experiences a force in accordance with equation (4.8) of

$$dF = \frac{\mu I_1 I_2 \sin \phi \sin \alpha \, ds \, dl}{4\pi r^2}. \tag{4.10}$$

Substitution of μ and integration yields

$$F = I_1 I_2 10^{-7} \int \int \frac{\sin \phi \sin \alpha}{r^2} \, ds dl$$

and

$$K_d = \frac{F}{I_1} = I_2 10^{-7} \int \int \frac{\sin \phi \sin\alpha}{r^2} \, ds dl. \tag{4.11}$$

In practice, using this expression, the forces can be calculated with satisfactory precision even on small home computers. Figure 4.26 shows the calculated and measured force between a ring magnet and a coil. We note the relatively narrow displacement range over which the variation of the force (and hence of K_d) is acceptable. This range is increased by applying two magnets and one coil or one magnet with two coils, because two peaks combined can form one broader curve (see figure 4.27).

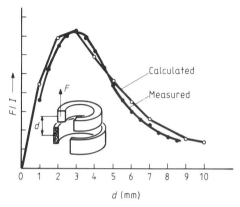

Figure 4.26 Calculated and measured force between a ring magnet and a coil.

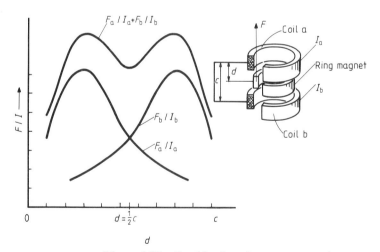

Figure 4.27 Combined peaks.

This combined peak method was used in the drive design of the 2-D actuator in use in a prototype of an LV player (see figure 4.28). The objective, suspended so that it can move vertically as well as radially, is provided at the upper and lower side with permanent magnet rings magnetised along the optical axis. Four coils, just below and above the two magnetic rings, either attract or repel the corresponding ring.

The small mirror, visible on the photograph, forms part of the built-in optical position detector. Between the coil pairs (the inner coils cannot be seen on the photograph) two banana-shaped coils are situated for the radial drive of the objective.

Figure 4.28   Prototype of a 2-D actuator for an LV player.

4.6.2   Mechanical transfer

Besides the optical position transfer K_{opt} and the drive transfer K_d, both discussed in the preceding section, the overall actuator transfer $K = \ddot{x}/I$ is also determined by the mechanical transfer $K_m = \ddot{x}/F$ of the moving part.

In the frequency range where the moving part behaves as a freely moving rigid mass (of value m), the mechanical transfer is constant. It is given by:

$$K_m = \ddot{x}/F = 1/m \tag{4.12}$$

which results in a total actuator transfer K of

$$K = K_d K_m K_{opt} = \frac{Bl \sin \alpha}{m} \tag{4.13}$$

for a coil in a magnetic field or

$$K = \frac{I_2}{m} \, 10^{-7} \int \int \frac{\sin \phi \sin \alpha}{r^2} \, ds \, dl \tag{4.14}$$

when a coil–magnet combination in air is considered.

The thermally determined maximum average spot acceleration $\ddot{x}_{\text{max av}}$ then follows from the equations (4.9) and (4.12)

$$\ddot{x}_{\text{max av}} = K \left(\frac{T_{\text{coil max}} - T_{\text{amb}}}{RR_T} \right)^{1/2}. \tag{4.15}$$

When the acceleration of gravity g may not be neglected, such as for instance with vertically moving parts, it follows that

$$\ddot{x}_{\text{max av}} = K \left(\frac{T_{\text{coil max}} - T_{\text{amb}}}{RR_T} \right)^{1/2} - g. \tag{4.16}$$

A mechanical equivalent of the aforementioned electrical cross-talk is formed by the reaction force due to the acceleration of the actuator mass m. This reaction force propagates through the entire player construction and can cause vibrations of large amplitude on the disc owing to certain mechanical resonances.

Instability arises when the amplitude of these resonances in the vicinity of the read-out spot is larger than the read-out spot itself. This type of instability is known as 'Jaulen', the German term for howling. A trivial solution to this problem is to diminish m, as the cross-talk is proportional to it. A better solution is formed by a dummy mass driven in antiphase. A related solution is to suspend the stationary part of the actuator drive movably so that its mass acts as dummy mass. The additional displacement of the 'stationary part does not influence the actuator transfer because it is driven by force instead of position.

In general the mechanical transfer is not as simple as the $1/m$ transfer. The mechanical part of the actuator transfer is negatively influenced by the effects of one or more mass-spring systems. Springs are always present because in practice the connections and transmissions show a certain amount of elasticity. The masses connected to such springs complete the mass-spring systems. In most actuators the parasitic mass-spring systems are easy to predict and locate and the corresponding resonance frequencies are relatively low. This observation can be generalised as follows: the more difficult the localisation of the mass-spring system, the higher the corresponding resonance frequency and hence the better the mechanical actuator transfer.

In the current LV objective actuator, of which figure 4.29 shows the principle, the parasitic mass-spring system can easily be recognised. In this case the suspension consists of a plain bearing. In most suspensions leaf springs are used instead of plain bearings. The stiffness of the relatively weak springs results in a deviation in K_m in the low frequency range ($f_{\text{res}} = 100$ Hz), which will be dealt with in the next section on suspensions.

It is important to realise that these suspension springs, owing to their finite mass, may behave as parasitic resonance mechanisms in the high frequency range.

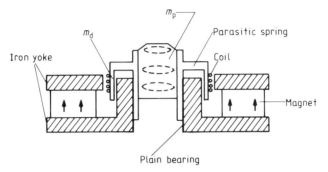

Figure 4.29 LV objective actuator.

Another example in which a number of parasitic resonances can easily be recognised is the rotatable arm construction (see figure 4.30) as used in the CD player for radial tracking. Figure 4.31 gives a very simplified representation of the arm. On both sides of the point of rotation in the middle of the arm driving coils are mounted. In the schematic diagram the mass inertia of the middle part is represented as a drive mass m_d on which a driving force F is exerted. To one side of the middle part, which is assumed to be non-deformable, the light pen with mass m_l is attached via an arm construction that acts as a spring G_l.

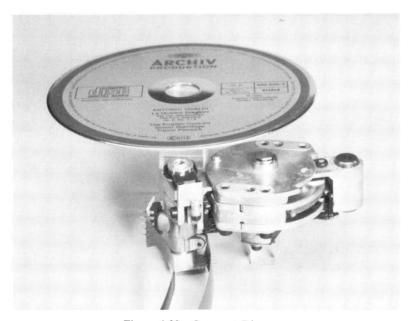

Figure 4.30 Compact Disc arm.

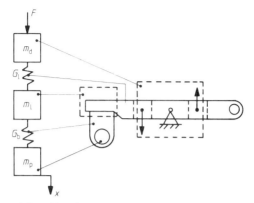

Figure 4.31 Simplified representation of the CD player arm.

An objective with driving magnet is attached to the light pen via two parallel leaf springs to permit focusing. The mass of objective and driving magnet is m_p. The stiffness between m_1 and m_p is formed by the buckling stiffness of the leaf springs (G_b). In the model of the mass-spring system shown in the left-hand side of figure 4.31, the rotational quantities have been replaced by translational quantities.

The proper functioning of the rotatable arm is determined by the parasitic resonances. These resonances have relatively low frequencies owing to the relatively large masses and the small stiffnesses caused by the shape of the arm. Figure 4.28 showed a 2-D actuator in which the parasitic resonance mechanisms are hardly discernable. Owing to the compact form the parasitic resonance frequencies are very high.

Two methods can be used for the determination of the parasitic resonances in an actuator construction.

(*a*) The so-called open loop method. In this the spot displacement is measured directly. If this is impossible, a displacement proportional to that of the spot has to be determined. As the displacements are in the submicron range, the signal-to-noise ratio of the measurement is important. This reduces the measurement range to some micrometres. Owing to this small range the actuator has to be suspended during the measurement in its own springs or auxiliary springs have to be used.

(*b*) The closed loop method. The same measurement set-up as with the open loop method is used but now the measured position signal is fed back, after electronic processing, to the driving coils. The $H/(1 + H)$ transfer is measured via this control system. For this measurement an additional summation point is provided in the closed loop (see figure 4.32). A sinusoidal voltage of constant amplitude and variable frequency is supplied to point p. The $H/(1 + H)$ transfer can now be measured at point b. A result of this measurement is shown in figure 4.33. In the frequency range above the control bandwidth where H is small it is found that $H/(1 + H) = H$. In the high frequency range of the spectrum, a parasitic resonance peak can be observed.

Table 4.3 gives five frequently occuring types of mass-spring systems with their corresponding Bode plots. The second type closely resembles the transfer of figure 4.33.

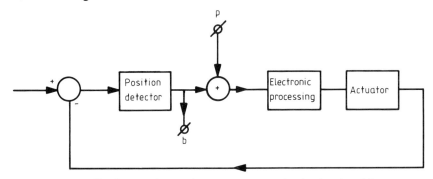

Figure 4.32   Summation and measurement point in the closed loop.

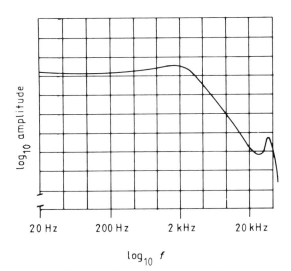

Figure 4.33 $H/(1 + H)$ transfer.

4.6.3   Suspension

In order to move the spot we use a moving optical component such as a mirror or an objective together with one or more drives.

The main purpose of the suspension is to restrict the displacement of the driven optical component to the direction into which it is driven. This holds especially for objectives, where only small angular deviations are allowed.

Table 4.3 Mechanical transfer.

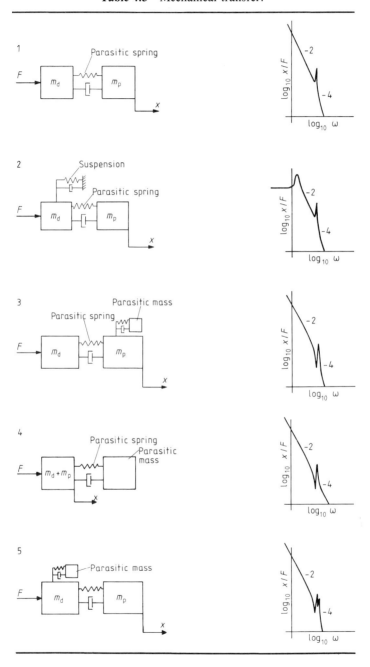

Displacements in the drive direction, however, must be freely possible. The concept of suspension as used in this section should be taken in its widest sense. All solutions fulfilling the above conditions are called suspensions. Suspensions may be of a plain bearing type, a spring type or an electromagnetic type. Examples of the first two have already been given. The electromagnetic type is sometimes misleadingly described as floating.

In the first example of the objective guiding via a plain bearing (see figure 4.29) the undesired tilting, radial and tangential displacements are limited by choosing the bearing clearance to be as small as possible. The focus movement, the desired degree of freedom, is, apart from a negligible bearing friction, not hindered. A condition is that the bearing clearance and the normal force on the bearing surfaces are small, thus implying a vertical use of the focus actuator.

A problem arises at switching on the focus control, when the objective has to approach the acquisition range of the focus error detection at low speed. This implies an extra speed control. If the objective is suspended on springs, this extra control can be omitted as for low frequencies the position is proportional to the drive current (see §4.5.1, equation (4.4)). Now we only have to apply a slowly increasing current.

Conversely, the low frequency part of the drive current can be used to measure the average position of the moving part with respect to its neutral position. This property of a spring suspension does away with the necessity for a position transducer for the focus, radial and tangential controls.

Besides other advantages, such as absence of play and friction, the spring suspension also has its drawbacks. Two of these we already have discussed, namely the decreased reduction in the low-frequency range and the addition of one or more resonance frequencies in the high frequency range as a result of high frequency vibration modes in the suspension springs. Possible solutions for the latter problem are a reduction of the Q factor and an increase of the parasitic resonance frequency. Reduction of the Q factor can be achieved by extra damping, for instance, by using suspension material with a high internal damping such as rubber. The resonance frequency can be increased by decreasing the corresponding parasitic spring mass. This results in an increase of the ratio between parasitic and driven mass so that the influence of the spring resonance on the actuator transfer decreases.

For a plain bearing suspension, usually applied in the vertical direction, a constant drive force is needed to lift the moving component. The resulting extra dissipation can be avoided by using a spring suspension. Then a constant acceleration of 1 g is not needed but an extra force has to be exerted to overcome the spring stiffness when the moving component is displaced. The magnitudes of both displacement and stiffness of the suspension springs determine which kind of suspension is to be preferred. For horizontal use or in cases where gravitational acceleration can be neglected, the use of springs always results in extra dissipation.

A special application of a suspension is that in which it has to guide a drive force. This is the case with the CD rotatable arm (see figure 4.30).

Owing to the radial tracking, the parallel leaf springs, which serve as suspension for the focus displacement, must have a high buckling strength. In the focusing direction, however, the bending stiffness has to be low.

The suspension resonance frequency in the focusing direction is 45 Hz. For a radial control bandwidth of 900 Hz the resonance frequency of the mass-spring system, formed by the buckling stiffness of the suspension springs and objective mass, should be about five times higher and hence must become about 4.5 kHz (see §4.5). As for the resonance frequency of the mass-spring system with mass M and spring stiffness G it holds that $f_0 = 1/2\pi\sqrt{G/M}$, the stiffnesses G_{vert} and G_{hor} are proportional to the square of the resonance frequencies. The resulting factor 10 000 can still just be realised in actual designs. In conclusion, we cannot expect a bandwidth higher than 1000 Hz in control systems with actuators driven via the suspension.

When the axis of the objective is not perpendicular to the disc surface, the read-out spot will be aberrated (coma, see p. 44) resulting in extra cross-talk of the neighbouring track. Coma is proportional to the third power of the numerical aperture. For LV players equipped with high NA objectives, as is necessary when an AlGaAs laser is used, this means that annoying interference patterns will be observed in the television picture. These interferences are caused by obliquity of the disc surface, due to its umbrella-like shape. This obliquity can be sufficiently overcome by using a tilting objective instead of a vertically moving one (see figure 4.34).

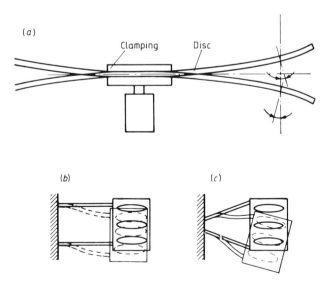

Figure 4.34 (*a*) Obliquity of the disc. (*b*) Vertically moving objective. (*c*) Tilting objective.

The automatic tracking of obliquity is a special feature of actuators equipped with electromagnetic rather than spring suspensions. The problems of this suspension method are closely related to those of 2-D and 3-D actuators that will be discussed in the next section.

4.6.4   2-D and 3-D actuators

A three-dimensional spot displacement is possible with an arrangement of actuators as used in the LV player (see figure 4.35). This arrangement consists of a vertically moving objective for focusing and two separate tilting mirrors.

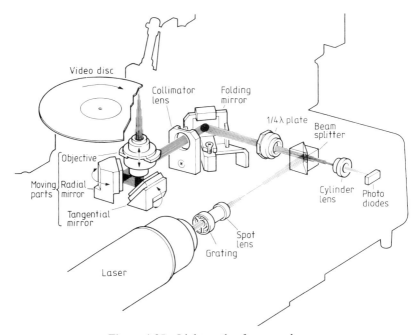

Figure 4.35   Light path of an LV player.

This method is attractive because of the possibility of choosing the optimum drive and suspension for each separate direction so that an optimum transfer function for each of the three actuators can be achieved. The use of separated actuators, however, implies that extra, optically high-grade components are required. In the case of the LV player this means two extremely flat mirrors with a reflective coating. Another disadvantage is the required space.

The alternative is one actuator that allows a three-dimensional spot displacement. The advantages of such a 3-D actuator are of a commercial rather than technical character as no expensive optical components are needed.

For three-dimensional manipulation of the spot with one component, only the objective comes into consideration. An alternative, which, however, uses more than one component, is the movement of the entire light path.

Before entering further into the possible designs of 3-D actuators we will discuss a number of technically less complicated 2-D actuators. For CD players a 2-D actuator (vertical and radial) is sufficient. A 2-D actuator for LV players has to be extended with an extra 1-D actuator.

The first 2-D actuator for optical recording was formed by replacing the two tilting mirrors for LV by one mirror that can rotate on two axes. The mirror was equipped with a point bearing, which in its simplest form consists of a rubber rod between the middle of the mirror and a fixed point. There are two drives allowing tilting round two perpendicular axes in the mirror plane. Mirrors have only these two tilting directions as relevant optical parameters so that no great requirements as to the degrees of freedom are imposed on the 2-D mirror suspension.

When an objective is used in a 2-D actuator, the close tolerances on angular deviations pose a serious problem and the suspension must prevent tilting of the objective. Figure 4.36 gives an example of such a 2-D suspension. The radial spot displacement is made possible by rotating the moving component in which the objective is mounted eccentrically. Focusing is achieved by sliding over the shaft. The counter-mass required for the dynamic balance is a drawback as the total mass is increased by a factor of 2.

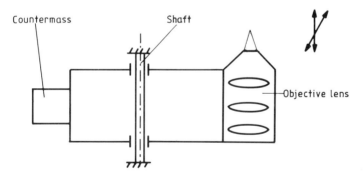

Figure 4.36 2-D actuator suspension with plain bearings on a shaft.

Another suitable 2-D suspension consists of four parallel flexible rods (see figure 4.37). The parasitic resonance of the rods can be compensated for by coating them with a damping material such as rubber. Tilting of the objective in one direction owing to the torsion weakness of the rods can be kept within acceptable limits by using a good symmetrical drive so that the torque in the tilting direction is kept as low as possible. The sensitivity to external rotational impulses remains unaltered.

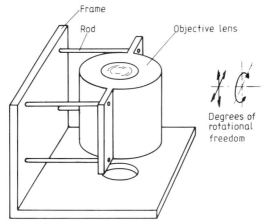

Figure 4.37   2-D tilting actuator suspended in four flexible rods.

A considerable gain in rotational stiffness is obtained when the flexible rods are set at a given angle (see figure 4.38). The larger rotational stiffness is caused by high buckling stiffness, because when tilted the rods would either have to stretch or contract.

An alternative 2-D actuator, the CD rotatable arm, has the advantage of a large stroke but, as usual with oblong constructions, its use is restricted to low bandwidths.

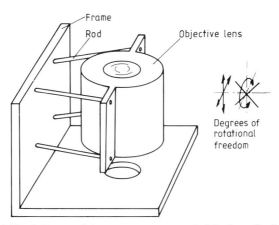

Figure 4.38   2-D non-tilting actuator suspended in four flexible rods.

The same holds for the 2-D actuator, developed for use in DOR, which also has a large stroke (20 mm, see figure 4.39). In this actuator a long coil is surrounded by an entirely closed magnet system. The movements of the coil are transmitted to the compact light path by two parallel rods that also serve as a radial suspension. The light path is suitable for reading as well as writing. Focusing is by a small objective actuator incorporated in the light path.

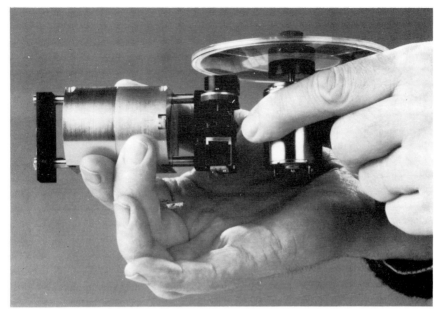

Figure 4.39 DOR actuator with a long radial stroke.

An alternative for the suspension is applied in a 2-D actuator that was also developed for use in a DOR player. An objective holder with two flat sides (see figure 4.40) can move freely in a vertical plane between two Rulon-coated gliding walls (see figure 4.41). Thus the objective floats with three degrees of freedom in a two-dimensional space. Of these degrees of freedom the two translations, in radial and vertical directions, are wanted. A striking feature of this method is that the unwanted degree of freedom, tilting, is controlled by an extra loop to a preset position. As an extra feature this preset position can be matched to the actual angle of the disc. The required angle position detector consists of a very narrow light beam which is split up into two beams (see figure 4.42) by the reflective prism, mounted on the objective holder (see figure 4.40). Both beams enter two dual photodiodes where they are converted into four signals from which the tilt signal is derived.

Besides the principle of this transducer figure 4.42 shows the objective with its drive coils and the three control loops. The radial drive is split up into an upper and a lower part so that a torque can be generated for the tilting correction. The corresponding static magnetic fields are generated by a number of magnets with iron yokes formed by the housing (see figure 4.41).

Figure 4.43 shows the components from figures 4.40 and 4.41 assembled in a robust actuator suitable for fast random access applications that will be discussed in §4.8 on carriages. A construction based upon this 'floating' actuator is the variant for LV discussed earlier (see figure 4.28).

Figure 4.40 Moving objective assembly of a 2-D actuator with plain bearings.

Figure 4.41 Housing of a 2-D actuator with plain bearings. The granular metal areas to the centre, left and right are the magnets and the smoother, polished areas on the left and central disc the iron housing.

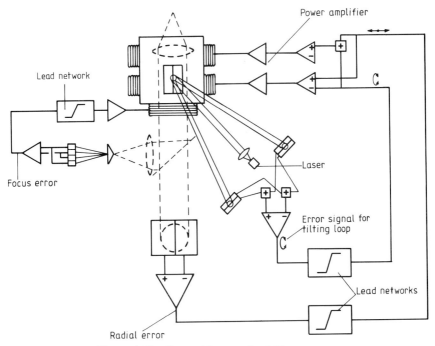

Figure 4.42 Control loops of a 2-D actuator.

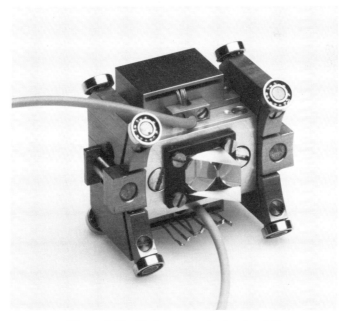

Figure 4.43 Fast-access actuator for DOR.

As with any rigid body, the objective has six degrees of freedom, namely three translations and three rotations. In a 3-D actuator the three objective translations are determined by the vertical, radial and tangential spot position control loops. One of the three other degrees of freedom, rotation round the objective axis, is optically of no importance and needs no control. For control of the other two degrees of freedom two suspensions are needed. At present electromagnetic suspensions are used because of their qualitative superiority over mechancial alternatives for 3-D actuators, due to, for instance, parasitic resonances.

Analogous to the extra control loop in the aforementioned 2-D variant two extra suspension control loops are required. This implies two extra angle transducers, two extra drives for the generation of the two torques and all the associated control electronics.

An extra feature is that, if the angle transducers measure the angle between the objective axis and the disc surface, the objective axis will remain perpendicular to the disc surface, in both radial and tangential directions.

A variant of the construction shown in figure 4.28 is suitable as an entirely electromagnetically suspended 3-D objective actuator. In this design the upper and lower part use three instead of two banana-shaped coils at an angle of $120°$. The mechanical suspension now has to be removed.

The excellent performance of a 3-D actuator such as the high control bandwidth is achieved by two favourable features: the use of a nonmaterial suspension resulting in very high parasitic resonance frequencies (> 20 kHz) thus allowing a very high control bandwidth and the use of moving magnets making disturbing and vulnerable electric leads unnecessary. As these advantages do not in all cases compensate for the disadvantage of the additional control loops, there is a need for a mechanical equivalent for the suspension. This equivalent has to be sufficiently free of resonances and must prevent two or three rotations. A solution to this problem has not yet been found although there is an alternative where one rotation and two translations are prevented by means of a membrane. A construction based upon this idea is shown in figure 4.44. This construction is called the light pen because the entire light path is incorporated in a pen-like construction. The artist's impression of this light pen (see figure 4.45) shows the four magnet systems for the drive above and the membrane below. The membrane forms the only suspension. The focus coil with its magnet system is mounted directly under the membrane. A ceramic ring above the membrane (see figure 4.44) provides the thermal insulation between light path and the focus coil in which heat is generated. Displacements of the top end of the light pen due to tracking causing angular deviations between disc and objective axis. To keep these deviations within limits (to limit the coma) the point of rotation, which in this case lies in the membrane plane, has to be far removed from the disc so that a high player design is the result.

In the above we have assumed the movement directions in 2-D and 3-D actuators to be mutually independent, i.e. a drive in one direction results in a displacement in that direction only. In general this will not be the case owing to imperfections of drive and suspension and cross-talk between the various drive directions will occur. This does not necessarily have to influence the control system negatively as undesired movements are compensated for by the corresponding control loops. If, however, cross-talk occurs in other parts of the controls, such as is especially the case in the position detectors, the combination of the various cross-talks can result in instability. For this reason the cross-talks in both optical detection system and actuator have to be controlled. The actuator cross-talk in the low frequency range is caused by inaccuracies of the suspension (e.g. obliquity of leaf springs in mechanical suspensions or obliquity of the detection components in electromagnetic suspensions). In the high frequency range cross-talk is mainly caused by a driving force that does not act on the centre of gravity.

Figure 4.44 Membrane-suspended light pen.

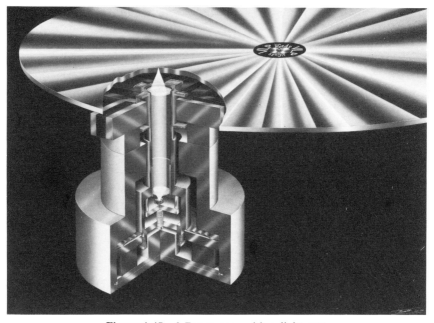

Figure 4.45   3-D actuator with a light pen.

4.6.5   *Jumping*

Among the features of LV are the possibilities of still pictures and slow or fast playback either in the forward or backward direction. The features are possible when one complete picture is recorded per revolution (CAV). In these modes the read-out spot is displaced quickly over one or more track-to-track spacings. When the displacement takes place within the flyback period of the TV picture the effects will not be visible. This implies that the displacement must be completed within one millisecond.

In an application of the LV player together with a games computer a moving picture is formed from pictures on tracks that are possibly some hundreds of tracks apart. In this case the spot has also to be displaced within one millisecond but now over a much larger distance. The games computer determines the sequence of spot displacements, thus allowing the build-up of various picture sequences.

A third application in which a fast displacement is required is the fast access procedure in DOR.

All these spot displacements are possible with a so-called jumping procedure. The radial control loop is opened and simultaneously a so-called jump pulse is supplied to the radial actuator. This jump pulse consists of two successive current pulses of equal amplitude and opposite sign (see figure 4.46). The spot now is accelerated and decelerated and thus is dis-

limitation determines the radial stroke, which generally amounts to some millimetres when the entire light path follows the track in the radial direction.

The CD arm (see figure 4.30) and the radial actuator of a DOR player (see figure 4.39), however, are examples where the radial stroke is sufficiently large for read-out of the entire disc. In other applications a carriage is needed to cover the entire radial stroke. When a fast access is required, such as in LV players to allow jumping to remote pictures, or in case of the CD player to allow the play-back of any piece of music within some tenths of seconds, a fast carriage displacement is needed. In DOR players in particular very fast access is essential.

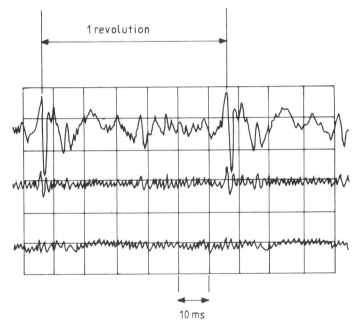

Figure 4.52 Top curve: original residual focus error signal (feedback only). Middle curve: idem using the additional memory feedforward loop. Bottom curve: idem using the obliquity feedforward signal. The horizontal distance between grid lines represents about 10 ms.

4.8.1 Guiding

The carriage has to be guided so that it can move freely in only one direction and, as always, a vertical control system is active; small vertical movements of the carriage due to impulses or vibrations are allowed. In this way only the vertical stroke of the focusing actuator is decreased.

Contrary to expectations the position of the stationary part of the focus actuator, which is mounted on the carriage, does not influence the vertical error spectrum because the objective is driven by force instead of via its position. Strictly speaking this only holds when the vertical suspension has no neutral position.

Tilting of the carriage, however, is important as the carriage must be parallel to the disc to within a small angle, e.g. within $\pm 0.5^{\circ}$.

Sometimes a partly stationary light path is applied, in which the light as a parallel beam is sent to the moving carriage. In this case the slide movement has to be parallel (within $\pm 0.2^{\circ}$) to the beam direction. These not very severe requirements can be fulfilled by a number of guiding systems. A frequently used method is to move the carriage via sleeve bearing bushes over two parallel rods. Variants in which the sleeve bearings have been replaced by roller or ball bearings have less friction. This advantage also holds for guides with V-grooves and balls as in carriage supports in typewriters.

4.8.2 Drive

With the exception of linear drives, the carriage drive consists of a rotating electric motor with a transmission and a rotation-to-translation conversion.

Driven in this way, the carriage assembly is usually self-braking. This implies that owing to internal friction it cannot be displaced by external forces. This has the advantage that external disturbances will not influence the carriage control so that no additional reduction has to be incorporated.

The drive motor can be a DC motor or it can be a stepping motor. An advantage of the stepping motor is its well defined angular rotation at a low cost price, which makes it suitable for positioning of the carriage without the use of a position detector. The DC motor is attractive because of its high efficiency and easy availability.

The transmission is often a gear drive, although, to achieve a lower noise level, a belt transmission is sometimes used.

For the rotation-to-translation conversion, many solutions are possible of which the most frequently used are a lead screw, toothed rack, geared belt, belt (either steel or synthetic material) and friction transmission.

For a stable carriage control with a sufficiently high bandwidth it is important that there is no play between motor rotation and carriage displacement. This backlash is mainly caused by play in the conversion. To reduce this play, pre-stressing in one direction can be used. When a lead screw or a toothed rack is used, the screw or pinion mesh can be pre-stressed by a spring force. The gear belt and other belts are already stressed and will show hardly any play.

Furthermore, the stiffness of the drive is important as, together with the carriage mass, it determines the frequency of the resonance that limits the bandwidth of the carriage control. Usually a bandwidth of about 5 Hz is chosen. This implies a resonance frequency greater than 25 Hz.

With a linear motor there are no problems of play and stiffness as the driving force can be exerted directly on the carriage. A drawback of the linear motor is the low efficiency due to the long stroke. The number of carriage displacements per unit of time, the carriage jump duration and the jump distance are thermally limited to low values (see §4.6.5, equation (4.20)), so a high efficiency of the drive is desired.

In the fast random access mechanism shown in figure 4.53, which was designed for DOR applications, rotating electric motors of high efficiency are used for this reason. Dead stroke and stiffness problems have been overcome in this case by using tightened geared belts made of synthetic material with a steel wire core. To achieve short access times the carriage resonance frequencies have been increased to above 500 Hz. The carriage consists of the 2-D actuator (see figure 4.43) with eight ball bearings for guiding. The high resonance frequency is obtained by having a low carriage mass (33 g), which, together with the powerful motors, allows very high accelerations up to about $1000\ \mathrm{m\,s^{-2}}$. Even with this low carriage mass a reaction force of 33 N will be exerted on the frame when the carriage is subject to this acceleration. To prevent the occurrence of too heavy vibrations we have developed a drive system in which the reaction forces and torques are compensated. The principle of this system is shown in figure 4.54.

Finally figure 4.55 shows the combination of a 2-D actuator, carriage, guiding and drive.

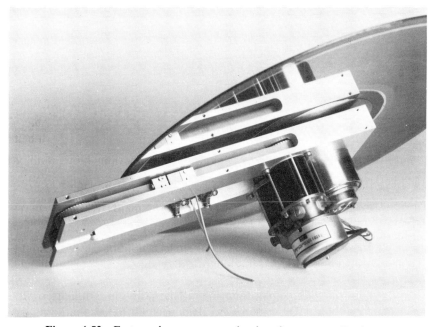

Figure 4.53 Fast random access mechanism for DOR applications.

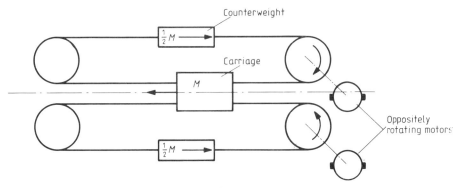

Figure 4.54 Compensation for forces and torques.

Figure 4.55 Detail of the fast random access mechanism.

4.8.3 Positioning

During continuous read-out of the disc the carriage position is controlled so that on the average the radial actuator acts around its neutral (middle) position. Thus a signal is needed that represents the distance of the actual position of the moving part of the actuator from the neutral position. When the moving part is freely suspended a position transducer is necessary.

For a spring suspension with a neutral position, the low frequency component of the drive current can be used as position signal, as in §4.6.3. When this signal or the signal of the transducer is supplied to the carriage drive, the carriage position can be controlled. The frequency range of the disturbances is so low that a sufficiently high reduction can be achieved with a control bandwidth of some hertz only. This low frequency carriage position control also can be used for the relatively slow access procedure for LV and CD, in which a large radial displacement is realised by means of a sequence of actuator jumps over some (or even one) tracks.

As in the game of golf, where the ball has to be directed from the tee to the hole in a minimum number of steps, the spot can quickly be directed to the desired track via a minimum number of jumps. In this fast access procedure, which exploits the features of the random access drive of figure 4.53, the carriage is slewed to the desired place by means of a feedforward control. The residual carriage position error is then measured by a carriage position detector, after which the carriage is sent to the desired position by a feedback control. The deviation of the spot position is now smaller than the tolerance of the carriage control. Next the spot is positioned accurately with the radial actuator control. During the carriage movement the objective retains its neutral position, after which the objective actuator completes the access procedure without a carriage displacement.

Figure 4.56 gives a schematic representation of the six controls from the fast random access control of figure 4.53. The numbers denote the various loops of which some properties are shown in table 4.5. In table 4.6 crosses indicate which loops are functioning for a given mode of the player.

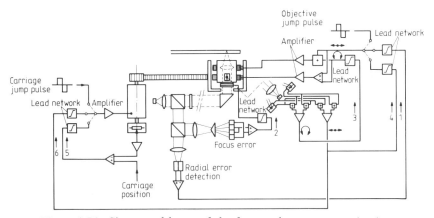

Figure 4.56   Six control loops of the fast random access mechanism.

The following worst case calculation shows the short access times that are possible. The access procedure uses one carriage and a maximum of three actuator feedforward jump pulses, each of them followed by a control and lock action of the corresponding feedback loop and a subsequent identification of the track by reading the address in the sector heading, which includes the track number. From §4.6.5 the jump duration appears to depend on the acceleration $\ddot{x}$ and the jump distance s. It is given by

$$t = 2\sqrt{s/\ddot{x}}.$$

Table 4.7 gives the numerical values of the jump times calculated by taking carriage and actuator accelerations of 1000 and 100 m s^{-2}, respectively. For the lock-in time of both feedback loops we take one period of the eigenfrequency associated with the corresponding bandwidth, i.e.

Table 4.5 Properties of the six controls used in the DOR carriage.

Loop number	Loop type	Measuring system	Actuator	Control bandwidth
1	Radial loop	Push–pull tracking error	Objective lens drive	6 kHz
2	Focusing loop	Foucault focusing error	Objective lens drive	2 kHz
3	Tilting loop	Optical position transducer	Objective lens drive	1 kHz
4	Objective lens centring	Optical position transducer	Objective lens drive	1 kHz
5	Carriage position with regard to frame	Potentiometer on motor shaft	Carriage motors	100 Hz
6	Carriage position with regard to objective lens	Optical position transducer	Carriage motors	100 Hz

Table 4.6 Functioning loops of the DOR player.

Mode	Loop number					
	1	2	3	4	5	6
Stand-by			×	×	×	
Focus		×	×	×	×	
Tracking	×	×	×			×
Carriage position change		×	×	×	×	

100 Hz and 6 kHz for carriage and actuator, respectively. Track identification introduces a delay of 0.3 ms at a maximum; this is the time necessary for one sector to pass, i.e. 1/128th part of the revolution time (40 ms) may occur before the read or write action in the desired sector can take place. From table 4.7 it can be seen that the maximum access time amounts to 76.5 ms.

Table 4.7 Jump durations.

Jump number	Max. jump distance	Max. jump duration (ms)	Max. lock-in time (ms)	Track number delay (ms)	Sub-total (ms)
1	80 mm	17.9	10.0	—	27.9
2	500 μm	4.5	0.2	0.3	5.0
3	100 μm	2.0	0.2	0.3	2.5
4	10 μm	0.6	0.2	0.3	1.1
				Revolution time	40.0 ms
				Max. access time	76.5 ms

4.9 Wobbling

Wobbling is an alternative method of error signal generation for both vertical and radial tracking if the wobble frequency is sufficiently high. However, when a low wobble frequency is used, there is still a suitable low frequency error signal which can be used to eliminate imperfections in the low frequency part of the optically-generated error signal such as offset.

This alternative error signal is generated via small periodical displacements of either spot or track (see §2.5). The latter solution has never been applied in consumer products because of standardisation of the disc specifications. Spot wobbling, however, is used successfully.

The spot can be moved by way of the objective, by a mirror or by moving the light source. All these methods have proved suitable.

4.9.1 Radial wobble
Proper radial tracking is possible with an error signal generated by a spot wobble of 0.3 μm. For smaller deviations the signal-to-noise ratio is too low. The wobble frequency has to be about 10 times higher than the control bandwidth. For a bandwidth of 3 kHz this implies a wobble of 0.3 μm at 30 kHz.

Because of the double-integrating function of all the actuators, energy problems arise because the amplitude of the wobble movement decreases with the square of the frequency of the drive current. However, we can successfully apply mechanical resonance. The mechanical resonance gain of more than 100 times ($Q > 100$) gives spot displacements of some tenths of micrometres and an acceptable heat generation in the drive.

The first radial wobble generator we used was a semi-transparent tilting mirror of which figure 4.57 shows a laboratory model. This mirror can be used both for radial tracking and spot wobbling. A resonance frequency of 33 kHz is achieved by means of two auxiliary masses which, in resonance, tilt in the opposite direction from the mirror tilt. The entire resonator consists of a glass plate with four saw cuts. The glass between mirror and auxiliary mass forms the torsion spring of the mass-spring system, the transfer of which is shown in table 4.3(4). The small internal damping obtained by using fused silica gives a mechanical resonance gain of at least 100 times.

Figure 4.57   Prototype of the wobble mirror.

The glass body is also used for radial tracking. To allow for the subsequent greater angular displacement, the total body is suspended in two rubber springs. To maintain the mechanical resonance, a piezo pick-up element is attached to one of the auxiliary masses. This pick-up element generates an acceleration signal that can be fed back to the radial tracking drive coils.

Figure 4.58 shows a 2-D version in which the tilting mirror can tilt radially as well as tangentially round a rubber suspension. The auxiliary mass at the underside together with the mirror mass at the upper side form the resonance mechanism.

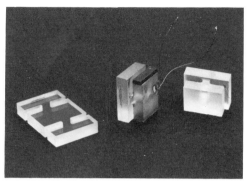

Figure 4.58   Laboratory model of a 2-D wobble mirror.

In figure 4.59 the interior of the bottom part of the LV light pen, which contains the laser (§4.1, figure 4.3) is shown. The spot produced by this light pen can wobble both vertically and radially by means of a wobbling AlGaAs laser. This laser is mounted on a metal rod about 3 mm in length, suspended in a membrane and driven with two piezoelectric drives. With these drives the resonances in two directions in the rectangular rod are excited, thus giving radial and vertical movement of the laser with different frequencies. The lead of the laser is glued to the rod to prevent breakage of the wire.

4.9.2   Focus wobble

Just as with radial wobble the problem is to achieve a sufficiently large wobble amplitude at a frequency of about ten times the required control bandwidth.

The light source actuator of figure 4.59 meets this requirement even though the vertical displacement of the spot on the disc as compared with the laser displacement is reduced by a factor of 4 owing to the longitudinal magnification of the light path.

This undesired reduction does not occur when the objective is wobbled. A possible construction of such an objective is given in figure 4.60. A countermass is provided concentrically around the objective mass in the form of a bus. Both masses are connected via a ring acting like a spring. In resonance the masses move in antiphase. Because this construction also allows large vertical displacements for focusing it is called a combi-objective actuator.

Figure 4.59   Interior of the bottom part of the LV light pen.

Figure 4.61 shows a construction for the generation of focus wobble integrated with a 2-D tilting mirror for radial and tangential tracking. The thin round mirror resonates in a convex–concave mode, thus causing the wobble. Only the mirror is connected under the node-line to a spacer to achieve a sufficiently large Q factor of the resonance. The spacer is attached to the frame via a rubber rod to permit tilting of the mirror and hence radial and tangential tracking.

The wobble resonance and the tilting in two directions are driven by four coils and a permanent magnet ring round the mirror. The wobble is maintained by applying to all coils a current derived from an acceleration signal which is supplied by a transducer on the mirror (positive feedback). Tilting is achieved by driving the pairs of opposite coils in antiphase.

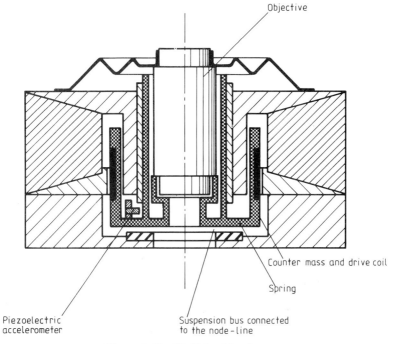

Figure 4.60 Wobble objective.

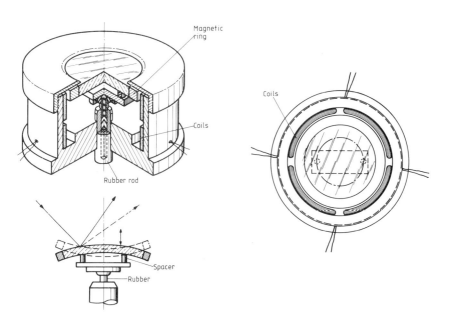

Figure 4.61 2-D tilting mirror combined with focus wobble.

References and bibliography

Bögels P W 1976 System coding parameters, mechanics and electromechanics of the reflective video disc player *IEEE Trans. Consum. Electron.* **EC-22** 309

Dorf R C 1980 *Modern Control Systems* (New York: Addison Wesley)

Harris C M and Crede C E 1976 *Shock and Vibration Handbook* (New York: McGraw Hill)

den Hartog J P 1956 *Mechanical Vibrations* (New York: McGraw Hill)

5 Mastering

J Pasman

5.1 Introduction

One of the principles the three major optical disc systems have in common is that they use discs on which information has been prerecorded in the form of a height profile. This height profile may contain the encoded video or audio information or it may serve to guide the read or write spot on data storage discs. It is through this profile that mass replication of the information is relatively simple.

The recording of the information from, for instance, a video tape into the surface relief pattern on the so-called master disc is performed in the mastering process, which therefore occurs at the beginning of the disc manufacturing process (Olijhoek *et al* 1981, Pasman 1983). The master is a flat glass substrate coated with a thin layer of photosensitive material (resist) about $0.12 \, \mu$m thick. The surface relief pattern is recorded by exposing the photoresist using a focused laser beam of which the intensity is modulated in accordance with the information (figure 5.1). In the exposed areas light is absorbed which has the effect of locally changing the solubility (Pacansky and Lyerla 1979). The height structure then appears in the development stage, when an alkaline solution is made to flow over the resist layer and dissolves the photoresist in the exposed areas.

Although the principles of exposure and development of photoresist on masters resemble well known techniques in optical microlithography used in the mass production of integrated circuits, there are some considerable differences. One such difference is the small size and the high optical quality of the light spot necessary to produce pits only about $0.6 \, \mu$m wide. This is only possible with diffraction-limited optics and a recording objective of high numerical aperture up to 0.8. When the blue $\lambda = 457.9$ nm line of an argon–ion laser is used as a light source, a recording spot can be obtained with a full width at half maximum (FWHM) of only 0.30 μm. For general purposes however a somewhat lower NA of 0.65 is used, resulting in a diffraction-limited spot of FWHM 0.35 μm.

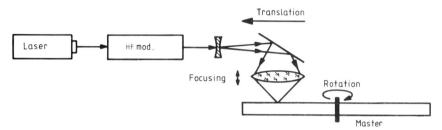

Figure 5.1   Schematic diagram of the laser beam recorder.

Unlike in microlithography, where the exposure time amounts to several tenths of a second, the exposure of one information element or pit on a master lasts only some 70 ns, when a 7 MHz video carrier is real-time recorded. This implies that the intensity in the light spot must be very high, which requires the use of a laser as a light source. The energy of a laser beam of typical intensity of 25 mW is concentrated into a spot of diameter less than 1 μm.

The resist layer thickness in the mastering process is about one order of magnitude smaller than usual in standard IC techniques. Moreover, not only is the absolute value of the thickness small but also the tolerances on the thickness are very tight. Fluctuations in resist thickness as well as in any other exposure and development parameter give rise to micro roughness and pits of varying volume resulting at read-out in extra noise or degradation of the signal. In practical applications the signal-to-noise ratio is usually limited by such effects as surface roughness and irregularities in pit dimensions of only a few nanometres (Heemskerk 1978).

Clearly a mastering process makes great demands upon reproducibility between different masters and upon homogeneity on any single master, which may contain up to 3×10^{10} information elements. This all requires professional apparatus in a climate-conditioned clean-room (class 100) environment and good process control.

5.2   The mastering process

5.2.1   Input processing

Before the actual recording on a master disc can take place, both the information and the substrate need to be prepared.

The master is a circular, polished glass substrate, about 0.5 cm thick and for video discs about 36 cm in diameter. The polishing is necessary to facilitate the focusing control and to reduce the surface noise. The disc is cleaned, inspected and coated with an organic adhesive layer over which the photoresist is spin coated (Jacobs 1978, Olijhoek *et al* 1981). The thickness of the resist layer can be varied by diluting the photoresist with a thinner. The thickness ranges between 100 and 170 nm for different applications. The resist stability is increased by a bake after which the layer thickness is measured with an interference microscope. Then the master is ready for recording.

Since each of the three main optical disc applications has its own characteristic recording signal the signal preparation in the mastering will be different in each case.

For video-disc recording a master tape is recorded which contains the complete video and audio signals encoded as described in §7.1 together with a cue code. This code is transferred to the disc in the form of digital picture addresses, necessary when special facilities such as still picture, reverse and slow motion are included.

A master tape is also required for digital audio disc recording. The tape includes the digital audio and subcode information (see §7.2). The signals are fed into an encoder which carries out the multiplexing, CIRC (Cross Interleave Reed–Solomon Code) encoding and EFM (eight-to-fourteen) modulation. The output signal is then recorded.

Unlike in video and audio disc systems, the information on data storage discs, which is recorded in the heading of the track sectors (see Chapter 6), is fully predetermined and can be generated by an electronic heading generator.

5.2.2 Exposure

In the recording stage the intensity of the recording laser beam is modulated by driving a fast electro-optical or acousto-optical modulator with the recording signal. In this way the information is stored as a modulation of the surface in the tangential direction only. Although the feasibility of extra storage capacity in the radial direction in the form of undulating tracks has been demonstrated (Braat and Bouwhuis 1978), it is not used in standard applications.

The video signal as described in §7.1 requires a large carrier-to-noise ratio (CNR) at read-out due to its analog character and large bandwidth. This implies a large modulation of the read-out signal, which is only possible when the modulation is also large at the recording side. Such a large modulation in the exposure of the resist at high spatial frequencies can only be obtained when the recording spot is relatively small compared with the tangential pit spacing. In other words, the MTF of the recording objective must be high even for high spatial frequencies. The pit spacing p is determined by the rotation frequency of the disc f_{rot}, the track radius r and the temporal frequency f_t

$$p = 2\pi r f_{rot}/f_t. \tag{5.1}$$

The smallest pit spacing is produced on LV video discs by a video carrier of temporal frequency $f_t = 7.9$ MHz (white screen). At an inner radius of 55 mm and a rotational frequency of 25 Hz, the minimum pit spacing is 1.1 μm and consequently the maximum fundamental spatial frequency $f_s = 900$ mm^{-1}. However, higher harmonics of this spatial frequency have also to be included to record the double sideband FM spectrum and to obtain a deeply modulated pit pattern.

The MTF of the recording objective of numerical aperture NA has a cut-off frequency f_{co} given by

$$f_{co} = 2NA/\lambda = 4370 \times NA \qquad (mm^{-1}). \tag{5.2}$$

Satisfactory CNR values for the above critical case of about 62 dB (measured with 30 kHz bandwidth) are obtained with an NA larger than 0.6.

The CNR is relatively tolerant with respect to the exposure level and development time. Even when the exposure is 30% too great, the CNR is hardly affected. Stricter limits are set however by the symmetry of the video signal. When the exposure level or the development time is off-optimum, the average tangential duty cycle of the pits as seen by the read-out optics deviates from the symmetry value of $\frac{1}{2}$ and intermodulation products are introduced in the read-out signal between the carriers of the luminance, colour and audio (§§7.1.5 and 2.4.2). Such intermodulation, giving rise to annoying interference patterns on the television screen, limit the tolerances in exposure energy and development to about ±10%. A test signal which is especially designed to measure the symmetry of the recorded pit pattern is the duty cycle modulation (DCM) test signal. It consists of a 'video' carrier of a fixed frequency $f_v = 7.1$ MHz of which the duty cycle is modulated by an 'audio' carrier of frequency f_a. After limiting a pulsewidth modulated square wave is produced of which the duty cycle varies between 30 and 70%. When this signal is recorded employing different exposure intensities, the asymmetry components in the read-out spectrum at the frequencies $f_v + f_a$ and $f_v - f_a$ can be measured relative to the video carrier level to give a plot as shown in figure 5.2. The best picture quality is obtained when the two asymmetry component levels are related in accordance with the read-out MTF. The difference between the level of the video carrier and the noise background is measured to give the CNR value.

Since the optical audio disc system differs in many respects from the video disc system, the mastering of CD masters is especially adapted to the CD requirements. Owing to the digital character and the smaller bandwidth of the CD signal (§7.2) lower CNR values of about 50 dB (carrier at 500 kHz, 400 mm^{-1}, 10 kHz bandwidth) are sufficient. Also the pit spacing, ranging from about 150 to 550 mm^{-1}, is smaller than usual on video discs by nearly a factor of two. This means that a lower NA of the recording objective can be used. Apart from making it easier to obtain a good spot quality and a larger depth of focus, this has the important advantage that in the radial direction the pits are wider and have smaller slopes. Such wider structures produce larger push–pull radial tracking signals without harming the HF CA signal (see p. 119). This is favourable for the CD player, which uses a PP tracking.

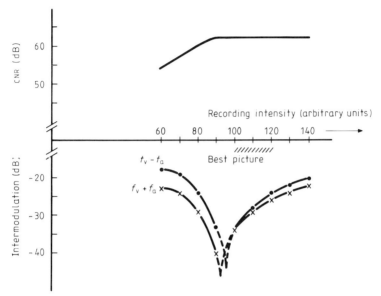

Figure 5.2 Example of measured CNR (top graph) and intermodulation terms as a function of the recording intensity for pits of highest spatial frequency.

An important pit geometry parameter, which also determines the quality of the read-out signal, is the symmetry level. In the player electronics a limiting action is performed on the read-out signal (see §7.2.1). The limiter level, also called the detection level, is taken in such a way that on average the produced digital signal has zero DC content. Since the cut-off frequency of the read-out optics is 1150 mm^{-1}, higher harmonics of the pit pattern are also detected. Even harmonic and in particular second harmonic contributions only occur when the pits are too long or too short. They have the effect of shifting the 'zero crossings' of the read-out signal resulting in a shift in the limiter level to compensate for the subsequent DC content. For spatial frequencies which are below half the read-out cut-off frequency, as is the case on CD discs, the shift in the detection level is independent of the frequency and as a consequence the flanks in the digital signal after limiting always coincide with the flanks of the original recorded signal. Deviations in exposure or development are therefore automatically compensated by the read-out electronics. The CD mastering is optimised so as to give the best signal-to-noise ratio and an acceptable asymmetry. It will be clear that second harmonics play a less dominant role in the CD system as do inter-modulation products in the LV system. In fact they both originate from the same source, namely pits of which the length is off-symmetry.

On masters for data storage discs the prerecorded structure is divided in the radial direction in tracks and in the tangential direction in sectors. Each sector consists of two parts, a relatively short sector heading, consisting of an array of pits containing the sector address and synchronisation patterns, followed by the area where users may record their data. Between the heading pits and in the user area a shallow pregroove is recorded to produce a push–pull tracking signal (see p. 114) This pregroove is recorded by reducing the intensity of the recording spot (figure 5.3). When this reduced intensity is harmonically modulated a clock pattern can also be recorded in the pregroove, which makes synchronisation easier. Unlike the recording of CD and LV masters, which are two-level recordings, we can see that intermediate levels are also recorded.

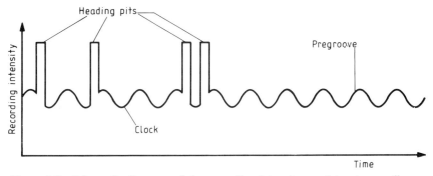

Figure 5.3   Schematic diagram of the recording intensity on data storage discs.

We will now look more closely at the recording apparatus, the laser beam recorder (LBR) of which the optical path is drawn schematically in figure 5.1. The beam of an argon–ion laser, of wavelength $\lambda = 457.9$ nm passes through a fast optical modulator, in general an electro-optical or an acousto-optical modulator, which modulates the beam in intensity in accord-ance with the HF signal of the processing electronics. For masters which rotate at a constant angular frequency in the CAV mode, the recording intensity should increase with the radius on the disc to preserve a constant exposure energy per unit surface. This slow variation in intensity can be executed by the same fast modulator or it can be separately performed by slowly rotating a $\lambda/2$ plate in the beam followed by a polariser. Part of the light is therefore coupled out by a beam splitter, measured by a detector and compared with the set point determined by the radius. In the extended play mode the master rotates at a constant linear velocity (CLV mode), which means that the exposure level should remain constant but the angular frequency decreases with the radius. After expansion of the beam by either a negative field lens or a telescope the light fills the aperture of the objective lens which is focused onto the rotating disc. When the lens assembly moves linearly in the outward direction a spiral track is exposed. The light reflected from the disc surface is collected by the objective and imaged onto a video camera to monitor the focus condition during recording. Due to the large NA of the objective lens, the depth of focus Δz, as given by

$$\Delta z \simeq \pm \frac{\lambda}{2\,NA^2} \qquad (5.3)$$

is only of the order of 0.5 μm and a dynamic focus control is necessary. A focus servo signal is obtained with the use of an auxiliary light source, a HeNe or an AlGaAs laser for which wavelength the photo laquer is insensitive. The light is coupled in with a dichroic mirror. A focus error signal is obtained from the reflected light either by the double-wedge Foucault method or by the skew beam method (§2.5.2 and Bouwhuis and Braat 1978). The objective is made to follow the vertical displacements of the master surface by driving a current through a coil wound around the objective, which is mounted inside a magnet (see Chapter 4).

Not only the focusing but also the linear translation of the objective and the rotation of the master disc must be controlled. Together they determine the track pitch which is usually in the range of 1.4 to 2.0 μm. For CD masters a pitch of 1.6 μm is specified. This track spacing is controlled to within 0.1 μm. In addition the track-to-track time-base error must be kept to within 25 ns. This is accomplished by using a direct drive rotation motor with an air bearing. The rotational velocity, as measured with a tachometer, is controlled by a phase-locked loop servo system. The linear translation is usually measured with an inductive speed transducer, but for special applications a more accurate laser measuring system is applied, which enables the radial error to be reduced to 30 nm.

When we consider the size of the pits it will be clear that the recording must take place in a dust-free environment. Also, as pointed out by Pacansky and Lyerla (1979), the presence of water is of importance in the photochemical exposure process and the humidity of the air is controlled.

Next we will consider some theoretical details of the exposure profile by which the geometry of the pits is determined. As an example we consider the aforementioned critical case of the highest spatial frequency present on masters. This frequency is found at the inner radius of video discs.

In Chapter 2 an expression was derived which gives the distribution of the complex light amplitude in the plane of focus of a lens. When a perfect lens is uniformly illuminated a circular intensity pattern is produced which is known as the Airy pattern (Born and Wolf 1975)

$$I(r) = \left(\frac{2J_1(2\pi NAr\lambda^{-1})}{2\pi NAr\lambda^{-1}}\right)^2 I_0(r=0) \tag{5.4}$$

where J_1 is the Bessel function of the first kind and order one. This pattern consists of a bright central spot surrounded by successive dark and bright rings. The width of the spot is determined by the wavelength of the light and the numerical aperture NA. Two ways of defining the spot width are the full width at half the maximum intensity (FWHM) and the diameter d of the first dark ring. The latter is given by

$$d = 1.22\lambda/NA. \tag{5.5}$$

Although for values of NA larger than about 0.5 the light spot starts to deviate from the Airy pattern (Hopkins 1943, Richards and Wolf 1959), the differences are not so large that we cannot use the simple Airy disc model

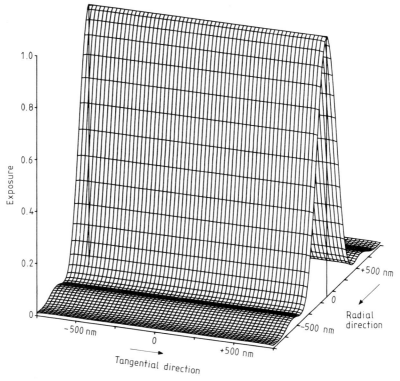

Figure 5.4 Exposure profile of continuous grooves recorded with NA = 0.6 and duty cycle DC = 100%. The first minimum lies at about 450 nm from the centre.

in this context. So when we take an objective lens of NA = 0.6 we consider the recording spot to have an intensity distribution with a first dark ring diameter of 930 nm. Suppose a rotating master is continuously exposed by this spot moving in the outward direction. Relative to the master the spot moves in a spiral over the surface with a tangential velocity v. The resultant local exposure profile can be calculated by integrating for each point the Airy pattern in the tangential direction. Since the absorption in the photoresist at the exposure wavelength is very low, the variation of the exposure in the vertical direction is neglected. The resultant exposure profile normalised with respect to the central exposure level is shown in figure 5.4. In the radial direction the effect of the first dark and bright rings is still to be seen. Of course there is no modulation in the tangential direction. This will be different when the spot is modulated. The exposure profile is then calculated by taking the convolution integral in the tangential direction of the spot intensity function $I(x,y)$ and the spot 'presence' function $H(t)$, which is unity when the modulator is on and zero when the modulator is switched off. In the case of a tangential period of 1100 nm and a

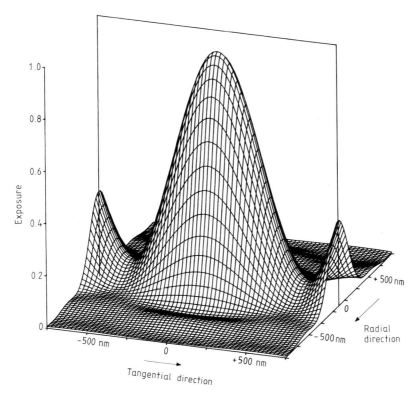

Figure 5.5 Exposure profile of pits recorded with NA = 0.6 and duty cycle DC = 50%. The tangential period $p = 1100$ nm.

duty cycle of 50%, $H(t)$ is unity in positions x' ($= vt$) where -275 nm $< x' - mp < 275$ nm

$$E(x,y) = \int_{-\infty}^{+\infty} I(x - vt, y) H(t) \, dt. \tag{5.6}$$

In figure 5.5 the profile is shown for the present case, normalised again by the central intensity in the case of continuous exposure. We note that in the centre of what is to become a pit the exposure level is less than 100% and in between the pits there is some unintended exposure. This is caused, of course, by the finite spot size, which is larger than the pit length. Only when the pit length, and the area between pits, are larger than the spot will the modulation in the exposure be 100%. This is an illustration of the concept of the MTF of a lens, acting as a low-pass filter for spatial frequencies. Only lower harmonics of the spot presence function $H(x)$ are transmitted to the disc and with a modulation depth smaller than unity. When we increase the bandwidth of the lens by taking a higher NA of 0.8 (figure 5.6) we see that the modulation depth increases.

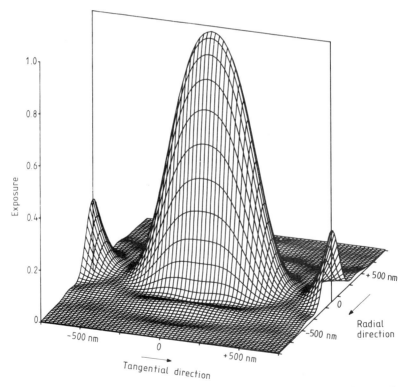

Figure 5.6 Exposure profile of pits recorded with NA = 0.8 and duty cycle DC = 50%. The tangential period $p = 1100$ nm.

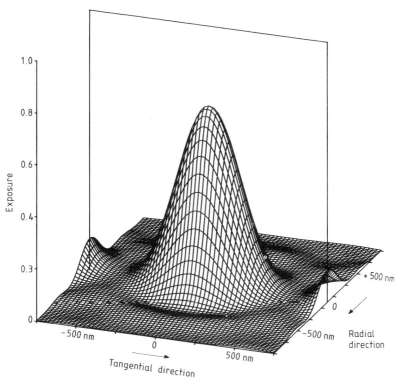

Figure 5.7 Exposure profile of pits recorded with NA = 0.6 and duty cycle DC = 30%. The tangential period $p = 1100$ nm.

Next the effect of duty cycle modulation is considered. We take the case of a duty cycle ranging from 30% to 70% as occurs in the DCM test signal (standard audio carriers only modulate the duty cycle between 45% and 55%). The exposure profiles when NA = 0.6 are shown in figures 5.7 and 5.8. We can summarise figures 5.4 to 5.8 by drawing in one figure the cross sections in the radial and tangential directions through the exposure centre $x = y = 0$ for different duty cycles (figure 5.9). We note that the gradient in exposure is weaker in the track direction than in the radial direction. As a consequence the pit walls will be steepest in the radial direction. Also, the effect of duty cycle modulation is not only to modulate the length of the pits but it also varies the width and the average depth of the exposure profile. This is an unwanted non-linear behaviour. In practice however two mechanisms ensure that this effect is not too severe. First, the top of the exposure profile, which would produce the deepest part of the pit in the photoresist if the resist layer were infinitely thick, is virtually truncated by the interface between the photoresist and the glass substrate. Any excessive exposure necessary to reach the bottom of the resist does not give any extra pit depth. Therefore the effect of different levels of the top of the exposure for different duty cycles is almost cancelled. Second, the development of resist in between pits which is suggested by the exposure level for larger duty cycles is reduced by the non-linear dependence of the development rate on the exposure. This development rate is defined as the rate at which the exposed resist thickness decreases during development. For the thin resist thicknesses, short exposure times and high exposure intensities used in optical recording the development rate is roughly a quadratic function of exposure. This means that between the pits, where the exposure is low, hardly any resist is removed during development.

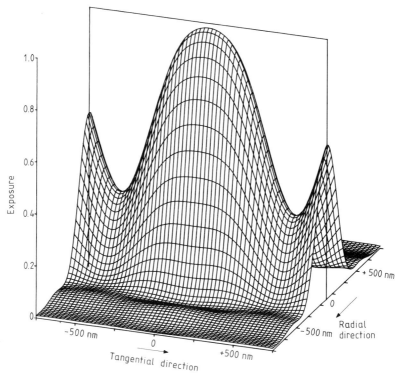

Figure 5.8   Exposure profile of pits recorded with NA = 0.6 and duty cycle DC = 70%. The tangential period $p = 1100$ nm.

The combined effects of finite resist thickness and quadratic development rate can be interpreted as a soft limiting action performed after the low-pass filter action of the objective lens.

5.2.3 Development

Once we have introduced the resist development rate and we know the exposure profile, we can calculate the resultant pit geometry during and after the development. To a first approximation the final depth profile

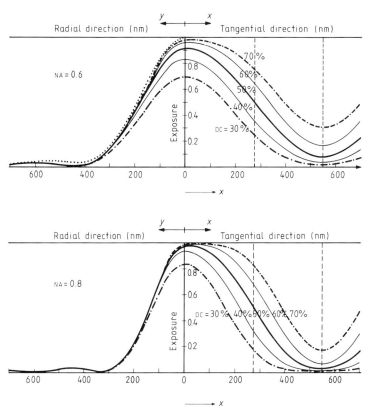

Figure 5.9 Cross sections in the exposure profiles through the profile centre in the radial direction (left-hand parts) and in the tangential direction (right-hand parts) when NA = 0.6 (top graph) and NA = 0.8 (bottom graph) for different values of the duty cycle.

equals the development rate profile obtained by just squaring the exposure profile. In figure 5.10 the radial cross section of the resultant development rate profile of continuous grooves recorded with NA = 0.6 is shown. We see that this profile is narrowed with respect to the original exposure profile. The model can be further refined when we assume that the removal of the resist during development is not directed in the vertical direction but perpendicular to the local resist–developer interface. This means that the development rate is not a scalar quantity but a vector quantity, always directed normal to the local interface and constantly changing when the developing structure evolves. This behaviour can be expressed mathematically by a non-linear partial differential equation, which can be solved to give the spatial depth profile at any instant of time during the developing process. A result of such a calculation is included in figure 5.10. The main effect is that the depth profile becomes wider where gradients in the development profile are large, as one would expect. The resultant groove width at the top of the resist is in this case seen to be about 550 nm.

The actual developing is performed by applying an alkaline developing fluid to the surface of the rotating master. The exposed areas are selectively dissolved in about 20 to 30 seconds. Because the development time, together with the exposure profile, determines the tangential symmetry, the developing should be stopped at the appropriate time. Inevitable small variations in photoresist properties, recording conditions and development parameters can be compensated for by altering the development time. The development process should therefore be monitored and stopped when the pit structure is optimal. This is performed by recording during development the intensities of diffracted orders produced when a specially exposed test band is illuminated by the beam of a HeNe laser. As we have seen in §3.3.1 the intensity of the first diffracted order is a measure of the volume removed and can therefore be used to indicate the progress of the developing. Depending on the proposed application, pit patterns or continuous grooves are recorded in the development test band. For general applications it is sufficient to record only the intensity of the first order relative to the zeroth order. Figure 5.11 shows a recorded plot of the intensities of the first and second orders for two orthogonal polarisation directions of the incident light, produced by continuous grooves.

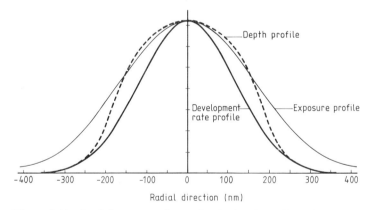

Figure 5.10 Radial cross sections of calculated profiles of exposure, development rate and depth of continuous grooves recorded with NA = 0.6.

5.2.4 *Further processing*

After development the intensities of both first and second diffracted transmission orders are measured over the programme area of the master disc to provide information on the quality and uniformity of the pit geometry.

After passing this test the master is evaporated with a thin metal layer (e.g. silver) which increases the reflectivity of the information structure. Next the master is played on a professional master inspection player where the signal quality can be electronically checked. Important electronic parameters are the CNR and SNR values, CA and PP amplitudes, intermodulation or second harmonic asymmetry terms and the occurrence of signal drop-outs. The signals are also decoded for a visual and aural inspection.

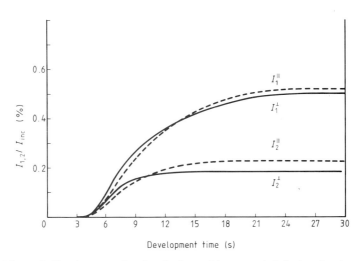

Figure 5.11 An example of order intensities recorded during development of continuous grooves. Both E polarisation (broken curves) and H polarisation (full curves) orders are shown.

For process control and trouble-shooting purposes diffraction measurements may be performed on the silvered master to indicate what geometries are recorded (see §3.3). The intensities of the diffracted orders and the phase difference between first and zeroth order are measured for two polarisations. The latter measurement is performed in the following way. The beam of a HeNe laser is normally incident on a rotating transmission grating (spoke wheel)(figure 5.12). The rotation causes the optical frequencies of the two first diffraction orders to be Doppler shifted by $+\omega_d$ and $-\omega_d$. A lens focuses both orders onto the grating structure on the master with such a magnification that for each of the two beams the direction of the negative first reflected order coincides with the direction of incidence of that beam (Littrow mount) and hence with the reflected zeroth order of the complementary beam. The negative first orders obtain a phaseshift ψ with respect to the zeroth orders. The light reflected in the two directions is coupled out and measured by two detectors which give time dependent signals produced by the interference of first and zeroth orders

$$I_1 \sim \cos(2\omega_d t + \psi)$$
$$I_2 \sim \cos(2\omega_d t - \psi).$$

(5.6)

Simple electronic phase measurement then yields twice the phase difference ψ.

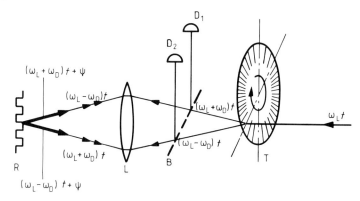

Figure 5.12 Schematic diagram of the phase meter set-up. T is the rotating transmission grating, B the beam splitter, L the lens, R the reflection grating and D_1 and D_2 are detectors.

5.3   Replication

After inspection the master leaves the mastering process and a nickel shell is electroplated onto the silvered surface of the master. When the nickel copy is separated from the master the information in the relatively soft resist on the master is destroyed. The nickel copy, which contains the negative of the master surface structure is called a father. The father may be used for low volume reproduction or it can be used in the generation of a family of nickel stampers. In the latter case, after a chemical modification of the nickel surface of the father, several mother positives are grown by electroplating. By the same process from each of the mothers several sons are produced. These negative masters are used as stampers in mass replication. In general different replication methods are used for video discs and audio discs.

The first method, the '2p' process (from photopolymerisation) has been developed especially for video-disc replication (Haverkorn van Rijsewijk *et al* 1982, Kloosterboer *et al* 1982). It has the technological advantage that high pressures and temperatures are not necessary. Besides, because there is no temperature cycle, no thermal stress is introduced in the replica after cooling, which might have introduced harmful double refraction. The principle of the replication of the information structure is the UV-light-induced polymerisation of a mixture of monomers with photoinitiator at the stamper surface (figure 5.13). The replica disc substrate is a 1.2 mm thick plastic (PMMA) substrate coated with an adhesive layer to increase the 2p adhesion. A few millilitres of the liquid 2p laquer are deposited around the middle of the nickel stamper and a PMMA substrate is lowered onto the stamper. The substrate is bowed by an over pressure into an inverted umbrella shape and reaches the stamper first in the centre. By further lowering the disc the 2p laquer flows to the outer rim thereby covering the

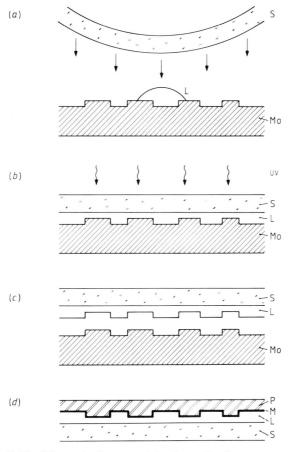

Figure 5.13 Schematic diagram of the 2p replication process. (*a*) The liquid 2p laquer is spread over the mould surface (Mo) by the bent substrate S. (*b*) UV exposure through the substrate which hardens the 2p laquer. (*c*) Separation of the substrate from the stamper. (*d*) The 2p layer is coated with a metal mirror (M) and a protective coating (P). Two such discs are glued together to form the final double-sided video disc. Diagram courtesy of *Philips Technical Review*.

stamper surface with a 10 to 30 μm thin film of liquid. Next the laquer is exposed through the substrate with UV radiation of wavelength of about 350 nm. The laquer polymerises and hardens. When the substrate is separated from the stamper the information-carrying 2p laquer adheres to the substrate and the stamper can be used for a new cycle. After a final exposure to fully harden the 2p laquer a reflective metal layer (aluminium or silver) is deposited onto the information structure. Next the vulnerable metal mirror is coated with a protective layer. Two discs are glued together and an airtight double-sided video disc is produced containing up to 2 hours of video programmes.

This principle of 2p replication is at present also used in the production of data storage discs. In that case, however, the reflective layer is a tellurium-based alloy. This aspect is treated in more detail in Chapter 6.

Compact Disc replica discs are manufactured by injection compression moulding, a method which resembles the conventional 'black' audio disc pressing. The base material consists of polycarbonate (PC) granules from which the whole disc including the information is pressed in one step. In this process the PC is heated in the press. The molten PC is then injected under pressure into a chamber formed by two moulds, one opposite the injection opening which contains the information and one blind matrix. The moulds are at a temperature well above the glass temperature of the polymer. Next the material is pressed into shape by the moulds followed by a forced cooling. The transparent PC disc is then ready for metallisation. A reflecting layer of aluminium is sputtered onto the information side. This mirror is in its turn coated by a protection laquer. After accurate punching out of the centre hole the discs are labelled. For process control purposes the presence of any harmful air bubbles or small particles in the discs and pin-holes in the reflective layer can be detected optically. Also optical properties of the disc material such as refractive index variations, double refraction and thickness are measured. Some discs are played to check the radial tracking signal, error rate etc.

5.4 Unconventional mastering

In this section the mastering process which is now commonly used within the Philips organisation is described. It satisfies all the system standards which are agreed upon by the different optical disc system manufacturers. Of course, new developments do not stop when standards are set. Such developments may be either improvements in the existing processes and systems which fall within the standards or they may comprise completely new possibilities or even new systems (see Chapter 8). An example of both kinds of developments in the mastering process, which have been realised at the Philips Research Laboratory, will be discussed in the next two sections. They also illustrate major aims of development, i.e. improvement and optimisation of the process, the disc structures, read-out signals etc and the increase of the information density on discs so as to increase playing time, recording capacity etc. Both examples have been made possible by simply extending a laser beam recorder with an extra, fully independent, light path which produces an extra recording spot.

5.4.1 Pregroove optimisation

As was discussed on p. 119 both the CA signal space and the PP tracking signal produced by pregrooves on data storage discs are optimum when shallow grooves about half the track pitch wide are recorded. Heading pits are detected in more or less the same way as CD and LV pits, which implies that their width should be about $0.6 \mu m$. In general the pregrooves are recorded by the same spot which exposes the heading pits, which means that a compromise must be made between the conflicting requirements of wide grooves and narrow pits. Such a compromise gives good enough (though off-maximum) read-out signals, certainly when the usual track pitch of $1.6 \mu m$ is recorded (Pasman *et al* 1985). This changes however when larger track spacings are required. Not only does the radial duty cycle of the groove decrease, resulting (see §3.3.2) in a smaller first-order amplitude and larger phase difference ψ, but also the effective overlap area S_{II} in figure 3.19 decreases due to a lower radial spatial frequency. All this may result in too low a PP signal (equation (3.20b)). A straightforward solution is to separate both functions of the recording spot and use two independent light paths and two spots. As was shown in §5.2.2 the width of the groove is to a large degree determined by the spot width, which can be changed by changing the aperture of the recording lens or, to be more precise, by changing the numerical aperture of the exposing focused light beam. So when the pregroove is recorded separately by the extra light spot, a wide groove is obtained by reducing the diameter of the extra light beam with a diaphragm before the beam enters the objective lens. When the exposure level of this spot is also independently controlled at a low level, the optimum wide-and-shallow-groove geometry is obtained without affecting the pit read-out. An extra advantage of this set-up is that it now becomes possible to record the heading pits, and therefore later the user holes, between the pregrooves rather than in the groove. As was explained on p. 115 the signal space is at a maximum between the grooves and at a minimum, though at an acceptable level, in the grooves (figure 3.18). In such a way recorded discs give, at a track spacing of even $2.4 \mu m$, a push–pull signal of 110% (peak-to-peak) and a central aperture signal space of 96%. Figure 5.14 shows a scanning electron micrograph of such a structure. Owing to the small contrast for electrons of the shallow, wide pregroove structure the pregrooves are hardly visible between the heading pits.

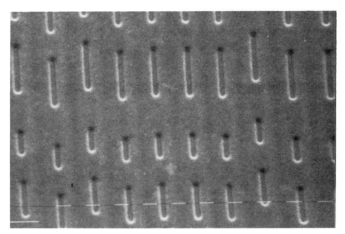

Figure 5.14   Scanning electron micrograph of an optimised pregroove and heading structure on data discs. Track pitch is 2.4 μm. 1 bar on the scale corresponds to 1 μm.

5.4.2   Tracks of alternating depth

The information capacity on optical discs can be enlarged by reducing the track spacing. Problems will arise however at the read-out. Since the reading spot is not infinitely small, the reduced track pitch will increase the cross-talk level. It was shown in §2.4.1 that this problem can be overcome to a certain extent. Neighbouring tracks are recorded with a different exposure level resulting in tracks with alternating depth. When deep and shallow pits are read in the CA and (tangential) PP mode respectively, the effective track pitch can be halved without increasing the cross-talk level. Using this principle, master discs have been recorded where, in between a conventional spiral of video pits with track pitch 1.8 μm, an extra spiral of shallow pits is recorded by the aforementioned, independently modulated, extra light spot. Figure 5.15 shows a scanning electron micrograph of such a structure. It is clear that the surface noise in the shallow pits, which do not reach the bottom of the resist in the development, is higher than usual, whereas the signal amplitude is lower, due to the small pit volume. As a consequence the CNR is insufficient for the analog video registration. Instead the extra spiral can be used for the registration of digital information such as computer programs or Compact Disc sound, accompanying the video programme. Since the video spiral is conventionally recorded such discs are fully backward compatible with ordinary video discs.

In this chapter we have seen how information, be it analog video, digital audio, preformatting or any similar future information format, can be recorded on master discs in a well defined way by exposing a photoresist layer by a focused laser beam of specific spot diameter of which the intensity is modulated. This information, being a coded height profile, can be transferred relatively simply and cheaply to replica discs in large quantities which is obviously of great importance when considering applications aimed at the all-important consumer market.

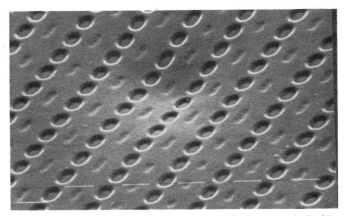

Figure 5.15 Scanning electron micrograph of a double spiral of Laser-Vision pits (deep pits) and Compact Disc information (shallow pits). Track pitch between deep tracks is 1.8 μm. 1 bar on the scale corresponds to 1 μm.

References

Braat J J M and Bouwhuis G 1978 Optical video discs with undulating tracks *Appl. Opt.* **17** 2022–8

Born M and Wolf E 1975 *Principles of Optics* (Oxford: Pergamon) pp. 395–8

Bouwhuis G and Braat J J M 1978 Video disc player optics *Appl. Opt.* **17** 1993–2000

Haverkorn van Rijsewijk H C, Legierse P E J and Thomas G E 1982 Manufacture of LaserVision video discs by a photopolymerization process *Philips Tech. Rev.* **40** 287–97

Heemskerk J P J 1978 Noise in a video disc system: experiments with an (AlGa)As laser *Appl. Opt.* **17** 2007–12

Hopkins H H 1943 The Airy disc formula for systems of high relative aperture *Proc. R. Soc.* **69** 116–28

Jacobs B A J 1978 Laser beam recording of video master discs *Appl. Opt.* **17** 2001–6

Kloosterboer J G, Lippits G J M and Meinders H C 1982 Photopolymerizable laquers for LaserVision videodiscs *Philips Tech. Rev.* **40** 298–309

Olijhoek J F, Peek T H and Wesdorp C A 1981 Eur. Conf. on Opt. Syst. and Appl. 1980, Mastering for Philips optical disc systems *SPIE* **236** 464–6

Pacansky J and Lyerla J R 1979 Photochemical decomposition mechanisms for AZ-type photoresists *IBM J. Res. Dev.* **23** 42–55

Pasman J H T 1983 Max Born Centenary Conference 1982, Rigorous diffraction theory applied to video disc geometries *SPIE* **369** 674–80

Pasman J H T, Olijhoek J F and Verkaik W 1985 Third international conference on optical mass data storage 1985, Developments in optical disc mastering *SPIE* **529** 62–8

Richards B and Wolf E 1959 Electromagnetic diffraction in optical systems II. Structure of the image field in an aplanatic system *Proc. R. Soc.* A **253** 358–79

6 Materials for On-line Optical Recording

A Huijser

6.1 Introduction

The development of the LaserVision video-disc system and its realisation in a practical device has been invaluable to the optical recording technology. Most of the optical and servo-mechanical solutions devised for that purpose are still being used today and are successfully applied in other systems like the Compact Disc digital audio system (see Chapters 7 and 8). These activities also made possible the practical implementation and thus the further development of a different type of optical storage technique: direct effect recording or optical direct read after write (DRAW) recording.

The LaserVision-based optical recording technology, also used in the Compact Disc, has been primarily developed for the purpose of data distribution. Data storage occurs 'off-line' in a so called mastering process (see Chapter 5). The information is not stored on a master disc in a direct readable fashion but the photosensitive layer on these discs needs further processing in the form of photolacquer development and metallisation to reveal the information carrying structures. Moreover, the master disc is just an intermediate storage medium in the mould-making process, necessary to enable mass replication of read-only discs for data distribution (see Chapter 8 for applications).

In optical DRAW recording, discs are being used in which data can be stored in a direct readable way. This on-line data storage is essential in the application of optical recording in storage devices such as for computer systems. In those applications stored information often has a proprietary character and replication of the DRAW disc for the purpose of data distribution is not an important feature.

An optical DRAW recorder is in essence nothing but an ordinary read-only device like a LaserVision or Compact Disc player. The only additional feature is the possibility of modulating the laser intensity to a much higher output than normally used in the read-out mode. At increased laser power it is possible to 'write' optically readable effects in the sensitive layer of a DRAW disc, thus enabling data storage.

Since the read-out of DRAW discs obeys all the rules derived in previous chapters we will in this chapter emphasise the materials aspects of DRAW discs. In the next section we introduce some of the important aspects of DRAW materials regarding system requirements. In §6.4 the various effects which are used in DRAW materials are described and illustrated with examples of actual applications. For typical system aspects and applications of the optical DRAW technology the reader is referred to Chapter 8 and references therein.

6.2 Aspects of DRAW materials regarding system requirements

As stated in Chapter 1, optical read-out principles can be applied to any type of effect that alters the state of the incoming light upon reflection or transmission (as it is rather impractical, we will disregard the transmissive mode of optical recording). Besides phase structures as used in LaserVision and Compact Disc media, DRAW media also exploit 'black and white' structures, i.e. intensity changers and polarising structures. These effects are observed in materials with a reasonable optical absorption at the wavelength of the laser to be used for writing. In all DRAW materials of practical interest, the effects are thermally induced, i.e. the effect is formed due to a local rise in temperature as a result of the absorption of the power in the laser spot being focused on the material. As a rule of thumb, an effect yielding optimum obtainable signal on read-out must be created within 50–100 ns with an incident power of 10 mW focused into a 1 μm sized spot, i.e. with an energy pulse of 0.5–1 nJ and with a power density of about 1 MW cm^{-2}. This restriction in energy is due to the limited laser power that can be delivered by semiconductor lasers. This type of laser is generally accepted as being the most suitable light source for optical DRAW recording (Bulthuis *et al* 1979). Their use implies that DRAW materials must have a reasonable optical absorption in the near infrared, i.e. at the emission wavelengths between 780 and 880 nm of today's AlGaAs semiconductor lasers.

In order to create effects with a minimum amount of energy, the volume to be heated must be as small as possible. Since the area of the spot cannot be reduced to much less than 1 μm^2, DRAW materials are used in the form of thin films. The optimum film thickness is not determined by the thermal requirements only. It also depends on the optical contrast between written and non-written areas and the technological problem of producing homogeneous (defect-free) thin films. Depending on the particular material–effect combination, layer thicknesses range typically from 5 to 100 nm.

These very thin layers have to be supported by a substrate to yield mechanical strength. Such a substrate acts as a heat sink with a negative effect on the sensitivity of the DRAW layer. This effect is minimised by trying to create adiabatic heating conditions through the application of short write pulses and by using substrate materials of low thermal diffusivity, such as plastic or glass or metals with plastic coatings. The influence of the substrate has to be taken into account in the optimisation of the film thickness. Temperature calculations (Kivits *et al* 1981) show that it is possible to raise the temperature in a 40 nm tellurium film on a PMMA substrate by about 1000 K with a 100 ns focused light pulse of 5 mW incident power, i.e. with 0.5 nJ. At that temperature a hole can be burned in such a layer which acts as a black spot (the DRAW effect) in a high reflecting surrounding (see §6.4). At pulse times below 100 ns the radial heat flow in the plane of the thin film is so small that the magnitude of the effect is completely determined by the diameter of the spot. This implies that, as with read-only applications of the optical recording technique, the storage density is determined by the inverse of the spot size or in other words by the optical cut-off frequency $2NA/\lambda$.

As already indicated above, sensitivity is not the only requirement to qualify a material–effect combination for optical DRAW applications. In the second place, written effects should exhibit a sufficient signal-to-noise ratio (SNR) in order to enable error-free read-out of stored information. The SNR value restricts the possible application of a DRAW material. For analog (frequency modulated) video storage a much higher SNR is required than for digital (pulse-length or pulse-position modulated) data storage.

Signal power is determined by the modulation depth of the effect, i.e. the optical contrast of the effect with respect to its non-written surrounding, and the amount of light reflected from the disc. When the signal power on the detector is low, 'shot-noise' will limit the SNR (Heemskerk 1978). This can be circumvented by increasing the light intensity in the read-out spot. However, this has its limits since the final result will be damage to the sensitive DRAW layer at the threshold for writing. Consequently, besides the high sensitivity, a DRAW layer should exhibit a threshold energy for writing below which the DRAW layer is not damaged at all. Obviously, this threshold energy must be fairly close to the normal writing energy in order to allow for enough read power.

In most practical DRAW systems, the SNR is limited by media noise (disc noise). Typical sources of disc noise are surface or layer/substrate interface roughness and irreproducible effect-formation due to an ill-conditioned writing process. In that respect, amorphous DRAW layers yield better SNR values than layers of coarse crystalline material while exhibiting the same contrast.

The third important aspect of DRAW materials is their aging characteristic. Since data storage is often performed for archiving purposes, the lifetime of DRAW media is an essential parameter. However, the effects of aging strongly depend on the system in which the DRAW media are being used. For instance, in digital data storage, error correction techniques can be applied to restore erroneous data deteriorating as a result of aging: the more powerful the error correction code, the longer the apparent lifetime of the disc. In analog video recording, deterioration of the signals due to aging results in 'drop-outs' in the video picture. Due to the high redundancy in a video picture, it is very difficult to determine the point at which it becomes impossible to interpret the picture information.

Another problem is to estimate the impact of aging effects. For archival purposes, the required media life ranges from 10 to 30 years (at present, information stored on magnetic tape has to be refreshed every two years). As a consequence, aging can only be studied in accelerated aging tests in which media are placed in an artificial climate of high humidity and high temperature. Various standardised aging tests are known but the translation of 'accelerated' life into 'real' life is (as yet) an uncertain step (Huijser *et al* 1983).

6.3   The optical DRAW disc

The sensitive layer supported by its substrate has to be worked up to a usable disc. The commonly adopted way is to do that in the form of the air sandwich (Kenney 1979) or a modified form of it. Two transparent substrates of plastic or glass are assembled in a way as shown in figure 6.1. The sensitive layers, in this particular case 30 nm thick tellurium alloy coatings on both substrates, are in that way protected against mechanical damage and dust. When the substrate material and the seal are made leaktight, the sensitive layer is isolated from the environmental atmosphere. This isolation helps prevent effects like corrosion of the sensitive layer— often the major problem regarding lifetime.

In the arrangement of figure 6.1 recording occurs 'substrate-incident' just as with the read-out of LaserVision and Compact Disc media. In cases where, for reasons explained in the next section, 'air-incident' recording is required, the same solution can be used: one of the substrates can be an uncovered blank through which the light is focused onto the air side of the sensitive layer of the other substrate. Of course, one can always use an unprotected surface for air-incident recording. In professional applications, the disc will almost certainly be kept in a protective cartridge to prevent mechanical damage. The one requirement then left is the corrosion resistance of the DRAW material.

Figure 6.1 reveals another (system—derived) option commonly applied in optical DRAW discs—pregrooved substrates (see §8.6). The pregrooved concept (Bulthuis *et al* 1979) is shown in figure 6.1 as a thin photopolymer (2p lacquer) supported by a thick glass substrate to yield the required mechanical strength. The pregrooved structure is moulded in the UV-curable 2p lacquer with a technique similar to that is used in the LaserVision disc production (see Chapter 5). Direct moulding in plastic, also used in optical disc production, is possible as well. Pregrooving is often combined with preformatting—prerecorded information which is replicated in the same way as the pregrooved 'tracks'. An example is shown in figure 6.2 where a scanning electron micrograph of a disc surface reveals 1.6 μm spaced tracks with, on the left-hand side, some replicated preformatted information and, on the right-hand side, DRAW effects in the form of tiny holes burnt in a thin layer of a tellurium alloy. This type of so-called ablative optical recording is explained in the next section.

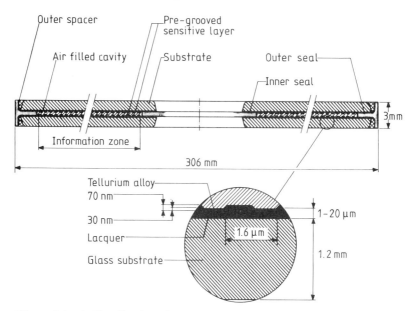

Figure 6.1 A Te alloy-based DRAW disc of the air sandwich type (from Rooijmans and Verhoeven 1983).

6.4 Optical DRAW effects

As stated in the previous sections, all DRAW effects of practical interest are thermally induced. Photon-induced effects, i.e. the optically detectable change of state of a material due to direct interaction of photons with

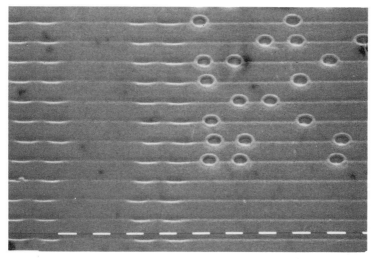

Figure 6.2 A scanning electron micrograph of the surface of a DRAW disc showing pregrooves, preformatted data on the left and written data ('holes') on the right. The scale indicates 1 μm steps.

matter, can in principle be used as well (Chen and Zook 1975). As such, attempts have been made to apply photochromatic and photodichroic materials to optical DRAW recording (Ralston 1983). However, up to now no practical implementation of any photon-induced effect in (prototype) optical DRAW media exists, and we will restrict ourselves here to the great variety of the commonly applied thermally induced effect–material combinations. Only those effect–material combinations which have shown their potential for practical application will be reviewed. This implies that the previously mentioned requirements regarding sensitivity and attainable SNR are met with in these solutions. However, lifetime aspects are often not fully investigated and this illustrates that optical recording technology is far from being mature (see §8.5).

Thermally induced effects can roughly be divided into three classes

(*a*) ablative recording
(*b*) phase-transition recording
(*c*) thermomagnetic or magneto-optic recording.

These different types of optical recording will be reviewed in the next sections and illustrated with typical examples.

6.4.1 Ablative recording
In ablative optical recording use is made of the effect that upon melting or evaporation of a thin layer, geometrical changes can be induced in that layer which give rise to optically detectable effects. Ablative recording is an

irreversible process so that this technique can be applied to write-once systems only (see §8.5).

Hole-burning.   The most studied phenomenon of this class is 'hole-burning' in thin metal or semi-metal films. Figure 6.2 shows an example of hole-burning in a tellurium–selenium alloy film. The effect is shown schematically in figure 6.3(*a*). For reasons of expected sensitivity, most studies on hole burning were performed with low melting-point materials like bismuth, indium and tellurium (Huijser 1984). However, a low melting point is not the only important parameter for the sensitivity in this type of recording. A molten domain in a thin layer on a substrate does not necessarily open to form a hole. The reason that a hole is formed at all lies in a lowering of the free energy of the thin-film–substrate system. It is due to the difference in layer and substrate surface energies (surface tension) which is released in the geometrical change from a locally molten film (initial state) into a hole (final state) (Kivits 1982).

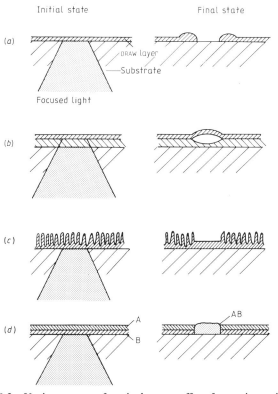

Figure 6.3   Various types of optical DRAW effect formation principles. (*a*) Hole burning (ablation); (*b*) bubble formation; (*c*) texture change; (*d*) alloying of bilayers.

Modelling of this geometrical change reveals an energy barrier between the initial and final state (Kivits 1982, Broer and Vriens 1983) which has to be surmounted before a hole can be formed. For times below 100 ns this cannot be realised at the melting point of the thin film. Experiments with Te, In and Bi films on PMMA substrates (Kivits 1982) show that at the onset of hole opening the temperature at the centre of the molten domain largely exceeds the melting point which shows no relation to the measured sensitivity. It is therefore concluded that hole formation must be initiated by some mechanism which lowers the barrier between initial and final state. Various mechanisms have been proposed for initiation (Broer 1983) such as blister formation, due to a pressure build-up at the layer–substrate interface, surface tension gradients (the Marangoni effect), surface and interface irregularities and recoil pressure from evaporating material.

The height of the barrier which prevents hole opening is a function of the layer thickness. This relation implies that very thin layers are relatively more sensitive. However, when the product of layer thickness and optical extinction coefficient of the DRAW material becomes less than unity, the absorbed power decreases proportionally and no net gain in sensitivity is reached. A solution to this problem is the incorporation of the sensitive layer in an antireflection configuration such as the so-called 'trilayer' (Bell and Spong 1978). Figure 6.4 shows such a trilayer structure. This quarter-wave antireflective structure is built up by the thin sensitive layer as the semitransparent mirror and a total reflector, e.g. aluminium, spaced by a non-absorbing dielectric spacer with refractive index n. The thickness of the dielectric must be tuned to the wavelength of the write laser. With a value near $\lambda/4n$, it is possible to produce an antireflective structure with a reflection near zero (zero reflection is not practical since the focusing system is based on reflected light). When a hole is burned in the sensitive layer, the antireflective structure is locally destroyed and the reflection increased to that of the metal mirror. So, the optical contrast of trilayer media can be made high.

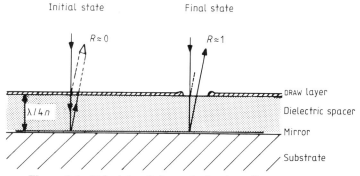

Figure 6.4 Principle of the antireflective trilayer structure.

The antireflective condition in a trilayer is reached with sensitive layers much thinner than those used in single-layer media. Nevertheless, the absorbed power in the thin sensitive layer is much higher. Since the dielectric spacer and the metal mirror are virtually free of losses, all non-reflected light, say 95% with a 5% reflecting trilayer, is absorbed in the sensitive layer. This is two to three times as much as is absorbed in optimised single layers. Trilayer media are indeed more sensitive than single-layer systems when the same low melting point materials are applied. For optimum sensitivity, the trilayer should be used 'air-incident'. When used 'substrate-incident', the sensitive layer is locked up between substrate and dielectric spacer. The heat loss to the surrounding material then becomes almost twice as high and recording sensitivity drops considerably.

The sensitivity of the trilayer configuration is often sacrificed to increase the resistance of the sensitive layer to corrosion. It allows for the application of high melting point elements like gold and titanium which benefits the lifetime of the disc. Nevertheless, it is possible to obtain sensitive media with lifetimes of 10 to 30 years with single layers of low melting point materials such as the Te–Se alloys (Huijser *et al* 1983, Terao *et al* 1983).

Besides metallic and semi-metallic materials, sensitive layers of organic dyes are also applied to the hole burning type of ablative recording (Howe and Wrobal 1981, Gravesteijn *et al* 1983, Sporer 1984). Organic dyes can be 'chemically' tuned to absorb very strongly at the wavelength of the write laser. Due to their low thermal diffusivity and low melting or decomposition temperature, these layers are very sensitive. Moreover, the signal-to-noise ratios that can be obtained are extremely high since disc noise of these 'amorphous' layers is virtually absent. It makes this class of materials very suitable for video recording and high density, high data-rate digital optical recording. Organic dyes offer another advantage—layers can be made by the simple and cheap spin-coating process rather than by the vacuum deposition techniques essential for the production of metallic- and semi-metallic-based optical recording layer structures. The same advantage is obtained with 'loaded' polymers which consist of a dispersion of very fine metal particles, e.g. silver, in a transparent polymer. The optical absorption is strong due to the scattering of light by the metal particles and the thermal characteristic of these layers is close to that of the pure polymer, i.e. excellent for optical DRAW. The reflection of these layers is low and a burnt hole yields a low contrast. This type of material is not only used in discs but is also applied in 'optical' tapes and cards (Drexler 1983).

Bubble formation.   Another important class of ablative recording effects is bubble formation (Freese *et al* 1982, Cornet 1983). The principle of this effect is shown in figure 6.3(*b*). The sensitive layer consists of a polymer–metal bilayer. Upon irradiation the metal is heated due to light absorption. This heat is transferred to the polymer which decomposes at elevated temperatures (a few hundred degrees centigrade). The resulting gaseous emission separates the metallic layer from the polymer and deforms the metallic layer into a bubble with a diameter almost equal to the spot size. By choosing the correct materials and metal layer thickness, blasting of the bubble can be prevented at writing conditions. The bubble, which has a permanent character, acts as a scatterer for light on read-out. Contrast ratios of up to 40% can be obtained with SNR values more than sufficient for digital recording (Cornet 1983).

Textured media. When a textured surface, such as that shown in figure 6.3(*c*), is heated locally above the melting point of the material, the molten area will re-solidify as a flat domain under the influence of surface tension. Originally, the textured surface is made to absorb strongly with its average periodicity much smaller than the wavelength of the incoming light. The straightened area reflects strongly when the material as such is a good reflector. The optical contrast of the effect in textured media can be high, but the disc noise is often high as well. Various ideas exist for producing textured media, the most studied one being the use of layers of germanium (Suh *et al* 1983). Another solution is the use of textured polymer layers coated with a metal reflector. Effect formation is not then by melting but by plastic deformation of the polymer at elevated temperatures.

6.4.2 Phase transition recording

In phase transition recording, the geometrical change of the sensitive layer is in principle absent. Instead, the optical constants of the sensitive layer are changed. This yields a change in reflection and thus an optical contrast. That optical contrast is often not very high since the optical constants are in general only slightly modified between initial and final state. A way to enhance this contrast is to use optical interference effects by tuning the layer thickness. The result of tuning is demonstrated in figure 6.5 for a polycrystalline TeSeSb compound which after recording (in this case melting of the alloy) is frozen into an amorphous state with slightly different optical constants. This compound can also be used for hole burning. Then, the optimum layer thickness would be about 25–30 nm, whereas in crystalline–amorphous phase transition recording the layer-thickness optimum lies at about 100 nm. This much thicker layer also helps to prevent hole formation in the molten area which, if it occurred, would introduce unacceptable noise in the written signal.

When irreversible geometrical changes of the sensitive layer do not occur, phase change media are candidates for reversible recording. The written state is a metastable state and the erased state, i.e. the initial state, is an intrinsically stable state at room temperature. In the reversed situation phase transition media are just like ablative materials for write-once application only.

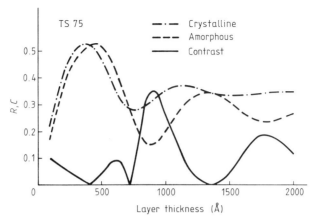

Figure 6.5 Reflection R of a TeSeSb alloy film as a function of the layer thickness and the derived optical contrast C between crystalline and amorphous states. $\lambda = 800$ nm.

Alloying of bilayers. Bilayer structures of elements or compounds of which the constitutents alloy as a result of laser heating, exist in great numbers. This type of optical DRAW (see figure 6.3(*d*)) is often very sensitive since one only needs to trigger the chemical reaction between the two constituents in order to release the 'chemically stored' energy of an exothermic reaction. Well studied examples are Pt–Si and Rh–Si bilayers (Ahn *et al* 1982).

Segregation. With vacuum deposition techniques it is possible to produce thin layers of multicomponent alloys which show segregation into two or more stable components under recording conditions. Well known examples are the suboxides (Akahira *et al* 1982) of which the tellurium suboxide TeO_x with $x = 1.1$ displays good optical DRAW properties. It segregates after melting into transparent TeO_2 and highly reflecting Te which crystallises immediately at room temperature. The written effects show a higher reflection than their surroundings.

Crytalline–amorphous recording. The third category of phase transition effects is that of crystalline–amorphous transitions. Many molten chalcogenides display a tendency to freeze into an amorphous state upon thermal quenching. In optical recording quenching rates of up to 10^9 K s^{-1} are obtained at which almost 'everything' becomes amorphous. Figure 6.6 shows amorphous domains in the coarse crystalline surroundings of a TeSeSb alloy. This phase change is also used in the reversed mode by writing crystalline domains in an amorphous thin layer. This type of switching has been demonstrated in Te_3Sb_2 and Se_3Sb_2 (Watanabe *et al* 1983). The amorphous layer is heated close to its melting point rather than above it as in the crystalline–amorphous recording. Writing is now in fact a local annealing of the unstable state of the amorphous layer. Although annealing is a well known phenomenon, in optical recording it is certainly not a trivial process since recrystallisation must occur on a time scale in the order of 100 ns, i.e. the length of the write pulse, whereas the amorphous effects have to be stable for many years at room temperature.

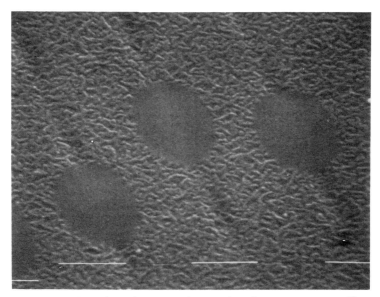

Figure 6.6 Scanning electron micrograph of a coarse crystalline TeSeSb alloy in which amorphous domains have been written by local melting.

Since crystalline–amorphous recording has been observed in both directions of the phase change, this type of recording is potentially reversible. In such a concept the writing step would be the crystalline–amorphous transition via local melting of the layer. Erasing of data would be the amorphous–crystalline annealing step. Since the peak temperatures in the write and anneal steps differ, the time required to anneal an amorphous domain is essentially longer than the time involved in the cooling down of a molten domain after a write pulse. However, the application of phase transition effects in reversible recording is only of interest when data erasure can be performed 'on-line', i.e. without changing the rotation speed of the disc. A solution to this problem is found in the application of separate write–read and erase spots. The write–read spot is the usual, about 1 μm diameter, spot found in standard optical recorders but the erase spot is an oblong spot of about 10 μm^2 projected through the same objective lens that forms the write–read spot. The erase spot, generated by a separate (semiconductor) laser, leads the write–read spot in the same track and with its longer axis parallel to the tracks. In that way it is possible to bridge the one order of magnitude difference in time scale between write and erase cycles. Nevertheless, the time to anneal is still very short e.g. a few hundred nanoseconds at normal disc spinning frequencies. Up to now, there has been only one compound reported in which this fast annealing step has been combined with the conflicting requirement of a good room temperature stability. This compound is a tellurium suboxide–germanium–tin alloy (Takenaga *et al* 1983) in which the switching probably occurs in small tellurium particles dispersed in a TeO_2 matrix. The addition of germanium influences the room temperature stability, whereas the tin obviously accelerates the recrystallisation process and is active at elevated temperatures only. The recording parameters such as sensitivity and obtainable SNR are up to standards—digital recording as well as low quality video recording is feasible. One possible problem is the repeatability of the write–erase cycle in crystalline–amorphous transitions. Since in the write step the material is temporarily molten, effects like segregation, evaporation of volatile components and irreversible material transport as in hole formation might result in a kind of 'fatigue' limiting the number of useful cycles. In the TeOx–Ge–Sn alloy this effect is indeed observed in the first few cycles as a degradation of the SNR. However, this degradation saturates at an acceptable level (~ 3 dB and less) and over a million cycles have been realised (Takenaga *et al* 1983).

6.4.3 *Magneto-optic recording*
Last but not least we will review the use of magneto-optic effects in optical recording. Magneto-optic recording is a combination of optical recording with the reversible characteristic of magnetic media. In fact it strongly resembles the technique of 'vertical' magnetic recording, the new trend in high density magnetic storage.

Instead of magneto-optic (MO) recording the term thermomagnetic writing is sometimes used. This is due to the recording mechanism involved which is schematically illustrated in figure 6.7. The magneto-optic medium consists of a thin film of a ferro- or ferrimagnetic material having a strong preference for magnetisation perpendicular to the film surface. Suppose this layer is magnetised in one of the two possible directions. Just as in the other types of DRAW systems, writing is done by heating the thin film with a laser pulse. Now, the critical temperature is the Curie temperature T_C above which the coercive magnetic field H_c of the material drops to zero. At that point the material can be polarised by a small external field H_u in a direction opposite to the original magnetisation. At the end of a write pulse the heated domain cools down and regains its permanent magnetic character, however with the opposite magnetisation, even without the external bias field H_u. The domain size is determined by the temperature profile which resembles the spot size when the laser pulse is short and the thermal diffusivity of the material is not too high. The external field H_u is of minor importance as long as it is much smaller than H_c at room temperature and there is no need to confine it to the domain size.

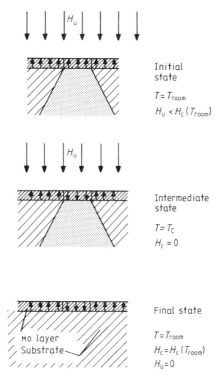

Figure 6.7 Schematic representation of the writing (and erasing) process in a magneto-optic DRAW layer.

The above method of recording is called 'Curie-point' writing and is used in ferromagnetic layers. Ferrimagnetic materials offer the possibility of what is called 'compensation-point' writing. It is based upon the different temperature dependences of the two magnetic sublattices in a ferrimagnet. Depending on the composition the ferrimagnet can have a compensation temperature T_{comp} at which the net magnetisation of the two sublattices is zero. Around T_{comp}, the coercivity H_c is inversely proportional to $T - T_{comp}$, i.e. a steep function of temperature. When the layer composition is chosen to have T_{comp} just below room temperature a sufficiently low H_c ($H_c < H_u$) can be obtained well below the Curie temperature. At room temperature, close to T_{comp}, H_c can be much higher than the value obtained in ferromagnets.

The vertical magnetisation is essential in magneto-optic recording for the retrieval of written data. Read-out is performed optically using the Kerr or Faraday effect. These effects manifest as a change in the state of polarisation of light upon interaction with a magnetised medium. These effects are a maximum when the magnetisation of the material aligns with the propagative direction of the light. In reflection the Kerr effect yields a small rotation of the plane of polarisation of linear polarised light. The direction of this rotation in either a positive or negative sense depends on the 'up' or 'down' direction of the magnetisation. In read-out, a disc with written domains will cause a modulated signal when the light reflected from the disc is analysed through a polariser normal to one of the two polarisation states. For small Kerr rotations, the modulation depth is then proportional to the Kerr angle θ.

Thermomagnetic recording differs very strongly in both the writing and reading process from magnetic recording where the domain size is determined by the external polarising field generated by the write head. In that case small domains can only be created with very small write heads close to the magnetic layer. In (video) tape recorders the write heads are in contact with the medium giving rise to wear of both heads and tape. In professional magnetic disc systems use is made of the so-called Winchester principle where the write head 'flies' very close (to the order of micrometres) to the surface without contact (Elphick 1983). The same principles are used in the read-out of magnetic media, obviously with the same consequences. Magnetic recording on the basis of the Winchester technology needs, for instance, a dust-free environment. This is created by giving each disc-drive unit its own sealed-off encapsulation. Therefore, high density magnetic disc systems are of the 'fixed-spindle' type with media and drive as an inseparable unit, i.e. very expensive and for many applications rather inconvenient.

Early experiments in magneto-optic recording were carried out on MnBi films (Unger and Rath 1971), but good recording characteristics could not be obtained. The coarse crystallinity of these films results in a disc noise level too high to be applicable in practice. Today's activities are concentrated on ferrimagnetic rare earth–transition metal (RE–TM) alloys like Tb–Fe, Gd–Fe or Gd–Co. For these $RE_{(1-x)}TM_x$ alloys with $x = 0.6-0.8$, it is possible to deposit amorphous thin films with the axis of easy magnetisation perpendicular to the surface (Biesterbos 1979). With regard to disc noise the advantage of the amorphous state of the thin layer is obvious. A disadvantage however, is that frequent heating (writing–erasing) at one location might result in recrystallisation which ruins the vertical anisotropy. For that reason use is often made of compensation-point writing rather than Curie-point writing which is possible in some of these alloys. In that case the temperatures reached during a write pulse can be kept much lower than the recrystallisation temperature for these amorphous layers at about 250 °C. The main problem in applying alloys with a compensation point is the strong dependence of T_{comp} on alloy composition. In the most popular material Gd–Fe, T_{comp} changes by about 100 °C with only a 1% change in composition (Biesterbos 1979). As a consequence, a highly developed deposition technology is required to attain sufficient homogeneity and reproducibility.

A low disc noise level is essential for these materials since the Kerr rotation angle is small, typically 0.2–0.4°. Even without disc noise, it is not possible with the shot noise limited SNR to perform high quality video recording (LaserVision standard). Consequently, magneto-optic recording is at present limited to digital recording with acceptable storage densities and data rates (Braat *et al* 1983) or low quality video. Increasing the shot noise limited SNR which is proportional to $R\theta^2$ in which R is the reflection coefficient of the magneto-optic layer, is made possible by incorporating the layer in a resonant structure like the trilayer configuration (Mansuripur and Cornell 1983). Multiple internal reflections enhance the Kerr rotation θ but at the same time R is lowered. Nevertheless, the net result is better but since R can only be lowered to a certain amount the SNR increase is not more than about 3–5 dB. This gain is possible only at the expense of a complex deposition technique and a much thinner magneto-optic layer. The thickness of the latter is about 10 nm instead of the 100 nm thick monolayers and this effects the lifetime of the storage layer. Rare earth and transition metal elements are easily oxidised and the thinner the layer, the shorter the lifetime. For practical applications the magneto-optic layer probably cannot do without encapsulation. In that case, the function of cladding layers and dielectric spacing of a trilayer can be combined. Dense materials like AlN, Al_2O_3, SiN and SiO_2 are currently being investigated for use as cladding layers.

Of special interest are the minimum domain size and the domain stability which are both related to the magnetic properties of the layer such as magnetisation M, coercivity H_c and wall energy σ (Huth 1974). Recently, it has been indicated (Kryder *et al* 1983) that the minimum domain diameter which is proportional to σ/MH_c, cannot be made much smaller than 1 μm in RE–TM alloys.

References

Ahn K, DiStefano T, Herd S, Mazzeo N and Tu K 1982 High-sensitivity silicide films for optical recording *CLEO Proc.* (1982) 140

Akahira N, Ohta T, Yamada N, Takenaga M and Yamashita T 1982 Sub-oxide thin films for an optical recording disk *SPIE Proc.* **329** 195

Bell A and Spong F 1978 Antireflection structure for optical recording *J. Quantum Electron.* **14** 487

Biesterbos J 1979 Properties of amorphous rare earth–transition metal thin films relevant to thermomagnetic recording *J. Physique* **40** C5-274

Braat J, Schouhamer-Immink K and Urner-Wille M 1983 High density magneto-optical recording *SPIE Proc.* **420** 206

Broer D and Vriens L 1983 Laser-induced optical recording in thin films *Appl. Phys.* A **32** 107

Bulthuis K, Carasso M, Heemskerk J, Kivits P, Kleuters W and Zalm P 1979 Ten billion bits on a disk *IEEE Spectrum* August issue

Chen D and Zook J 1975 An overview of optical data storage technology *Proc. IEEE* **63** 1207

Cornet J 1983 Deformation recording process in polymer–metal bilayers and its use for optical storage *SPIE Proc.* **420** 86

Drexler J 1983 The Drexon product family for laser recording and digital-data storage; a status report *SPIE Proc.* **420** 57

Elphick M 1983 Winchester disk technology spins into new orbits *Computer Design* (January) 89

Freese R, Willson R, Wald L, Robbins W and Smith T 1982 Characteristics of bubble-forming optical direct-read-after-write (DRAW) media *SPIE Proc.* **329** 174

Gravesteijn D, Steenbergen C and van der Veen J 1983 Single wavelength optical recording in pure, solvent-coated infrared dye layers *SPIE Proc.* **420** 327

Heemskerk J 1978 Noise in a video disk system: experiments with an (AlGa)As laser *Appl. Opt.* **17** 2007

Howe D and Wrobel J 1981 Solvent-coated organic materials for high density optical recording *J. Vac. Sci. Technol.* **18** 92

Huijser A 1984 Optical recording *Physica* **127** B 90

Huijser A, Jacobs B, Vriens L, Markvoort J, Spruijt A and Vromans P 1983 Ageing characteristics of digital optical recording (DOR) media *SPIE Proc.* **382** 270

Huth B 1974 Calculations of stable domain radii produced by thermomagnetic writing *IBM J. Res. Develop.* **18** 100

Kenny G 1979 *US Patent* 4 074 282

Kivits P, de Bont R, Jacobs B and Zalm P 1982 The hole formation process in tellurium layers for optical data storage *Thin Sol. Films* **87** 215

Kivits P, de Bont R and Zalm P 1981 Superheating of thin films for optical recording *Appl. Phys.* **24** 273

Kryder M, Meiklejohn W and Skoda R 1983 Stability of perpendicular domains in thermomagnetic recording material *SPIE Proc.* **420** 236

Mansuripur M and Cornell G 1983 Magneto-optical recording *SPIE Proc.* **420** 206

Ralston L 1983 An evaluation of photochromic and photodichroic materials for write, read, erase applications *SPIE Proc.* **420** 186

Rooijmans C and Verhoeven J 1983 Characteristics of the Optical Media Laboratory disk *SPIE Proc.* **420** 18

Sporer A 1984 Laser marking process in an oriented dye film *Appl. Opt.* **23** 2738

Suh S, Craighead H, Howard R and Schiavone L 1983 Morphology dependent contrast measurements of microscopically textured germanium films *SPIE Proc.* **382** 199

Takenaga M, Yamada N, Ohara S, Nishiuchi K, Nagashima M, Kashihra T,

Nakamura S and Yamashita T 1983 New optical erasable medium using tellurium suboxide thin film *SPIE Proc.* **420** 173

Terao M, Horigome S, Shigematsu K, Miyauchi Y and Nakazawa M 1983 Resistance to oxidation of Te–Se optical recording films *SPIE Proc.* **382** 276

Unger W and Rath R 1971 Thermomagnetic writing in homogeneous MnBi films *IEEE Trans. Mag.* **MAG-7** 885

Watanabe K, Oyama T, Aoki Y, Sato N and Wiyaoka S 1983 New optical recording material for direct-read-after-write (DRAW) disks *SPIE Proc.* **383** 191

7 Channel Coding for Optical Disc Systems

K Schouhamer Immink

7.1 Coding Formats of the PAL and NTSC LaserVision video

7.1.1 Requirements for the read-out system

The modulation and coding format to be used has to be chosen in such a way that it matches the special requirements of the optical channel. The main characteristics of the channel are bandwidth limitation and asymmetry of the recording process. The bandwidth restricting element is found by combination of the finite spot diameter and the tangential velocity of the track. The length of the track is determined by the diameter of the disc and track pitch, so that the tangential velocity is directly related to the playing time. As discussed in Chapter 2 the ideal spot diameter is determined by the wavelength λ of the laser beam and the numerical aperture NA of the objective lens. The absolute bandwidth of the optical read-out is given by

$$\nu = 2\text{NA}/\lambda.$$

The spatial frequency ν on the disc and the tangential velocity of the track define the frequency of the electrical signal

$$f = v_\text{T}\nu = 2\pi R f_\text{r}\nu$$

where R is the radius of the scanned track and f_r is the angular revolution frequency of the disc. Having chosen a fixed angular revolution frequency then the frequency characteristic is clearly a function of the radius.

Figure 7.1 gives the amplitude against frequency characteristic of the playback system for some radii, corresponding to a numerical aperture of 0.4 and a wavelength of 633 nm (HeNe laser). The angular velocity of the

228

disc is 25 Hz, which is the chosen frequency in the PAL video format (30 Hz in the NTSC case). The cut-off frequency at the inner radius ($R = 55$ mm) is 10.9 MHz increasing to 29 MHz at the outer radius ($R = 145$ mm). For recording a shorter wavelength and a higher numerical aperture are used. For example, with $\lambda = 458$ nm and NA $= 0.7$ the writing frequency characteristic is expanded in frequency by a factor of 2.5 with respect to the read-out characteristic (Chapter 5).

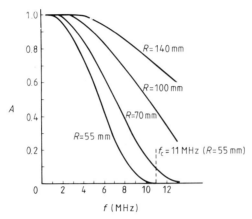

Figure 7.1 Amplitude characteristic of the playback system as a function of the (electrical) frequency with the radius of scanning as a parameter. Cut-off frequency $f_c = (2\mathrm{NA}/\lambda)v_T$; tangential velocity $v_T = 2\pi R f_r$; revolution frequency $f_r = 25$ Hz; numerical aperture NA $= 0.4$; laser wavelength $\lambda = 0.63 \times 10^{-6}$ m

An important effect in the design of a modulation system is the occurrence of noise and non-linearities of the transmission channel. There are three main sources of noise (see Heemskerk 1978)

(*a*) disc noise originating from surface roughness of the disc and irregularity of the pit dimensions
(*b*) pre-amplifier noise
(*c*) laser noise.

In the transmission channel a number of non-linearities occur (de Haan and Velzel 1977, and see Chapter 2). The two-level writing signal is usually generated by a hard-limiter in the FM modulator. An asymmetrical off-set of the limiter results in a non-zero time average of the writing signal which generates intermodulation products from different source frequencies. Further non-linearities are present in the writing, development and replication steps. The reading mechanism itself also introduces a non-linearity.

7.1.2.   Examples of signal encoding schemes

The colour signal used in broadcasting is basically composed of the black and white (luminance) signal with the colour (chroma) information added by means of a sub-carrier. In the PAL 625 lines format the sub-carrier frequency is 4.43 MHz, in the NTSC 525 lines the sub-carrier is 3.58 MHz. We shall see later that in most encoding systems the composite colour signal is again separated in luminance and chroma. The luminance is low-pass filtered to relieve the bandwidth requirements of the storage medium thus increasing the playing time. The disadvantage of this technique is the decreased resolution of the video picture both in luminance and chroma.

A property of optical disc recording is that in general two levels are recorded, called pit and land. We conclude that only frequency, phase and/or pulsewidth modulation can be applied in the video disc. Vaanholt (1982) gives as examples of basic modulation systems now in use in the different video disc systems listed below.

(*a*) Line sequential systems. An example is the TRIPAL system (Bruch 1967) used in the Teldec video disc system. The recording system is basically a line sequential recording the colour information R(ed), G(reen) and B(lue) with a bandwidth of 600 kHz then extended to 3 MHz to include the luminance information.

(*b*) Colour-under or crossband system. Here the chroma sub-carrier is transposed to a lower frequency and added to the FM modulated luminance signal by means of pulsewidth modulation (Kenney and Hoogendijk 1974). All consumer VTR recorders use this principle.

(*c*) Buried sub-carrier system. The RCA and VHD video disc systems use the so-called buried sub-carrier modulation system. (Clemens 1978, Pritchard 1981) The term 'buried sub-carrier' refers to a technique by which the chrominance sub-carrier and its modulation sidebands are placed at a relatively low frequency range within the wider band luminance channel in such a way as to cause minimum interference and such that the luminance and chroma may easily be separated at the player and converted to standard NTSC (or PAL) format.

(*d*) The direct or composite modulating system. In the direct or composite system used in the LaserVision formats, the standard PAL or NTSC formatted signals are directly frequency modulated and recorded on the disc (Vaanholt 1982).

In the composite modulation system the colour sub-carrier does not need to be separated (yielding picture quality degradation) and the video signal can be decoded in the player by only one frequency demodulator. Hence the main reasons for choosing the composite signal encoding in the LaserVision system are the picture quality and the simplicity of the decoding electronics. Another reason for the choice of the unmodified CCIR composite format is that special features such as teletext can now be easily incorporated in the system making the LaserVision a very attractive video source.

In the following section we study in more detail the difficulties encountered when dealing with a direct composite frequency modulated (FM) signal.

7.1.3 Direct frequency modulation

The difficulties that arise in a direct FM system are mainly due to the peculiar spectrum of the composite PAL or NTSC video signal. In general the spectrum decreases with increasing frequency. We observe a peak at the colour sub-carrier frequency. The direct frequency modulation causes, as we shall see, many sidebands that may interfere in the video picture after demodulation. Early experiments showed that, in particular, sidebands caused by the colour sub-carrier have a deteriorating effect such as moiré patterns on the picture quality. The study of the interference sources can be based on the simple model of a main carrier FM modulated with a sine wave signal with frequency ω_0 at the colour sub-carrier. We follow the analysis of Vaanholt (1982).

When a main carrier J_0 with frequency f_0 is modulated in frequency with a sub-carrier frequency f_s then the spectrum after limiting is given by the infinite sum

$$f(t) = J_0(m) \cos \omega_0 t - J_1(m) [\cos (\omega_0 - \omega_s) t - \cos (\omega_0 + \omega_s) t]$$

$$+ J_2(m) [\cos (\omega_0 - 2\omega_s)t + \cos (\omega_0 + 2\omega_s)t] \ldots$$

where $J_0(m)$, $J_1(m)$, ... etc are Bessel functions whose argument is the so-called modulation index m. Although this series represents a spectrum with an infinite width, it is well known that the sideband amplitudes determined by the Bessel functions $J_0(m)$, $J_1(m)$, ... etc fall off sharply with the modulation index m. The modulation index m can be found as follows. In the NTSC case the FM modulator has a black-to-white frequency deviation from 8.1 to 9.3 MHz. The sync level is found at 7.58 MHz. In figure 7.2 the spectrum of the NTSC encoded video signal is shown. We note the main carrier and the two first-order sidebands of the colour sub-carrier at distances of 3.58 MHz. Also included in the figure are two carriers A_1 and A_2 used for audio transmission (see §7.1.4). Pre-emphasis is used to enhance the signal-to-noise ratio of the demodulated video signal. The maximum amplification a of the higher frequencies at recording is 2. The resulting modulation index for the chrominance sidebands is given by

$$m = \frac{a\Delta\omega}{\omega_c} \frac{V_c}{V_{bw}}$$

where $2\Delta\omega$ is the black-to-white deviation (1.2 MHz), V_c the peak-to-peak amplitude of the chrominance and V_{bw} the black-to-white amplitude of the luminance. For $V_c = 675$ mV (75% saturated cyanic or red colours) we have $m = 0.32$, $J_1(m) = -16$ dB and $J_2(m) = -38$ dB.

The PAL situation is quite different. In this case to relieve the bandwidth requirements (for PAL the sub-carrier frequency is 4.43 MHz) the main carrier frequency is decreased to 7.6 MHz. The reasons for this choice will be given later. The decrease of the main carrier frequency causes the second-order sideband to 'fold back' to the positive frequency $2 \times 4.43 - 7.6 = 1.22$ MHz. The colour sideband $J_2(m)$ interferes with the high frequencies of the luminance when the signal is demodulated again. A restriction on the carrier frequency f_0 is easily derived: $f_0 = 2f_s - f_0 + B_v$, where B_v is the video bandwidth (set to 5.5 MHz) and f_s is the PAL sub-carrier ($= 4.43$ MHz). We find $f_0 > 7.18$ MHz. The frequency spectrum of the PAL encoded video signal is depicted in figure 7.3. The audio carriers A_1 and A_2 are discussed in the next section.

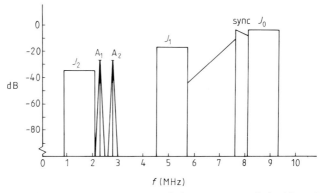

Figure 7.2 Frequency spectrum of the NTSC encoded video signal. Note the main carrier J_0 and the first and second order sidebands J_1 and J_2. Only the low frequency components are shown.

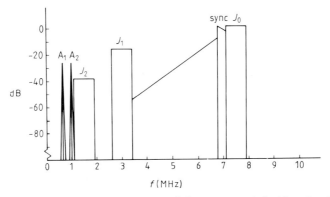

Figure 7.3 Frequency spectrum of the PAL encoded video signal.

7.1.4 Sound processing in the video disc

Figures 7.2 and 7.3 showed the spectra of the NTSC and PAL video signals, including the audio signals. The stereo audio signals are frequency modulated on two carriers and added to the frequency modulated video by means of pulsewidth modulation. As shown in figure 7.4 the frequency modulated stereo signals $x_1(t)$ and $x_2(t)$ are linearly added to the output of the video FM modulator and then applied to a limiter. This results in a pulsewidth modulation as indicated in figure 7.5. The level of the audio carriers is -26 dB below the unmodulated video carrier for both the PAL and NTSC systems. In NTSC the audio carrier frequencies are 2.31136 MHz $(146\frac{1}{4} \times F_h)$ for channel I (left) and 2.812499 MHz $(178\frac{3}{4} \times F_h)$ for channel II (right) (F_h = horizontal line frequency = 15734 Hz). These audio carrier frequencies are interleaved with the video carrier so that during periods of low modulation their sidebands cause a minimum of intermodulation in the decoded video signal. The audio signals are pre-emphasised before encoding resulting in a maximum deviation of 150 kHz.

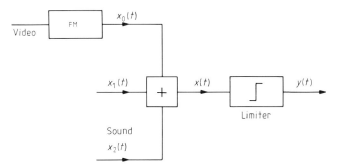

Figure 7.4 Generation of the pulsewidth modulated signal.

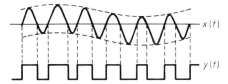

Figure 7.5 Principle of pulsewidth modulation in the time domain (see figure 7.4 for the nomenclature).

7.1.5 New developments

As discussed in the preceding section in the current LaserVision (LV) format the analog audio stereo channels are frequency modulated and added to the encoded video by means of pulsewidth modulation. The maximum audio signal-to-noise ratio of the LV 525 lines NTSC format is at present approximately 70 dB, which includes the 15 dB improvement using the CX noise reduction system (see Badger and Allen 1982). In the 625 lines PAL and SECAM formats of the LV the audio signal is approximately 10 dB superior to the NTSC format. People who enjoy audio-oriented video programmes such as concerts or operas would welcome any improvement in audio quality. The Compact Disc digital audio system has a superior audio quality (see §7.2). These considerations motivated us to investigate the feasibility of combining the LaserVision video signal with Compact Disc audio on one disc (see Immink *et al* 1983).

We first go back to the preceding section where the spectrum of the Laser-Vision formats was derived. In figure 7.2 we plotted the spectrum of the NTSC encoded LV disc. The frequency range from DC–2 MHz is not used in this format. The first audio component is at 2.3 MHz. We find that in the range < 2 MHz the second-order colour (spurious) sideband J_2 is not needed for decoding. This J_2 component can be sufficiently removed by means of an electronic circuit. A basic circuit description is given in figure 7.6 (Coleman 1977). The method is basically a compensation method, first the chroma band is filtered out from the composite video signal. The second harmonic of this signal is generated by means of a squarer circuit and band-pass filtering. The frequency-doubled chroma signal is now added, with the correct phase and amplitude, to the original composite video signal. After frequency modulation the chroma component J_2 will be cancelled. We now have the whole spectrum ranging from DC to 2 MHz at our disposal. The bandwidth needed for PCM encoded audio, for example the Compact Disc format, 16 bits linear quantisation at 44.1 kHz sampling frequency, needs a bandwidth of approximately 1.4 MHz (see also the next section). The addition of the digital audio signal is now in principle quite simple, and pulsewidth modulation is again used. The two-level, modulated signal (e.g. EFM (eight-to-fourteen) modulation can be applied as used in the Compact Disc) is low-pass filtered to suppress interference in the video picture, pre-

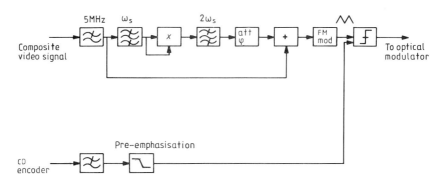

Figure 7.6 An embodiment example of the compensation of the second-order sideband J_2. The (att)enuation and the phase (φ) shifter are adjusted in such a way that they compensate J_2

emphasis is added and forwarded to the pulsewidth input of the video encoder. The extension of the encoder is straightforward (see figure 7.7). The figure shows a standard video encoder extended with an additional pulsewidth modulator input. The resulting spectra of the NTSC and PAL video formats are depicted in figure 7.8 and show clearly the frequency band that is occupied by the digital audio signal. Only minor modifications are needed for an LV player (see figure 7.9): we just have to low-pass filter the photodiode signal and feed it to a standard PCM audio decoder such as the Compact Disc decoder, that can be applied in unmodified form. We observe that the newly developed system is compatible with players that rely on the old format. Unfortunately this is only possible in the case of the NTSC coding format. In the PAL case the analog audio carriers are located at 0.5 and 0.7 MHz. In other words we have to remove these analog audio carriers if we want to add the digital signal.

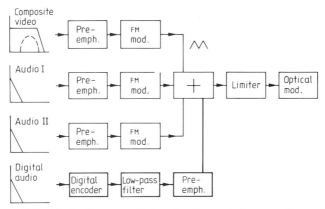

Figure 7.7 Block diagram of the signal processing encoding of the combined video and digital audio encoder. The block diagram holds for the PAL and NTSC video formats with some altered parameters. Note that the analog carriers have to be removed in the PAL case. The FM modulator is extended with a J_2 compensation (see figure 7.6).

Many experiments were carried out to measure the signal-to-noise ratio of the sub-band coded digital signal. In laboratory environments the read-out under non-ideal optical situations (defocusing and mistracking) was investigated. The experiments showed that the error rate before error correction is larger than can be measured under normal conditions of the Compact Disc, but that after error correction only a few unreliable audio samples were found.

The digital signal is not only restricted to applications in the audio field, but it can also be used to store digital data. If it is remembered that an LV disc contains 50 000 pictures in CAV mode it is easily found that the sub-band coded digital channel has a capacity of 0.5 Gbyte for half an hour.

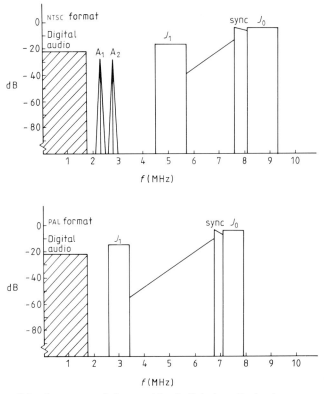

Figure 7.8 Spectrum of the combined digital audio in the NTSC and PAL video formats.

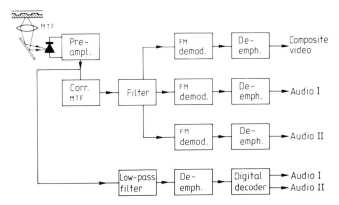

Figure 7.9 Block diagram of the signal processing of the LaserVision player. The digital data (audio) can be reconstructed by linear filtering.

In other words 10 kbyte of information per picture. This offers tremendous possibilities for information storage.

7.2   The Compact Disc digital audio system

In the mid 1970s investigations concerning the feasibility of storing high-quality audio information on an optical disc were begun. The first experiments applied frequency modulation with a large modulation index to improve the demodulated signal-to-noise ratio of the audio signal. The experiments showed that the system based on frequency modulation did not lead to satisfactory results. The main reason for this is that small imperfections on the disc, called drop-outs, result in clearly audible clicks. The only solution was to apply 'digital audio'. In this signal format the studio audio signal is measured at fixed time intervals (sampled), quantised and further processed with digital circuitry well known in digital computers. The advantage of the digital formatting is that we can apply error correction control circuitry that corrects most of the errors that occur. Error correction combined with interleaving schemes can cope with almost any imperfection of the detected signal. A disadvantage of the use of digital audio is the enormous increase of the bandwidth needed to transmit or store it. The digital audio as used in the Compact Disc has a bit rate of approximately 2 Mbit s^{-1}. Optical disc recording has, as we shall see, an information density of up to 1 bit μm^{-2}, so that a playing time of more than one hour is possible on a single side of a 12 cm diameter disc. This gigantic capacity should be compared with, for example, a mini 'floppy disc' frequently used in small office and personal computers. These floppies have a capacity of say 1–2 Mbit being equivalent to only 0.5–1 s of playing time.

Another special feature is that 'control and display' information is recorded, as C&D bits. This includes first of all information for the listener, such as playing time, composer and title of the music. The C&D channel has a capacity of approximately 70 kbit s^{-1} and is completely separated from the audio channels.

In the LaserVision system the signal is recorded using frequency modulation. Each transition from land to pit and vice versa contains information for the video decoder. In fact any distance between a minimum and a maximum value of the lengths of the pits and lands may occur. This is not the case with the Compact Disc formatting. Here the intervals between transitions can only take nine values and all interval lengths are integer multiples of a predefined unity.

In the Compact Disc system the analog audio signal is sampled at a rate of 44.1 kHz, which according to Nyquist's sampling criterion is sufficient for the reproduction of the maximum audio frequency of 20 kHz. The number of bits per sample is 32, i.e. 16 for the left-hand and 16 for the right-hand stereo channel. This corresponds to a signal-to-noise ratio, as a result of the quantisation, of more than 90 dB. A simple calculation shows that the net bit rate is $44.1 \times 1000 \times 32 = 1.41 \times 10^6$ audio bits per second. The audio bits are grouped into so-called frames, each containing six of the original stereo samples.

Error correction bits are added in accordance with the CIRC (see Vries *et al* 1980). The resulting bit rate (for every three original audio bits an extra bit is added) is $\frac{4}{3} \times 1.41 = 1.83$ Mbit s^{-1}. Eight bits of C&D information are added per frame and the whole bit stream is now modulated according to the rules of the EFM modulation (see Heemskerk and Immink 1982, Ogawa and Immink 1982). In EFM code blocks of eight data bits are transformed into seventeen channel bits with special properties that make them suitable for the optical channel. After adding synchronisation sequences the channel bit rate equals 4.3218 Mbit s^{-1}.

The two-level signal produced in this way is used during mastering (Chapter 5) to switch the laser beam that exposes the master disc on and off.

The read-out of the disc is in principle accomplished in the same way as with LaserVision discs. The photosignal from the photodiode in the player is demodulated by the EFM decoder. The demodulated information reaches the error correction and detection circuitry where most disc errors are removed.

Speed variations of the disc, for example, due to disc eccentricity, cause wow and flutter. This problem can easily be solved by using a buffer memory (see Carasso *et al* 1982). The input data enter the buffer memory with a speed dependent on the disc velocity. The data stream leaves the buffer with a rate synchronised with a quartz clock generator. The average velocity of the disc is controlled by using the average content of the buffer memory. After leaving the buffer memory the data with quartz precision now enter the digital-to-analog converters (Goedhart *et al* 1982, Plassche and Dijkmans 1982) which reproduce the stereo sound. In the next sections the background to the choice of EFM modulation system is described. Furthermore we describe how, by adding extra bits, error correction or parity bits, it is possible to detect and correct disc errors.

7.2.1 *System aspects and modulation*

As discussed in the preceding section the data from the error correction circuitry are transferred to a modulator. The modulator has the task of transforming the data bit stream into a two-level signal with special properties.

The choice of a channel code can be a complex affair taking into account the physical properties of the transmission channel. One important factor is space efficiency, i.e. the number of bits per unit surface that can reliably be stored on the disc. Another factor is the reliability of the information read-out. The reliability of the system can be expressed by the tolerances that can be allowed in the optical light path. It will be shown that a particular choice of a coding system has an influence on the manufacturing tolerances of the disc and player. The most important parameter of a transmission channel is the bandwidth. In optical disc systems the bandwidth is directly determined by the diameter of the read-out spot and the scanning velocity. The spot diameter d, defined as the full width at half maximum (FWHM) of the light intensity, can be calculated by

$$d = 0.5 \, \lambda/\mathrm{NA}$$

where λ is the wavelength of the laser light and NA is the numerical aperture of the objective lens. To obtain a high information density in the radial and tangential directions d must be as small as possible. The laser chosen for the CD system is the small solid state AlGaAs diode laser with a wavelength of approximately 800 nm. This means that the NA must be made as large as possible. With increasing NA, however, the manufacturing tolerances of the optical light path rapidly become smaller. For example the tolerance in the local skew of the disc relative to the optical axis is proportional to NA^{-3}. The tolerance for the disc thickness is proportional to NA^{-4} and the depth of focus is proportional to NA^{-2}.

After considering all these factors in relation to one another a value of 0.45 was chosen for the NA. This gives a value of about 1 μm for the FWHM spot diameter.

We shall now deal with the bandwidth properties of two-level channel codes. There are many codes and no code is universally accepted as 'best'. For this reason we shall base our study on theoretical sequences, called max-entropic run-length-limited sequences, that play a key role in channel code designs for information storage applications. The choice of the Compact Disc modulation system EFM is fully based on the theory the so-called binary run-length-limited sequences. This theory goes back to Kautz (1965) and Tang and Bahl (1970). Adopting Tang's notations we define a binary (dk) sequence as a sequence that simultaneously satisfies the following two conditions.

(d) constraint: two logical ones are separated by a number of consecutive logical zeros of at least d.

(k) constraint: the number of consecutive logical zeros is at most k.

A sequence satisfying the (d) and (k) constraints is called a (dk) sequence. Sequences satisfying only the (d) constraint are called (d) sequences. From a (dk) sequence we derive a run-length-limited binary sequence with at least ($d+1$) and at most ($k+1$) consecutive zeros (or ones) by summing modulo 2 the (dk) sequence. In this way the ones of a (dk) sequence indicate the position of a transition zero to one (or one to zero) of a run-length-limited sequence. Tang and Bahl (1970) derived simple recursion relations for the number of distinct (dk) sequences of block length n as a function of the constraints d and k. If for convenience we restrict ourselves to (d) limited sequences, the number of distinct binary sequences $N(n)$ of block length n is given by

$$N(n) = \begin{cases} n + 1 & 1 \le n \le d + 1 \\ N(n-1) + N(n-d-1) & n > d + 1. \end{cases}$$

The asymptotic information rate R, defined as the number of information bits (< 1) per channel bit that can maximally be carried by the run-length-limited sequence, on average, is determined by the specified constraints and is given by

$$R = \lim_{n \to \infty} \frac{1}{n} \log_2 N(n).$$

For large n the number of distinct (d) sequences $N(n)$ equals

$$N(n) \sim \mu^n$$

where μ is given by the largest root of

$$z^{d+1} - z^d - 1 = 0.$$

The maximum information rate R is then simply

$$R = \log_2 \mu.$$

Similar relations can be derived for sequences with a d and/or k constraint. As an example in the case $d = 1$ we simply find for the number of codewords of length n: $N(n) = 2, 3, 5, 8, 13, 21$ etc, being the sequence of Fibonacci numbers.

The process of modulation maps the input data stream onto the run-length-limited output stream. In general a block of m consecutive data bits is mapped onto n consecutive channel bits. This format is called block-based channel codes. The existence of a maximum information rate merely states that $m/n < R = R(d,k)$ for any finite m and n. If one wishes to transmit (store) a certain fixed amount of information per time unit then the channel clock should run at least $1/R$ times faster than the data clock to compensate for the d and k constraint. In other words, a channel bit takes a time which is shorter by a factor of at least R than that needed for a data bit. The minimum physical distance per data bit length of the run-length-limited sequence generated by modulo 2 integration of the dk sequence is now given by

$$T_{\min}/T = (d+1)R(d,k)$$

where T is the data bit time.

Table 7.1 lists R and the minimum distance $T_{\min}/T$ for various d for some values of practical interest. Both R and $T_{\min}$ are specified per data bit length. The values of R and $T_{\min}/T$ in the table are theoretical maxentropic bounds. An inspection of the table shows that with increasing d the minimum distance between transitions T_{min} can be increased. The rate R decreases with increasing d. Qualitatively we may state that T_{min}/T is related to the highest relative frequency which should pass the channel with no distortion. The table shows clearly the trade-off between T_{min}/T, i.e. the highest frequency to be recorded, and the timing accuracy R. The importance of the study of maxentropic sequences is that they do not depend on a particular embodiment of a channel code. A property that makes this study even more practically attractive is that embodiments of channel codes with finite hardware can easily reach 90–95% of the maximum values of the table (see Beenker and Immink 1983). A rescaling of the maxentropic sequence-based computer simulations results in a generally applicable theory independent of a typical embodiment of a modulation system.

Table 7.1 Maximum rate R and T_{min}/T for various d.

d	R	T_{min}/T
1	0.69	1.38
2	0.55	1.65
3	0.46	1.84

The quality of a digital channel is usually evaluated by means of an 'eye-pattern', which is obtained by observing the signal on an oscilloscope synchronised with the clock of the bit stream. The signals originating from different pits and lands are superimposed on the screen. The demodulator in the player determines whether the signal is positive or negative at the clock moments (the broken curves in figure 2.41) and hence reconstructs the bit stream. The lozenge pattern around a dash is called the 'eye'. The eye can become obscured owing to channel imperfections. The signals in figure 2.39(a) were calculated for a perfect optical system. Figure 2.43 shows the effect of severe defocusing of 4 microns and a useful indication of the bandwidth properties of channel codes is the eye height against tangential information density. The minimum value of the signal at the sample moments is defined as the worst-case eye opening or eye height. If we assume a linear read-out process the output of the optical channel is the convolution of the channel (optical read-out) impulse response and the pit pattern on the disc. If we assume the pit pattern to be ideal two-level and, for example, a Gaussian shaped impulse response of the optical read-out, we can quite easily calculate the eye height against tangential information density (Immink and Aarts 1983).

Figure 7.10 shows the minimum worst-case eye height against normalised information density with d and consequently T_{min} as parameters. All these calculations are based on the theoretical maximum rates of the maxentropic codes. The eye heights of practical codes can be found by rescaling the horizontal axes with a constant, the ratio of the practical and maxentropic rate. The figure reveals the following important results. The eye opening decreases with increasing information rate for all d values. For a value $d' > d$ we notice that the eye opening is initially smaller at lower densities, but decreases more slowly. The result is that at a certain density both eye openings are equal and for a still larger density the eye opening is larger for $d' > d$. It is quite clear from this figure, that if we want to design a high density modulation system then the choice of a certain d depends on both the minimum tolerable eye opening and the information density We note that it is only worthwhile considering a $d = 2$ system over a $d = 1$ system if we can tolerate a minimum eye opening smaller than 28% (-11 dB) of the top eye opening.

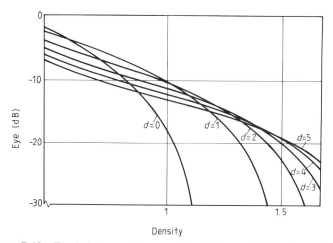

Figure 7.10   Eye height against normalised information density with d as a parameter.

Another conclusion of the calculations is the observation that for larger d the slope of the curves is smaller. In other words the system becomes less sensitive for variations in the bandwidth of the transmission system. This parameter is particularly important for the optical disc where defocusing and disc skewing have a detrimental effect on the bandwidth of the read-out. The reader can quite easily verify that a choice of a modulation system has a great influence on the tolerances of the disc and the read-out system.

The parameters discussed above are only two of many that play a role in the consideration of the total system concept. Another parameter is the energy at low frequencies of the read signal. This has to be as small as possible, the reasons for this requirement being threefold.

Firstly the servo systems for track following and focusing are controlled by low frequency components of the information signal, so that low-frequency components can interfere with the servo systems. The second reason is illustrated in figure 7.11, where the read signal is shown for a clean disc (7.11 (*a*)) and for a disc that has been soiled, e.g. by fingerprints or scratches (7.11 (*b*)). The imperfections cause the amplitude and the average level of the signal to fall. The fall in level causes a completely incorrect read-out if the signal falls below the decision level. Errors of this type are avoided by filtering out the low frequency components. This filtering (AC coupling) is only permissible provided the information signal itself is not distorted, in other words does not contain low frequency components. Thirdly the circuitry used for regeneration of the binary signal can be simple and reliable if the design is based on the assumption that on the average an equal number of ones and zeros are received. The decision level can then be found by averaging the photodiode signal.

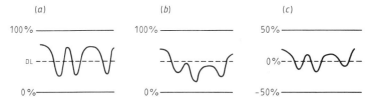

Figure 7.11 The read-out signal (*a*) for a disc, (*b*) for a soiled disc and (*c*) a soiled disc after high-pass filtering. DL = decision level (courtesy *Philips Tech. Rev.* **40** 1982).

The EFM modulation system. After many experiments, and having considered system aspects of many channel codes, we came to the following preferred embodiment—EFM. Figure 7.12 gives a schematic general picture of the bit streams in the encoding system. The information is divided into 'frames'. One frame contains six stereo samples or $2 \times 16 \times 6$ bits. These are divided into symbols of eight bits. The bit stream B_1 thus contains 24 symbols per frame. In B_2 eight parity symbols are added and one C&D symbol, resulting in 33 'data symbols'. The modulator translates each symbol into a new symbol of 14 bits using a fixed code book (look-up table). Added to these are three 'merging bits', for reasons that will be explained shortly. After the addition of a sync pattern of 27 bits to the frame the bit stream B_i is obtained. The sync pattern is added so that in the player the correct sequence of characters can be found. The sync pattern is unique and will not occur in other bit positions. It can easily be verified that an EFM frame contains 588 channel bits. Finally, B_i is converted into a control signal for the write laser. It should be noted that in figure 7.12 the sequence B_i does not mean 'pit' or 'land', but a '1' indicates a pit edge (a(dk) sequence).

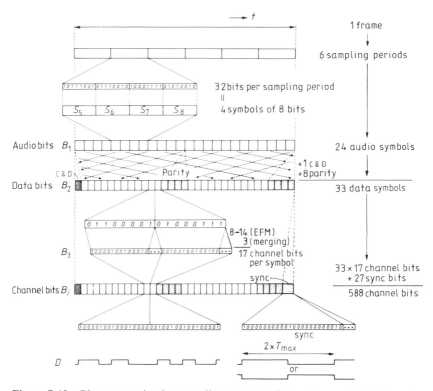

Figure 7.12   Bit streams in the encoding system of the Compact Disc (courtesy *Philips Tech. Rev.* **40** 1982).

The code book of EFM is designed with a T_{min} of 3 and a T_{max} of 11 channel bits (this means in the notation of the preceding section a code with $d = 2$ and $k = 10$). A simple computer search shows that at least 14 channel bits are needed for the reproduction of all the 256 possible 8-bit symbols under the condition $d = 2$ and $k = 10$. The computer search showed that for the given constraint more than 256 14-bit symbols are possible. This surplus is omitted. Given the 256 channel symbols we still have the degree of freedom to choose the dictionary. The dictionary was compiled with the aid of a computer in such a way that the translation of the channel symbols onto the data symbols can be done with minimum hardware in the player.

The merging bits between the 14-bit symbols are needed for the following reasons. The run-length conditions can only be satisfied if at least two merging bits are added between the channel symbols. If the run-length is in danger of becoming too short we choose '0' for the merging bits; if the run-length is too long we choose a '1' for one of them. If we do this we still retain a large measure of freedom in the choice of the merging bits, and we use this freedom to minimise the low frequency content of the signal. Two merging bits would be sufficient for continuing to satisfy the run-length conditions. However, a third was added to give sufficient freedom for effective suppression of the low frequency content, even though it means a loss of 6% of the information density on the disc. All information is contained in the 14-bit symbols, the merging bits do not contain any information and are removed from the bit stream in the demodulator.

Figure 7.13 illustrates the principle of selection of the merging bits. Our measure of DC content is the DSV (digital sum value). The DSV is defined as the difference between the totals of pit and land lengths accumulated from the start of the disc. The figure shows the translation of two data symbols onto two EFM symbols. From the T_{min} constraint the first of the merging bits in this case should be zero; this position is marked 'X'. In the two following positions the choice is free; these are marked 'M'. The three possible choices for the merging bits are '000', '010' and '001', and in figure 7.13 the DSV against time for the three possible merging bit choices have been plotted. The calculation is based on the assumption that the DSV is zero at the beginning of the first symbol. The modulator is designed such that it chooses the merging bit combination with a resulting DSV that is minimum at the end of a symbol. In the example of figure 7.13 we simply find that '000' will be chosen. When this simple merging strategy is applied, we find that the noise in the servo band frequencies (< 20 kHz) is sufficiently suppressed.

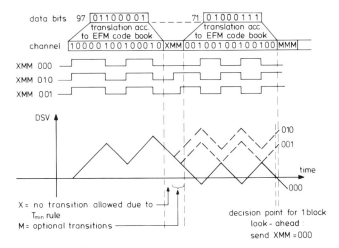

Figure 7.13 Strategy for minimising the low frequency content of the EFM signal. As a criterion the digital sum value (DSV) is used. In the figure the DSV is plotted as function of time for three possible merging bit combinations (one combination '100' is forbidden by the T_{min} constraint in the merging of the left symbol). The merging bits yielding a minimum DSV at the end of a symbol are chosen.

This simple algorithm has, however, some distinct disadvantages. There are combinations of channel symbols where no choice exists. In such cases it might not be the best choice in the blocks preceding these combinations to aim for the lowest DSV, but to minimise the DSV excursions over a longer period of transmission. In other word some short term results have to be traded in for longer term success. In some cases different possible merging bit combinations give the same DSV at the end of the symbol in question. In such cases our simple algorithm with a short look-ahead period (17 channel bits) can only make an arbitrary choice. Because the two alternatives might end up with a different polarity there might be a difference further up between them. Immink and Gross (1983) have given algorithms that look-ahead over more than one symbol. They used a microcomputer to evaluate this more sophisticated procedure. Figure 7.14 gives a time plot of the encoder output DSV at the end of each transmitted symbol for four different look-ahead intervals. We note that the curves with longer look-ahead intervals are centred more around the zero value and there are several places where it can be seen how the further look-ahead strategies allow a greater excursion in order to have a smaller deviation at the later stage.

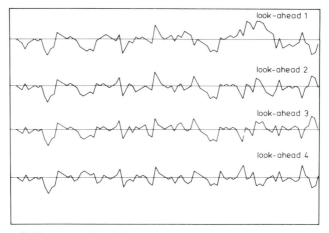

Figure 7.14   Examples of the digital sum value against time (arbitrary units) for 1-, 2- and 4-symbol look-ahead strategy. The plots show examples where short term profit is sacrificed to achieve an improved DSV in the longer term.

Figures 7.15 (*a*) and (*b*) show power density functions of the modulated output in the frequency range 0 to 50 kHz. The comparison is done for the look-ahead intervals of 1, 2 and 4 channel symbols as shown in figure 7.15. The net improvement in total power integrated over the servo frequency band is for the four-symbol look-ahead approximately 10 dB enhanced with respect to the simple one-symbol look-ahead strategy. Though the experiments showed an enhancement when using more complex merging strategies the international standard for the Compact Disc opted for the simple one-symbol look-ahead strategy.

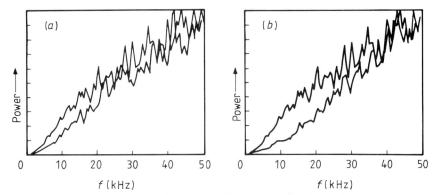

Figure 7.15 Power density function of EFM at the low frequency range (< 50 kHz). Curve (*a*) compares the 1-symbol look-ahead with a 2-symbol look-ahead. Curve (*b*) shows a comparison between a 1- and a 4-symbol look-ahead strategy. The power is plotted on a linear scale.

7.2.2 *Error correction and concealment,* CIRC

The major advantage of using digital audio techniques is that in the digital domain we can apply error correction systems that can cope with almost any deterioration of the signal. As discussed in the introduction the first experiments for audio storage on optical disc used wideband frequency modulation, which improved the signal-to-noise ratio of the demodulated audio. Drop-outs (a relatively long interval of erroneous signals), however, still produced audible clicks. We have to keep in mind that the bit density on the Compact Disc is in the sub-micron range making it almost impossible to store and read-out the information without errors. Major causes of imperfection are: dust and scratches on the master disc; non-optimum mastering; bubbles and irregular diffraction in the plastic substrate; scratches or fingerprints on the plastic substrate and a non-optimum laser spot during read-out, caused by mistracking or defocusing. The error correction that is added to the format of the Compact Disc enables the mass production of Compact Disc records that can be played without noticeable noise. We shall go on to discuss the principles of error correction and the way it is implemented in the Compact Disc code, CIRC.

Principles of error correction. A full mathematical treatment of the basics of error correction is outside the scope of this book. The reader is referred to the textbooks of Berlekamp (1968) and Lin (1970) with their many references. Here we shall deal only with a basic understanding coming as close to reality as possible.

Assume we want to send a certain number of digits over an unreliable channel. Let us be more specific and assume that we want to send the ages of say three children over the UK cable. The ages are 5, 6 and 8 years. If for any reason one of the digits is changed then the receiver of the message will not be able to detect (or even correct) the error. A very simple way to make error detection possible is the following. We simply add all digits and send the sum, 19, as well. If one of the four numbers is received in error then the receiver by checking the sum will be able to detect this error. He will not be able to correct it and has to ask the sender to repeat the message. We also note from this example that only one of the four digits may be in error. If more than one digit is wrong then we are not always able to detect an error. An improved version of our simple error detection code can be made by adding again all the (four) digits and also transmitting this second check sum.

This simple example teaches us two important points:

(*a*) If we want a more reliable communication then we have to pay more (in our example we have to pay the Post Office for four words instead of three).

(*b*) There is a certain bound on the number of wrong digits that can be detected.

In the preceding example we were only able to detect the errors; it is however even possible to correct them.

Assume we want to transmit k data numbers, $X(1)$, $X(2)$, ..., $X(k)$. We add $(n-k)$ check digits: $X(k+1)$, ..., $X(n)$ called parity check symbols. The ratio k/n is called the rate of the code. In our example we had $k = 3$, $n = 4$ and $R = k/n = 3/4$. Error correction is possible if $n - k > 1$ parity symbols are added in a clever way. Let us assume $n - k = 2$ and choose $X(k+1)$ and $X(n)$ such that

$$X(1) + X(2) + \ldots + X(n) = 0$$

$$X(1) + 2X(2) + \ldots + kX(n) = 0.$$

We define the received symbols $R(j)$ $(1 \le j \le n)$ and assume that during transmission only one error was made in symbol $X(i)$, such that

$$R(i) = X(i) + E(i)$$

where $R(i)$ is the erroneously received symbol and $E(i)$ is the error made in that symbol. The receiver of the message calculates the following two checks, so-called 'syndromes'

$$S1 = R(1) + R(2) + \ldots + R(n)$$

and

$$S2 = R(1) + 2R(2) + \ldots + nR(n).$$

If no error has occurred during transmission, i.e. $E(i) = 0$, we simply find $S1 = S2 = 0$. If, however, $E(i)$ is non-zero, we find by substitution

$$S1 = E(i) \qquad \text{and} \qquad S2 = iE(i).$$

By inspection of this result we find surprisingly that we can correct the error that was made during transmission: the first syndrome $S1$ equals the error $E(i)$ and the position of the error can be found by $i = S2/S1$. By a simple substitution we can reconstruct the symbol $X(i)$.

We can come to important conclusions from this example.

(a) We can not only detect errors, but also correct errors made during transmission.

(b) In the given example with two parity check symbols we can apply different strategies of decoding: detect errors only and correct errors, if possible.

If we correct the error we will not detect the fact that more than one error could have occurred. The reader can see that if more than one received symbol is in error the whole method is useless. Detecting is possible if not more than two symbols are in error. We note a certain trade-off between a strategy of being on the safe side, i.e. detecting only, or less safe by correcting errors. We shall see in the next section that the same situation will arise with the actual implementation of the Compact Disc error correcting code CIRC. A generalisation of the given example will show that a code able to correct t errors in a codeword sequence needs $(n - k) = 2t$ parity checks. It can be seen that at the receiver we need to know the magnitudes of the t errors and their position in the sequence, so that $2t$ independent equations are needed for solving them.

In the examples discussed in this section we used 'normal' arithmetic of the type learnt in primary school. In practical codes we use finite-field or Galois-field arithmetic (name after the 19th century French mathematician Galois, who developed finite-field arithmetic). Practical error correcting codes, using Galois-field arithmetic, are often based on so-called Reed–Solomon codes, after their inventors (see Berlekamp 1968 and Lin 1970).

Interleaving. We can as we have seen correct errors in a sequence of symbols if not too many errors are to be expected in the sequence. Errors never happen alone so that simple single or double error correcting codes are useless if we do not add 'interleaving'. Interleaving is a way to disperse the original sequence (with parity check symbols), spreading the errors over more code words. The reverse process is called de-interleaving.

The process of interleaving can best be explained using a simple example. Figure 7.16 shows a circuit using three delay lines, with 0, 1, 2 and 3 word delay. At the input we notice a multiplex switch that synchronously passes an input symbol into one of the delay lines. The output switch again serialises the symbol stream for transmission. We assume two errors were made, marked with an x, during transmission. When de-interleaving we note that the errors are spread out so that in the given example the two errors are in two different codes enabling us with a one-error correcting code to correct two errors. We can easily verify that we can correct longer 'bursts' of errors if we use more and longer delay lines. In the Compact Disc system a more sophisticated way of interleaving is applied, making it very useful for audio applications.

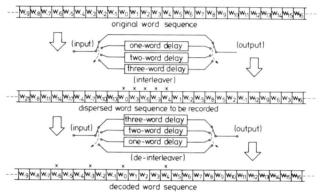

Figure 7.16 Simple interleave and de-interleave scheme using delay lines. The example shows that correction of two consecutive errors is possible even with a one-error correcting code.

Cross-interleaved Reed–Solomon code (CIRC).   The error correcting code used in the Compact Disc system employs not one, but two codes C_1 and C_2, which are interleaved 'crosswise'. For code C_1 we have $n_1 = 32$, $k_1 = 28$ and for C_2 $n_2 = 28$, $k_2 = 24$. The rate of the CIRC code is $(k_1/n_1)(k_2/n_2) = 3/4$. In other words 25% of the stored information on the disc is used for parity checking. Both C_1 and C_2 can correct up to $(n_1 - k_1)/2 = (n_2 - k_2)/2 = 2$ symbols in each codeword. The structure of the CIRC encoder is shown in figure 7.17. Basically CIRC consists of a cross interleave (see Doi 1982) and two Reed–Solomon codes. The sequence of encoding is described in the next paragraph.

Scrambling plus delay of two symbols. For the encoder, 16-bit data of 12 words is input per frame (six complete stereo samples). The number 12 is chosen (Vries and Odaka 1982) because it has as its least common multiples 2, 3 and 4 enabling easy expansion of the system into three or four channels

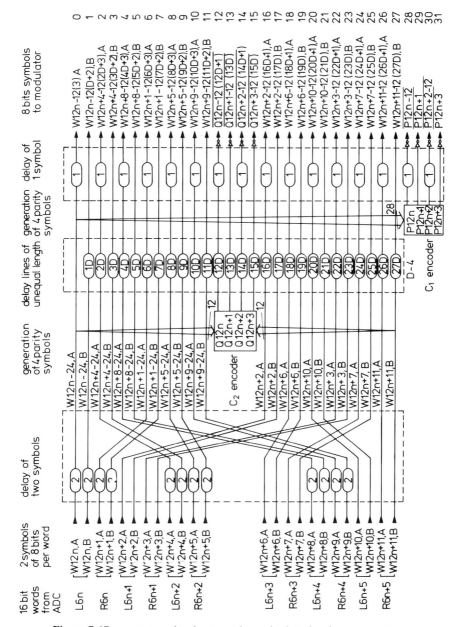

Figure 7.17 CIRC encoder for two channels: interleaving sequence.

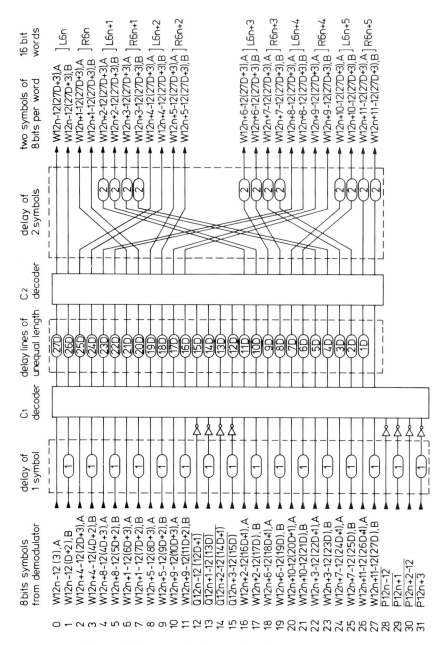

Figure 7.18 CIRC decoder: de-interleaving sequence.

in the future. The input data, 12 16-bit samples, are divided into 24 symbols of eight bits and form a frame of symbols that are processed. A delay of two symbols is added to the 12 symbols, which are used for concealment when no error flag is generated by the C_1 decoder but an uncorrectable error exists at the C_2 decoder The symbols are then scrambled and four parity-check symbols are generated, resulting in $24 + 4$ symbols at the C_2 level. The 28 symbols are delayed using delay lines with unequal delays, 'cross interleave'. The delay was chosen presuming the use of a 16 kbit RAM (random access memory) for storage. After this interleave code words are again formed and parity symbols are calculated according to the C_1 code. Four parity symbols are added, resulting in a total of 32 symbols at the C_1 level.

If the output of the C_1 encoder is recorded directly on the disc, symbols within the same correction block become adjacent to each other causing the error generated at the boundary to become a two-symbol error, thus reducing the error correction capability. To avoid such an error a one-symbol interleave is added. The eventual recording is made after inverting the parity symbols. As error control with CIRC is made on an eight-bit symbol basis, the EFM modulation method described in the preceding section is also expected to generate errors in symbol units without error propagation of small errors.

Performance of the CIRC code.   The CIRC decoder is shown in figure 7.19.

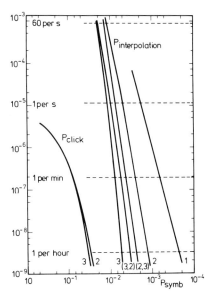

Figure 7.19 Performance curves for several decoding strategies. The calculations were performed assuming random errors.

The C_1 and C_2 codes are Reed–Solomon codes with four parity checks enabling two-symbol error correction per code. Given the C_1 and C_2 code format it is possible to use in the decoder different strategies of decoding. In figure 7.19 we have plotted, assuming random errors, the performance of the CIRC code for different strategies (Vries and Odaka 1982). In table 7.2 the performance of the code for burst-error operation is shown. The table shows the correction length, being the length of a string of burst error bits, that can be corrected. The table also shows the concealment length, being the length of a burst, that can be completely corrected, but can be reconstructed using interpolation of the audio samples.

Table 7.2   Performance of CIRC error correction code.

Aspect	Specification
Maximum completely correctable burst length	$\simeq 4000$ data bits (i.e. $\simeq 2.5$ mm track length on the disc)
Maximum interpolatable burst length in the worst case	$\simeq 12\,300$ data bits (i.e. $\simeq 7.7$ mm track length)
Sample interpolation rate	One sample every 10 hours at $\text{BER} = 10^{-4}$ 1000 samples per minute at $\text{BER} = 10^{-3}$
Undetected error samples (clicks)	Less than one every 750 hours at $\text{BER} = 10^{-3}$ Negligible at $\text{BER} = 10^{-4}$
Code rate	3/4
Structure of decoder	One special LSI chip plus one random access memory (RAM) 2048 words of 8 bits
Usefulness for future developments	Decoding circuit can also be used for a four-channel quadraphonic reproduction

References

Badger G and Allen R 1982 The audio side of the Laser video disc *72nd Convention AES, Anaheim, Preprint* 1935 (F-5)

Beenker G F M and Schouhamer Immink K A 1983 A generalized method for encoding and decoding run-length-limited binary sequences *Trans. Inform.* **IT-29** 751–4

Berlekamp E R 1968 *Algebraic Coding Theory* (New York: McGraw-Hill)

Bogels P 1976 System coding parameters, mechanics and electro-mechanics of the reflective video disc player *IEEE Trans. Consum. Electron.* **CE-22** 309–17

Bruch W 1967 Das TRIPAL verfahren *Funkschau* **18** 563–5 (in German)

Carasso M G, Peek J B H and Sinjou J P 1982 The Compact Disc digital audio system *Philips Tech. Rev.* **40** 151–5

Clemens J K 1978 Capacitive pickup and the buried carrier encoding system for the RCA video-disk system *RCA Rev.* **39** 33–59

Coleman C H 1977 Moiré interference reducing circuit for FM video recorders *US Patent* 4, 052, 740

Doi T T 1982 Error correction codes for digital audio *Proc. AES Premier Conf., Ryetown* (New York: Audio Engineering Society) pp. 147–77

Goedhart D, van de Plassche R J and Stikvoort E F 1982 Digital-to-analog conversion in playing a Compact Disc *Philips Tech. Rev.* **40** 174–80

de Haan M R and Velzel C H F 1978 Intermodulation and moire effects in optical video recording *Philips Res. Rep.* **39** 436–59

Heemskerk J P J 1978 Noise in a video-disk system *Appl. Opt.* **17** 2007–21

Heemskerk J P J and Schouhamer Immink K 1982 Compact Disc: system aspects and modulation *Philips Tech. Rev.* **40** 157–64

Hoeve H, Timmermans J and Vries L B 1982 Error correction and concealment in the Compact Disc *Philips Tech. Rev.* **40** 166–72

Immink K A Schouhamer and Aarts R M 1983 Maximization of recording density in Te-alloys *Proc. Int. Soc. Opt. Eng., Geneva* (*SPIE* **396**) 181–8

Immink K A Schouhamer and Gross U 1983 Optimization of low-frequency properties of eight-to-fourteen modulation *Radio Electron. Eng.* **53** 63–6

Immink K A Schouhamer, Hoogendijk A H and Kahlman J A 1983 Digital audio modulation in the PAL and NTSC LaserVision video disc coding formats *74th Convention AES, New York Preprint* 1997 (also *IEEE Trans. Consum. Electron.* **CE-29** 543–51)

Kautz W H 1970 Fibonacci codes for synchronization control *IEEE Trans. Inform. Theory* **17** 436–61

Kenney G C and Hoogendijk A H 1974 Signal processing for a video disc system (VLP) *IEEE Trans. Broadcast. Telev. Recep.* **BTR-20** 217–29

Lin S 1970 *An Introduction to Error-Correcting Codes* (Englewood Cliffs, NJ: Prentice Hall)

Ogawa H and Schouhamer Immink K A 1982 EFM – The modulation for the Compact Digital audio disc *Proc. AES Premier Conf., Ryetown* (New York: Audio Engineering Society) pp. 117–24

van de Plassche R and Dijkmans E C 1982 A monolithic 16-bits D/A conversion for digital audio *Proc. AES Premier Conf., Ryetown* 54–62

Pritchard D H, Clemens J K and Ross M D 1981 The principles and quality of the buried-subcarrier encoding and decoding system *IEEE Trans. Consum. Electron.* **CE-27** 352–9

Tang D T and Bahl L R 1970 Block codes for a class of constrained noiseless channels *Inform. Control* **17** 436–61

Vaanholt H 1982 The coding format for composite PAL video signals and stereo sound in the LaserVision optical videodisc system *4th Int. Conf. on Video and Data Recording, Southampton* (London: IERE) pp. 351–65

Vries L B, Immink K A, Nijboer J G, Hoeve H, Doi T T, Odaka K and Ogawa H 1980 The digital Compact Disc system: modulation and error correction *67th Convention AES Preprint* 1674 (New York: Audio Engineering Society)

Vries L B and Odaka K 1982 CIRC—The error-correcting code for the compact disc digital audio system, *Proc. AES Premier Conf., Ryetown* (New York: Audio Engineering Society) pp. 178–88

8 Applications

A Huijser

8.1 Introduction

The optical recording principles as presented in the previous chapters have been incorporated in actual systems. The characteristics of some of these systems have already been described in the appropriate places. In this chapter these systems will be reviewed in a more general way and existing or future applications will be discussed.

Optical recording technology has found its way into both professional and consumer products. This differentiation between consumer and professional applications is rather artificial since a professional character is inherent in optical recording systems. A better way to distinguish between the various applications is to consider their data storage function, i.e. their use as a memory device. In that way we divide the systems into read-only memories (ROM); write-once memories (PROM) and erasable memories (EPROM, RAM). The abbreviations in parentheses are those commonly used for silicon ICs with almost similar functions. Other terms are often used for optical recording systems having the PROM or EPROM function. Such abbreviations or names are mostly used to emphasise one of the typical features of the optical recording technology such as DRAW for the direct read after write function; DOR for digital optical recording and Add-On Disc, typical for write-once media. The distinction between consumer and professional systems is now simply the fact that present consumer applications of the optical recording technology are all of the ROM type for which media can be mass-replicated at low cost (see Chapter 5).

In the consumer area, the LaserVision video disc system and the Compact Disc digital audio system have already been introduced on the market. Licensees all over the world have adopted these systems, and system specifications have become world standards. This standardisation is essential for a consumer product since the market demands a large range of software, available from various sources.

In the professional field of storage devices, the need for standardisation is hardly present for the systems as long as they are 'plug compatible'. Media standardisation would only be driven by such concerns as 'second-sourcing'. Moreover, optical recording systems for professional applications are at the forefront of market introduction and feedback from users will certainly change the present specifications. As a consequence, it is not possible to present more than some rough outlines of these systems. Moreover, no reference will be made with respect to erasable systems in which the advantages of optical recording are combined with the erasability of magnetic media. Although these systems overcome any remaining scepticism about optical recording, they will certainly not be introduced soon.

8.2   The LaserVision video disc system

The present boom in optical recording technology has been initiated by the 'Video Long Play' optical disc system presented to the international press at a conference held at the Philips Research Laboratories on 5 September 1972 (Compaan and Kramer 1973). Further development led to its introduction to the US market in 1976. Since then the name of the system has been changed from 'VLP' to 'LaserVision'. This is in order to distinguish it from other video-disc systems based on non-optical pick-ups, developed during the same decade (McCoy 1978).

For the introduction to the European consumer market in 1982, the original NTSC based system had to be redesigned to the PAL video format, commonly adopted in Europe. The main difference is the video frame frequency—30 Hz for NTSC as opposed to 25 Hz for the PAL system. These values determine the maximum spinning frequency of a video disc which contains at least one full video picture per revolution.

On the standard 30 cm diameter disc, the spiral of the continuous information track starts at a radius of 55 mm and ends at a radius of 145 mm. Besides the 30 cm disc, a version with the same inner-track radius but with an outer diameter of only 20 cm is accepted by all LaserVision equipment. Between the inner and outer tracks, the information can be stored in either the constant angular velocity (CAV) mode or in the constant linear velocity (CLV) mode, both starting with one complete video frame per revolution on the inner track.

In the CLV mode, optimum use is made of the storage capacity due to a constant areal density all over the disc. This implies that the tracks at the outer radius contain about 2.5 video pictures per revolution, yielding a playing time of almost one hour per disc side for running video such as in the play-back of feature films. While scanning the information from inside to outside radii, the spinning frequency of the disc decreases to maintain a constant track velocity with respect to the read-out spot.

In the CAV mode, the spinning frequency of the disc is kept constant independent of radius. Each track contains just one video picture per revolution. With over 50 000 tracks per disc side, this yields about 30 minutes of running video or, more importantly, over 50 000 randomly accessible pictures. The CAV mode is particularly useful for interactive use of the video disc, such as (programmable) instruction in educational applications. For interactive play-back of CAV discs use can be made of LaserVision player features like 'still-picture', at any track and unlimited in time; 'slow-motion', in both forward and backward direction; 'fast-scan' and 'go-to', an automatic picture search on picture number. Standard LaserVision equipment can play back both CAV and CLV discs.

Figure 8.1   Exploded view of a LaserVision player based on a HeNe laser.

8.3   Professional applications of LaserVision

An important trend in interactive LaserVision (ILV) players is to interface them with (personal) computers. For that purpose a special disc format has been designed in which the computer program that accompanies the inter-active video disc can be stored in the standard audio channels on the disc. In this way, the computer software to be used with the disc can be loaded into the computer directly from the video disc itself. Thus, no additional media are needed to run the ILV program under computer control.

The incorporation of the Compact Disc digital audio format in the Laser-Vision video disc standard (Schouhamer Immink *et al* 1984) is of special interest to ILV applications. Besides the 50 000 high quality video pictures, such a disc can contain over 500 Mbytes of random accessible digital data, i.e. 10 kbytes per picture. With that combination a very powerful database can be created for a variety of applications in the field of information systems, in some of which slides or microfiches are now being used.

A special application of ILV is found in video games and in motion-picture editing. With the use of galvano-mirror actuators it is possible to perform the so-called 'instant jump', a random access over a few hundred tracks within the short period of the frame-sync pulse between successive pictures. With this feature it is possible to create lively video scenes without visible interruptions from pictures which are rather randomly distributed over the disc. In ILV video games, the player will see a sequence of pictures according to the rules of the particular game and the reactions of the player to them.

Besides entertainment, LaserVision-based video games have a professional application in systems like link trainers and flight simulators, in creating realistic visual effects.

8.4 The Compact Disc digital audio system

It was recognised in the early period of VLP research that the optical recording technology could well be used for the storage and play-back of audio signals. Obvious advantages were thought to be absence of wear and, with respect to existing 'black' audio records, an extremely high capacity and thus playing time per disc. Although essential to it, the present success of the optical recording technique in audio play-back cannot be ascribed totally to these two properties. The incorporation of digital signal processing, made possible by the huge storage capacity of an optical disc, has proved to be essential for the audio play-back quality of the Compact Disc digital audio system.

Just as with the LaserVision system, the Compact Disc digital audio system has been initiated and developed at the Philips Research Laboratories. In the final stage before market introduction Philips and Sony agreed after a joint development programme to settle in the summer of 1980 for a standard to be offered to third parties. Meanwhile, almost 100 licensees have adopted these specifications and Compact Disc has become a world standard (Compact Disc digital audio 1982).

Besides the high signal-to-noise ratio of over 90 dB, the flat frequency response up to 20 kHz and the absence of wow and flutter, the digital signal processing makes possible error correction and interpolation of damaged signals. Also, an advantage from a system point of view is the possibility of incorporating non-audio information in the form of the so-called control and display bits. They can contain additional system information for the listener such as music title, playing time, etc, as well as information for internal use within the play-back system itself, such as pre-emphasised recording, pause and non-audio application (see §8.5).

Figure 8.2   The optical pick-up of the Philips Compact Disc player. The height of the optical stylus based on a solid state laser is just over 40 mm.

In contrast with LaserVision, where the system is more or less determined by the practical limits of the optical recording technology, the Compact Disc system has been designed with ample tolerances for both disc and player. An important difference between LaserVision and Compact Disc players is that the CD system is completely designed around the GaAlAs double heterojunction laser. Semiconductor lasers emit at about 800 nm, in contrast to the 633 nm wavelength of the HeNe laser commonly applied in the first generation LaserVision players. These tiny semiconductor lasers allow for a very compact construction of the light path, which harmonises entirely with the small (120 mm) diameter of the Compact Disc, and thus of the play-back apparatus.

8.5 Professional applications of the Compact Disc system

The storage capacity of a Compact Disc amounts to almost 1 Gbyte of digital information. Together with the advantage of the fast random accessability inherent to disc systems, Compact Disc offers the possibility of application as a gigantic ROM for data distribution in fields other than audio information. As the CD audio format, the CD–ROM format has been standardised. Since this CD–ROM format is compatible with the CD audio standard, CD–ROM discs can be played back on standard CD audio players having a digital output.

Applications of CD–ROM are first of all the distribution of computer software, now being distributed using magnetic tape or (floppy) discs. The advantages of the Compact Disc for that purpose are obvious for both software distributor and user—low media costs due to mass replicability combined with an enormous capacity. Moreover, Compact Disc is easy to distribute; it can be mailed at virtually no cost and without the precautions necessary for magnetic media. It also offers well protected data which do not degrade with time.

Another application is the distribution of (large) databases which can be easily encoded digitally, such as telephone directories, catalogues, manuals, etc.

Although LaserVision and Compact Disc in general can be employed in the same professional applications, the small size of the Compact Disc is often the winning feature. For instance in the storage of road maps, Compact Disc in combination with a video memory is preferred to LaserVision, i.e. the typical picture medium. Such an application is being developed for in-car use and thus a small player volume is an obvious requirement.

8.6 Write-once systems

As mentioned in the introduction to this chapter, professional systems other than those based on the ROM function of LaserVision and Compact Disc, are not yet available on the market. A few manufacturers have announced a recordable system or even sold a few prototypes. All the systems announced so far belong to the class of write-once memories (PROMs). They are divided, just as the ROM products, into two categories namely picture (analog) storage and digital data storage systems. Typical storage capacities are about 50 000 video pictures of 'analog' data or 1 Gbyte of digital data on discs having the generally accepted diameter of 30 cm. Digital data rates are up to 10 Mbit s^{-1}.

The write-once systems are all based upon the application of semiconducting GaAlAs lasers for both writing and reading. Moreover, most systems employ discs that are pregrooved for tracking purposes and preformatted to facilitate random access. The application of GaAlAs lasers and pregrooves is essential in the development of small, cheap and reliable optical recording systems (Bulthuis *et al* 1979).

The advantage of GaAlAs laser diodes in optical recording systems is that their light intensity can be modulated by modulating the electric current through their diode structure. Gas lasers require external light modulators such as acousto- or electro-optic light modulators. The advantages of using a GaAlAs laser over a gas laser/modulator combination are so great in both price and volume that they simply outweigh the drawback of their rather long wavelength of about 800 nm. The latter limits both the data storage capacity of the disc which is inversely proportional to the square of the wavelength, as well as the data rate, scaling with 1/wavelength.

Pregrooving of the disc allows for a simple player concept such as the LaserVision and Compact Disc players. It avoids the need for high precision spindles as in mastering equipment. From a system point of view, pregrooving offers the possibility of preformatting the disc. Preformatting is most often used in digital recorders. It enables the location of a written block of data or of an empty area on the disc to record data, which is essential for random access to the disc in both write and read actions. A simple way of preformatting is to divide the pregrooved tracks in a number of sectors. Each sector consists of an (initially) empty area for data storage, i.e. the data field, and a header with preformatted information such as track and sector number or other data to be used in the system—synchronisation words, subcodes, etc. A special form of preformatting is the incorporation of a small in-depth modulation in the pregroove (Carasso and Huijser 1982). This modulation is used as a pilot signal to synchronise the data in the data field during write as well as read actions. Pregrooves and header information are moulded into the disc substrate in a similar way to which data are replicated in LaserVision and Compact Disc disc production. Moulds are replicas from master discs for which recording processes are reviewed in Chapter 5

The main application of write-once systems is in long-term 'archival' data storage. For that application the lifetime of the stored information must be at least 10 years and for some applications even 30 years. The information stored on the discs is affected by aging of the sensitive layer and its substrate. Aging occurs mostly in the form of small localised defects such as pinholes and tiny cracks in the storage layer (Huijser *et al* 1983). These defects, called drop-outs, deteriorate the HF signal on play-back.

An important figure for the media in archival storage is 'end of life'. This is a difficult to define quantity for video recordings. Video pictures can contain a number of drop-outs before the picture can no longer be recognised. This is due to the large amount of redundancy in a picture. For digital data, end of life is in principle the moment that anywhere on the disc a single bit cannot be retrieved properly. A more common definition is to express it as the chance to read bits erroneously, the so-called uncorrectable bit error rate (UBER). Figures for UBER range from 10^{-10} to 10^{-14}, depending on the kind of data.

These extremely tight requirements can be met in digital optical recording systems by applying a combination of 'rewrite' procedures and error correction codes (ECC). The initial bit error rate of optical data discs typically lies in the range of 10^{-6} to 10^{-4}. These BER values can be corrected using a powerful error correction strategy to UBER values in the range mentioned above. However, correcting the data errors caused by initial defects would substantially consume the finite error correction capacity of the ECC. Thus, hardly any capacity would be left to deal with errors caused by aging of the disc and end of life would come shortly after data were written on the disc. A solution to this problem is found in rewriting initially erroneous data. Written data can be checked for errors by comparing them with the original data block in a direct read after write procedure. Depending on the block length, i.e. the sector length of 1–5 kbit, an initial BER of 10^{-5} yields a rewrite rate of only a few per cent. That will hardly affect the storage capacity of the disc or the transfer rate with which data can be written. Data to be rewritten are stored in the next sector on the same track. The rewrite action is of course subjected to the same data check as a normal write action.

The data check can be performed after or even during the write action. Three methods are in use.

(*a*) Written data are read when they pass the read/write spot after one full revolution of the disc. Retrieved data are then on-line compared with the original message as temporarily stored in a buffer memory.

(*b*) Direct read during write (DRDW) with an on-line check on errors as mentioned above. The method is based on the fact that a write pulse is short compared to the time that the read/write spot 'sees' the location where the readable effect has been written. It is then possible to detect whether an effect has been created or not (see figure 8.3). To perform DRDW, one needs a detection circuit which can recover very fast from overloading as induced by the high intensity write pulse.

(*c*) Direct read after write by a second (read-only) spot which is trailing behind the write spot at only a few microns distance (see figure 8.4). The main problem is to prevent cross-talk by light from the high intensity write spot scattered into the read-only detection optics. Lasers of different wavelength, combined with interference filters are used to reduce this cross-talk to an acceptable level (Carasso and Huijser 1982).

These three methods all have their specific advantages and disadvantages. The first method is inexpensive and reliable. However, the data transfer rate for writing is enormously decreased, at least by a factor of two when the message length spans a complete track, but more generally by a factor of

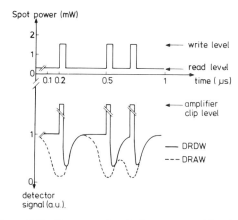

Figure 8.3   Detector signals in DRDW verification.

$(s + 1)$ where s equals the number of sectors per revolution. The two-spot method does not suffer from a decrease in data transfer rate and is reliable. The player is of course more complex with almost twice the amount of optics plus detection circuitry, and is thus more expensive. The DRDW method seems to be a good alternative since it combines the advantages of a simple player design and no reduction of data transfer rate for writing.

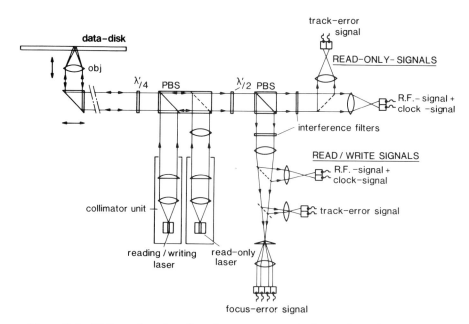

Figure 8.4   Write and read optics of a two-spot optical recorder. The two lasers operate at different wavelengths.

The reliability can be good when tracking velocities and thus data rates are not too high.

8.7 Applications of write-once systems

Since write-once optical recording systems have not really been introduced on the market, many of their applications have yet to be devised. Most system and media development has been concentrated on digital data recording in devices like on-line and back-up storage peripherals for computer applications. Nevertheless, some write-once optical recording media are capable of storing 'analog' data, i.e. video information, with a quality comparable to LaserVision standards.

Write-once video recording will be used where random picture access is essential and media distribution is not important. The strong link with ILV applications (see §8.3) is evident. Examples are picture archiving and video and film editing. The latter application in particular will find rapid acceptance since it saves a lot of time and money. In that application, video or film shots (typically 4 to 6 hours for a film of one and a half hours) are all stored on a number of write-once video discs. A battery of read-only ILV players, hooked to a computer offers the director the possibility of composing the film or television programme under computer control.

As mentioned in the preceding paragraph, write-once optical recording systems will be used in data storage systems in which archival aspects or mass storage requirements prevail. Both aspects are often combined in (document) filing systems, where at present a variety of different media are applied.

The most common form of filing is still storing the original documents or copies of them. This method requires a lot of space and document retrieval is very difficult, time consuming and labour intensive. A less bulky method is to copy the documents on microfilm. Although microfiche sytems find many applications, they cannot be considered as user friendly and storage is rather complicated due to the photographic process.

A more modern method is to transfer the documents into digital data which can be electronically stored, transmitted by cable, reproduced on printers or plotters and displayed on high resolution CRTs. Computer-generated documents and documents made on word-processors are already available in digital form. Other documents like hand-written letters, drawings and photographs can be digitised using optical scanners. As storage media for these digital data, write-once optical discs offer the combination of a large capacity and fast random access. The storage capacity of a 1 Gbyte optical disc is equivalent to approximately 500 000 A4 documents when the data are computer or word-processor generated. When documents have to be scanned, the number of pixels per document determines the storage capacity expressed in number of documents.

In mass storage systems based on optical recording techniques such as the Megadoc system (de Vos 1982) document storage occurs in the way described above. The system consists of various peripherals such as a scanner with a resolution of 4 million pixels on any A4 document, an image printer and a high resolution CRT. The heart of the system is a write-once optical disc recorder, integrated in a juke-box configuration in which 64 discs can be stored. Average access time on a disc is 150 ms, whereas the time to load a disc from the juke-box is less than 20 s. The whole system is operated from a keyboard and controlled by a computer. Although the system can be extended with more juke-box units, the storage capacity of the basic unit is already beyond imagination—30 million documents which can be retrieved at random within seconds.

These systems based on optical recording can be applied successfully in environments where huge amounts of data have to be stored for longer periods of time (Goldberg 1983). Those large databases are found for instance in hospitals where medical x-ray images have to be stored for many years. A typical hospital (100 beds) produces about 30 000 x-rays annually. This requires roughly 10^{12} bits per year when stored in a digitised form. With an average of 10 years' storage this forms a data bank of over 10^{13} bits. Even larger data banks are found in libraries (up to 10^{14} bits), electronic imagery, as for instance with weather satellites which require 10^{14} annually and land mapping (the US National Map database would occupy in a digitised form about 5×10^{14} bits).

It must be noted here, that devices based on magnetic recording can also be applied in the field of filing systems. At present they rarely are, especially magnetic tape. The drawback of magnetic tape is its very clumsy access. Magnetic disc systems, on the contrary, offer the same accessibility as optical discs. However, high capacity Winchester-type magnetic disc memories are very expensive and are of the fixed-spindle type (Elphick 1983). Both aspects are unacceptable when considering storage costs per bit, the essential parameter in electronic filing. The lack of erasability of write-once optical recording systems, often said to be their major drawback, is certainly not essential and not even desirable in most filing applications. When this is added to their superior price/performance ratio, it is beyond doubt that write-once optical recording systems will in the future be applied more often in data storage than envisaged today.

References

Bulthuis K, Carasso M, Heemskerk J, Kivits P, Kleuters W and Zalm P 1979 Ten billion bits on a disc *IEEE Spectrum* **16** 26

Carasso M and Huijser A 1982 Principles of optical recording systems with AlGaAs lasers and pregrooved discs *Proc. Conf. on Lasers and Electro-Optics, Phoenix* p. 30

Compaan K and Kramer P 1973 The Philips VLP system *Phillips Tech. Rev.* **33** 178

Compact Disc digital audio Special issue 6 1982 *Philips Tech. Rev.* **40** 150–80

Elphick M 1983 Winchester disk technology spins into new orbits *Computer Design* (January) 89–102

Goldberg M 1983 Large memory applications for optical disks *SPIE* **382** 20

Huijser A, Jacobs B, Vriens L, Markvoort J, Spruijt A and Vromans P 1983 Ageing characteristics of DOR media *SPIE* **382** 270

McCoy D 1978 The RCA SelectaVision videodisc system *RCA Rev.* **39** 7

Schouhamer Immink K, Hoogendijk A and Kahlman J 1984 Digital audio modulation in the PAL and NTSC optical video disc coding formats *J. Audio Eng. Soc.* **32** 883

de Vos J 1980 Megadoc, a modular system for electronic document handling *Philips Tech. Rev.* **39** 329

Subject Index

Author Index